MW00442861

THE SOLICITOR GENERAL AND
THE UNITED STATES SUPREME COURT

The U.S. government, represented by the Office of the Solicitor General, appears before the Supreme Court more than any other litigant. The office's link to the president, the arguments it makes before the Court, and its ability to alter the legal and policy landscape make it the most important Supreme Court litigant bar none. As such, scholars must understand the office's role in Supreme Court decision making and, more important, its ability to influence the Court. This book examines whether and how the Office of the Solicitor General influences the U.S. Supreme Court. Combining archival data with recent innovations in the areas of matching and causal inference, the book finds that the Office of the Solicitor General influences every aspect of the Court's decision-making process. From granting review to cases to selecting winning parties, writing opinions, and interpreting precedent, the solicitor general's office influences the Court to behave in ways that it otherwise would not.

Ryan C. Black is an assistant professor in the Department of Political Science at Michigan State University, where he studies the federal judiciary, with a particular emphasis on the U.S. Supreme Court and the U.S. Courts of Appeals. His work has been published in the *Journal of Politics*, *Political Research Quarterly*, *Journal of Law, Economics and Organization*, *American Politics Research*, *Presidential Studies Quarterly*, *Justice System Journal*, *Law and Social Inquiry*, and a variety of law reviews. He is also a coauthor of *Oral Arguments and Coalition Formation on the U.S. Supreme Court: A Deliberate Dialogue*.

Ryan J. Owens is a Lyons Family Faculty Scholar and assistant professor in the Department of Political Science at the University of Wisconsin. His work analyzes the U.S. Supreme Court, the U.S. Courts of Appeals, and American political institutions. His work has appeared in the *American Journal of Political Science*, *Journal of Politics*, *Political Research Quarterly*, *Judicature*, *William and Mary Law Review*, *Law and Society Review*, and *Justice System Journal*.

The Solicitor General and the United States Supreme Court

EXECUTIVE BRANCH INFLUENCE AND JUDICIAL DECISIONS

RYAN C. BLACK

Michigan State University

RYAN J. OWENS

University of Wisconsin

CAMBRIDGE
UNIVERSITY PRESS

CAMBRIDGE UNIVERSITY PRESS
Cambridge, New York, Melbourne, Madrid, Cape Town,
Singapore, São Paulo, Delhi, Mexico City

Cambridge University Press
32 Avenue of the Americas, New York NY 10013-2473, USA

Published in the United States of America by Cambridge University Press, New York

www.cambridge.org
Information on this title: www.cambridge.org/9781107680999

First published 2012
First paperback edition 2013

A catalogue record for this publication is available from the British Library

Library of Congress Cataloguing in Publication Data
Black, Ryan C., 1982–
The Solicitor General and the United States Supreme Court : executive branch influence and
judicial decisions / Ryan C. Black, Ryan J. Owens.
    p.   cm.
Includes bibliographical references and index.
ISBN 978-1-107-01529-6 (hardback)
1. United States. Solicitor General – Influence.   2. United States. Supreme Court.   3. Judicial
process – United States.   I. Owens, Ryan J., 1976–   II. Title.
KF8792.5.B58   2012
353.4'2293–dc23   2011046675

ISBN 978-1-107-01529-6 Hardback
ISBN 978-1-107-68099-9 Paperback

To my dad, for his endless generosity and unwavering support
– R.C.B.

To Karen, Wyatt, and Henry for their love, patience, and
understanding; to my brother Jason,
for his gracious help over the years; and to my parents,
Tom and Jan, for their love of learning and guidance
– R.J.O.

Contents

Acknowledgments

This book is the culmination of a lengthy project that began several years ago. Along the way, we received comments and feedback from a number of colleagues and friends. Tim Johnson and Patrick Wohlfarth both read the full manuscript and provided helpful comments, which we very much appreciated. Steve Ansolabehere took the time to read various components of the book and offered valuable insight. James Fowler and the participants at the University of California–San Diego American Politics and Institutions Project provided useful comments as well. Justin Wedeking and Tony Madonna were also there with helpful perspectives. We also appreciate the comments we received from former solicitor general Seth Waxman, who helped us broaden our focus. Discussants at assorted political science conferences both endured our presentations and offered helpful comments. For taking on these typically thankless tasks, we thank Saul Brenner, Paul Collins, Kevin McGuire, Rich Pacelle, Marie Provine, Isaac Unah, Tom Walker, and Justin Wedeking (again).

We also benefited from outstanding research assistants. For their often clutch performances, we gratefully thank Amanda Bryan, Rachel Schutte, Nick Snavely, and Dan Thaler.

For providing financial support, Owens thanks the Lyons family and the University of Wisconsin for their generous support of his research as well as Dan Carpenter and the Center for American Political Studies at Harvard University. We both thank the Center for Empirical Research in the Law at Washington University in Saint Louis.

Last, but not least, we would like to thank our spouses, Krista Black and Karen Owens. We could not have written this book without their support and patience, which we most certainly tested at various times throughout the process.

1

The Solicitor General and the Supreme Court

In 1992, the National Organization for Women (NOW) and two abortion clinics filed a petition for a writ of certiorari[1] asking the U.S. Supreme Court to hear their case and apply the Racketeer Influenced and Corrupt Organizations Act (RICO)[2] against a group of abortion protestors. NOW alleged the protestors broke that law by seeking to put abortion clinics out of business.[3] The claim faced an uphill battle. Both lower federal courts that heard the case decided against NOW, holding that to violate RICO, one must engage in economically motivated behavior. The lower courts stated that because the protestors sought to limit the *availability* of abortions rather than to gain abortion-related *business*, RICO did not apply. Had the litigation ended at the circuit court of appeals – as most appellate cases do – that would have been the end of the road for the litigants, and federal racketeering law would have looked very different today. But the litigation did not end there. NOW sought Supreme Court review to settle whether RICO imposed such an economic motive requirement.

Supreme Court review was improbable. The Court hears fewer than one hundred cases each year, granting review to less than 1 percent of all requests

---

[1] A petition for certiorari is a formal request asking the Supreme Court to review the decision of a lower court. When the Supreme Court issues a writ of certiorari, it orders the lower court that heard the case to send up the record of that case so that it can review that court's determination. As we discuss later, the Supreme Court grants such requests on a discretionary basis; that is, it is not obligated to grant certiorari to any particular type of case or legal issue, although there are a handful of *appeals* the Court must hear – these are largely election-related cases and constitute only a small fraction of the Court's cases each term.

[2] See, generally, 18 U.S.C. §1961, et seq.

[3] We obtained information on this case and others throughout the book from the cert pool memos, private docket sheets, and other archival data collected by us and others (Epstein, Segal, and Spaeth 2007) at the Library of Congress Manuscript Reading Room in Washington, D.C. We would like to extend a gracious thank-you to the staff of the reading room for their assistance while we collected our data.

(Owens and Simon 2012). During the 1992 term (in which NOW sought Supreme Court review), the Supreme Court heard only 97 petitions out of more than 7,200 requests. In line with the general tendency to hear only the fewest of cases, the law clerk tasked with summarizing the case for the justices privately urged them to deny review.[4] He pointed out that none of the traditional reasons to grant review, such as legal conflict or judicial review exercised by the lower courts that heard the case, applied to the petition. There was only minimal conflict among the lower courts regarding whether RICO required an economic motive. What is more, the Court had denied review to a similar certiorari request just three terms earlier. On top of all that, the clerk suggested the case might be too politically sensitive for Court review:

> Whenever a case involves abortion, there is a risk that the parties will become distracted, and that the real issue will be distorted. The risk seems especially great in a case in which [one] of the plaintiffs (NOW) is a leading proponent of the "pro-choice" position and [one] of the defendants (Operation Rescue) is a leading proponent of the "pro-life" position. (Cert Pool Memo 92-780)

Another factor mitigating against review was that a merits decision had unclear downstream consequences. What would the decision do to RICO? What effect would it have on abortion doctrine? What would the decision do to the Court's broader standing among the public? Justice Blackmun's law clerk summed up the uncertainty that the justices surely faced when he wrote to Blackmun:

> It's very hard to predict what this Court would do with a case like this, and it's equally hard to tell what unintended consequences would flow from a precedent one way or another. (Cert Pool Memo Markup 92-780)

Put plainly, none of the typical rationales for granting review seemed to apply, and so review was improbable – but not impossible.

During the Court's conference vote on whether to hear the case, a handful of justices formally requested the views of the U.S. solicitor general (SG) – the attorney for the U.S. government; that is, before determining whether to hear the case, justices wanted the SG's opinion of the petition. Was the issue important enough to merit review? Did RICO require judicial

---

[4] As we explain more fully later, each Supreme Court justice (except Justice Alito) pools his or her clerks together to write memos summarizing petitions for certiorari and to make recommendations as to whether the Court should grant or deny review to the case. They employ this mechanism as a time-saving device. In this case, the clerk recommended that the Court deny review, in part because of a lack of conflict among the lower courts. As we explain later in the book, one of the Court's primary responsibilities is to unify the law. Thus it often grants review to clear up conflicting legal interpretations among the lower federal courts.

fine-tuning? Did the lower courts need Supreme Court guidance? To answer
these questic   justices turned to the Office of the Solicitor General (OSG).
The d   isi   o call for the views of the SG turned out to be consequential.
The OSC rec   mended that the Court grant review to the petition, reverse
the lower court decision, and declare that RICO contained no economic
motive requirement. This recommendation appeared to have changed at least
one justice's mind – and the course of law. As Figure 1.1 shows, after the
justices received the SG's grant recommendation, Justice O'Connor changed
her vote. Her first vote (in the initial round of voting) was to deny review,
yet her second vote – which came after the OSG's recommendation – was
to grant review. Her grant vote (technically a join-3 vote) became the fourth
vote to hear the case (along with Justices White, Blackmun, and Stevens) and
triggered full Court review.[5]

At the merits stage, the OSG performed ably, making a series of persuasive
arguments. First, OSG lawyers argued that the economic motive requirement
failed as a matter of statutory construction. Neither the plain meaning of
RICO's text nor its legislative history evinced any such economic motive
requirement. Second, they claimed that such a requirement would make it
difficult for U.S. Attorneys to prosecute acts of violence based on political or
religious reasons. Forcing prosecutors to show that a defendant had economic
rather than political goals would impose unnecessary hurdles for them to
obtain guilty verdicts. Third, requiring federal judges to determine whether an
act was economic or noneconomic in nature would pose a practical problem.
Could judges really determine how much economic benefit would be needed
to make an act economic rather than political? Without objective criteria,
judicial capacity would be stretched.

The Court agreed. On January 24, 1994, every justice – even those opposed
to the Court's abortion jurisprudence – ruled that RICO contained no economic motive requirement. The decision thus cleared the way for courts to
apply RICO to actors with noneconomic motives. This included, of course,
abortion protestors like Scheidler, the Pro-Life Action Network, and others.[6]
And though the ruling did not mean that pro-life activists would necessarily
be held to have violated RICO (as future litigation would reveal),[7] it did mean

---

[5] When granting review to a petition of certiorari, the Court operates according to a Rule of
Four. If at least four of the nine justices vote to grant review, the case will be placed on the
Court's plenary (merits) docket. Technically, the Court will grant review to a case with three
grant votes plus a join-3 vote (Perry 1991). O'Connor's vote in *Scheidler* was a join-3 vote, which
triggered review.

[6] See *National Organization for Women v. Scheidler*, 510 U.S. 249 (1994).

[7] *Scheidler v. NOW, Inc.*, 547 U.S. 9 (2006).

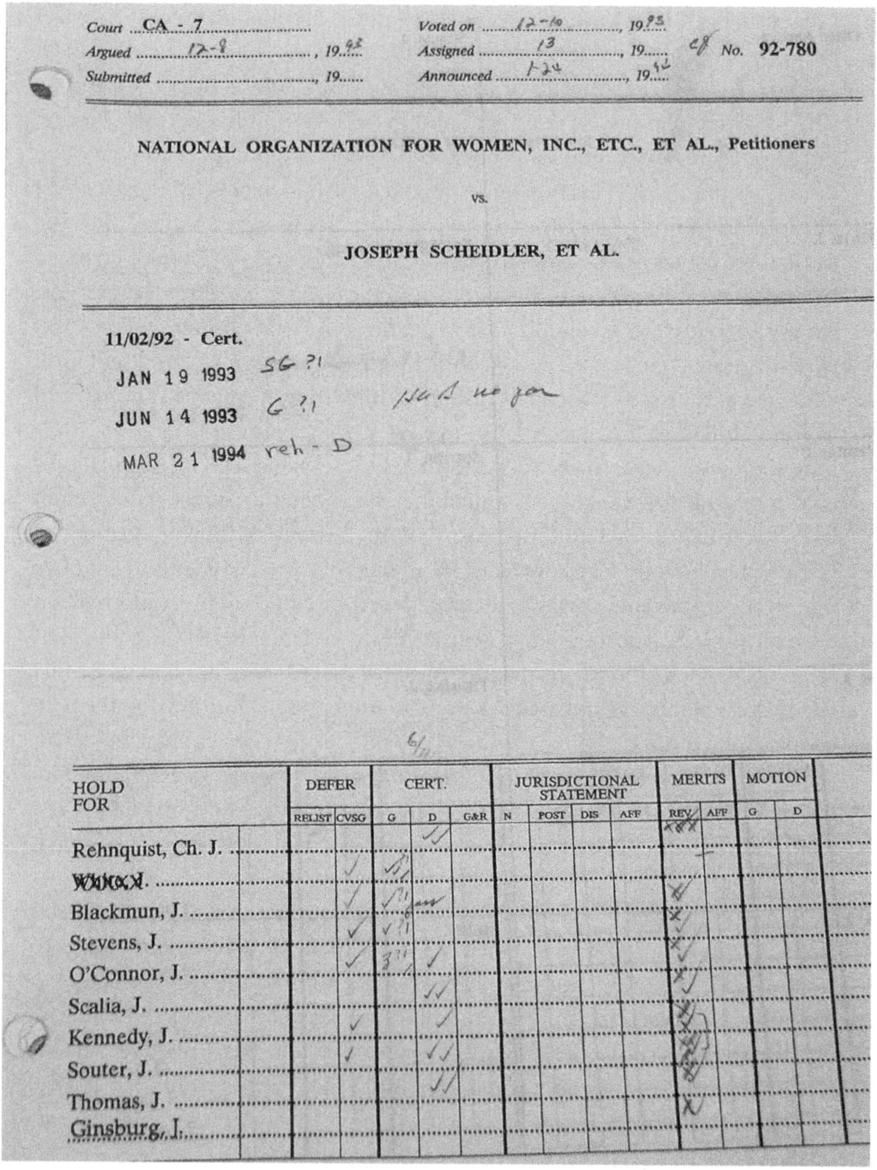

Court CA - 7 Voted on 12-10, 19 93
Argued 12-8, 19 93 Assigned 13, 19 No. 92-780
Submitted , 19 Announced 1-24, 19 94

NATIONAL ORGANIZATION FOR WOMEN, INC., ETC., ET AL., Petitioners

vs.

JOSEPH SCHEIDLER, ET AL.

11/02/92 - Cert.

JAN 19 1993 SG ?!

JUN 14 1993 G ?!

MAR 21 1994 reh - D

HOLD FOR	DEFER		CERT.			JURISDICTIONAL STATEMENT				MERITS		MOTION	
	RELIST	CVSG	G	D	G&R	N	POST	DIS	AFF	REV	AFF	G	D
Rehnquist, Ch. J.													
XXXXX.													
Blackmun, J.													
Stevens, J.													
O'Connor, J.													
Scalia, J.													
Kennedy, J.													
Souter, J.													
Thomas, J.													
Ginsburg, J.													

FIGURE 1.1. Justice Blackmun's docket sheet in *NOW v. Scheidler* (92-780), obtained from Epstein, Segal, and Spaeth (2007). The Court's initial round of voting occurred on January 19, 1993. The second round of voting occurred on June 14, 1993, after the Court received the SG's recommendation.

that they would have to defend themselves against RICO challenges, draining them of much-needed resources that might have been spent more profitably elsewhere.

In sum, the SG and his staff of lawyers persuaded the Court in the following ways:

- To hear the case, though six justices initially opposed review
- To overturn two lower court rulings in a politically sensitive case
- To rule unanimously that noneconomic actors, including pro-life protestors, could be charged with violating federal racketeering laws

GOAL OF THE BOOK

Were the events that took place in *Scheidler* typical? Does the OSG influence the U.S. Supreme Court, or did the OSG simply get lucky? This is the phenomenon we scrutinize: SG influence. We examine one central question throughout this book: does the OSG influence the U.S. Supreme Court? We provide a multifaceted empirical analysis of SG influence throughout the Supreme Court's decision-making process. We examine the Court's agenda stage, its brief-writing stage, and its merits termination stage, all with the goal of determining whether the OSG influences the Court. Of course, while our goal is to determine whether the OSG influences the Court, we also seek to make broader connections regarding the source(s) of that influence. In other words, not only do we seek to provide a rigorous analysis of OSG influence but we also hope to bring clarity to the overall picture of what drives OSG influence.

To be sure, we are not the first to examine the SG's relationship with the Court. A long train of well-respected empirical and qualitative studies show that throughout the Court's decision-making process, SGs succeed frequently (Wohlfarth 2009; Nicholson and Collins 2008; Bailey, Kamoie, and Maltzman 2005; Deen, Ignagni, and Meernik 2003; Pacelle 2003; Days 1995; Salokar 1992; Caplan 1987). These and other studies have pointed out a number of features that all highlight OSG success before the Court. From them, we know, for example, that the Court grants review to far more government certiorari petitions than petitions filed by any other party (Black and Owens 2009a; Caldeira and Wright 1988). We know that the OSG wins an astonishingly high percentage of its Supreme Court cases (Epstein, Segal, Spaeth and Walker 2007). We know that when the OSG participates as an amicus curiae, the side it supports usually wins (Collins 2004; Segal 1988). We even know that the

Court may be more likely to borrow language from the SG's brief than from briefs filed by all other litigants (Corley 2008).

Of course, if SG *success* implied SG *influence*, we would not hesitate to assert that the OSG influences the Court at every turn. In fact, we would not need to write this book! Success, however, does not necessarily imply influence. SGs may succeed before the Supreme Court for reasons that have nothing to do with influence. For example, if justices were inclined for ideological or legal reasons to support the OSG's argument – even before the office provided its argument – could we contend that the OSG influenced them? We think not.

Rather, to determine OSG influence, one must examine judicial behavior *but for* the presence of the SG; that is,

> the measure of a Solicitor General's advocacy [i.e., influence] is not how often the Court agrees with him, but how often he has persuaded the Court to take a position it would not have taken without his advocacy. (McConnell 1988, 1115)

Only if judicial outcomes look different because of the OSG can one infer influence.

Put plainly, although scholars and journalists have produced high-quality research on the SG – and we wholeheartedly recommend these works to our readers – our understanding of OSG influence over the Court remains shrouded in mystery. Our goal here is to remove the mystery.

Why is SG influence important to study? Why should OSG influence matter to legal scholars, political scientists, politicians, and the public? Jeffrey Segal answered this question over twenty years ago, when he stated: "Our understanding of the Supreme Court will not be complete until the role of the solicitor general is better understood" (Segal 1988, 142–43). More specifically, there are at least four reasons why readers should care about OSG influence. First, as the lawyer for the U.S. government before the Supreme Court, the SG's behavior can affect millions of us. The OSG appears before the Court more than any other litigant. If the OSG could influence justices, its powers would be extensive. Indeed, national policy might turn on the position taken by the SG. So if we care about Supreme Court policy outcomes, we must understand the OSG.

Second, it is almost exclusively through the SG's office that presidents interact with the Supreme Court. The president's only direct link to the Court is through the SG. To be sure, the president nominates justices, and with that dynamic comes some indirect control over Court outcomes. Once on the bench, however, all bets are off; the president can exercise no direct control over them (Epstein, Martin, Quinn and Segal 2007). Simply put, to understand executive–judicial relations, one needs to understand the intermediary – the OSG.

Third, if the SG could influence the Court, presidents might circumvent Congress and use the OSG to make policy. When faced with hostile legislators, presidents have three choices: they can moderate and work with Congress, they can pursue their agendas within the executive branch through regulation, or they can seek policy victories in the judicial branch through Supreme Court litigation. If they succeed in the judiciary, presidents can make an end run around Congress, and if their success is tied to the OSG, that office becomes crucial to understand in a separation-of-powers context.

Finally, the OSG employs highly skilled lawyers who often go on to become Supreme Court justices themselves. It is no surprise that three of the last four justices confirmed to the Supreme Court once worked in the OSG. Justice Kagan was SG from 2009 to 2010, Justice Alito was assistant to Solicitor General Rex E. Lee from 1981 to 1985, and Chief Justice John Roberts served as principal deputy solicitor general from 1989 to 1993. A number of other justices throughout the Court's history also had served in the OSG (Epstein, Segal, Spaeth and Walker 2007). Because so many justices were once OSG lawyers, knowledge of the OSG may actually provide useful background information about the Court.

OUTLINE OF THE BOOK

Before we get ahead of ourselves, though, we briefly outline our strategy in this book. Chapter 2 starts off our investigation of OSG influence by providing important background information on the OSG. We examine when and why Congress created the office as well as the critical functions the SG fulfills today. We then provide a host of descriptive data on OSG success before the Court.

Chapter 3 discusses existing theories that seek to explain SG success. We examine a number of theories such as the (poorly named) agent of the Court theory, attorney experience, attorney quality, ideological and separation-of-powers considerations, and the OSG's possible strategic case selection. We discuss the observable implications of each of these theories and examine whether they – and their accompanying studies – can tell us anything about SG influence.

Chapter 4 is the first of four empirical chapters that examine OSG influence. It analyzes whether the OSG influences the votes justices cast during the agenda-setting stage. We analyze how justices respond to OSG recommendations to grant or deny review to certiorari petitions, taking advantage of unique archival data that allow us to peer inside justices' private conferences and observe how they voted. Using research-backed methods of vote prediction, we predict how a justice will vote in a case and then compare her actual agenda vote to her predicted agenda vote. This research design allows us to examine whether the OSG influences justices to cast agenda votes that they might not otherwise cast.

In Chapter 5, we search for influence by comparing the probability of an OSG victory with the probability of a non-OSG victory in cases where the two attorneys are otherwise identical. The chapter employs a unique matching technique to investigate whether arguing on behalf of the OSG causes an attorney to be more victorious before the Court. More specifically, we seek out lawyers and cases that are as identical as possible in terms of experience before the Court, resources, ideological position vis-à-vis the Court, and the like. We then split the data into two groups: cases in which an OSG lawyer participates and cases in which someone other than an OSG lawyer participates. After matching these cases so that they are as similar to each other as possible, save for our treatment (the presence of an attorney from the OSG), we examine whether the OSG attorney is more likely than the non-OSG attorney to win before the Supreme Court.

Chapter 6 searches for OSG influence by examining whether Court opinions borrow more language from OSG briefs than from otherwise identical non-OSG briefs. Our approach in Chapter 6 employs the same matching methodology as used in Chapter 5. We take two briefs that are nearly identical in all relevant manners and ask whether the Court borrows more language from the OSG brief than from the non-OSG brief. Once again, by matching on all relevant characteristics but for the treatment, we can determine if OSG status drives up the probability of favorable treatment by the Supreme Court.

Chapter 7, our final empirical chapter, analyzes OSG influence by examining whether the Court's treatment of legal precedent is a function of the OSG's recommendations. We examine whether the Court is more likely to positively or negatively interpret precedent when the SG recommends such treatment of it. To do so, we once again employ matching. We compare cases in which the OSG recommends a particular treatment to the Court with cases in which the OSG does not make such a recommendation. By so doing, we can determine whether the Court is more likely to treat precedent positively or negatively as a result of the OSG's recommendation.

Chapter 8 concludes the book. In it, we review our results and discuss what OSG influence means for Supreme Court decision making, the separation of powers, and nomination politics more broadly.

So that there is no confusion over our results, we highlight our major findings at the outset. Our results all point toward one unmistakeable finding;

the OSG does not simply succeed before the U.S. Supreme Court, it actually influences the Court throughout its decision-making process. The OSG influences justices to grant review to cases they otherwise would prefer not to hear; it influences the Court's rulings (who wins and loses); it influences the language of Court opinions; and it influences the evolution of doctrine by supporting and opposing Supreme Court precedent. In all facets of the Court's decision-making process, the OSG influences the Court.

We pause to offer a note to the reader about our approaches and methods. We employ a mixed-methods approach that includes archival data, large-n quantitative analysis, and cutting-edge empirical methods. At all times throughout this book, however, we aim to describe clearly our data sources, our methods for coding variables, and our hypotheses. We do so, of course, to meet the stringent demands of social science (which require that data be valid and reliable and that future researchers be able to replicate our study) but also to aid the reader's understanding of our work. As such, while we seek to provide a systematic treatment of SG influence over the Supreme Court, we also strive to make our approach readable, entertaining, and accessible for readers of all backgrounds.

As a further note, we understand that a broad empirical approach such as the one we take here necessarily forces us to ignore some of the nuances inherent in each case before the Court. We recognize, for example, that personal characteristics unique to justices and SGs might lead to outcomes in particular cases, and we remain cognizant that there may well be some variables that influence the OSG's relationship with the Court that are simply impossible to measure. Still, these are issues that affect all quantitative studies, and scholars have decided – quite correctly, we believe – that those trade-offs are worthwhile to pursue answers to broad, general questions. The approach we take, in short, although not perfect, allows us to generalize from our data to all issues, all SGs, and all justices. Put simply, we hope that our approach – which raises theoretical questions and answers them using rigorous but clearly explained empirical analyses – is one that our readers will enjoy and that advances our understanding of the Supreme Court and the SG.

Former SG Erwin Griswold once stated, "I think a strong solicitor general can have very considerable influence on the Court" (quoted in Salokar 1992, 98). Was this comment merely the hopeful wish of a Supreme Court practitioner or the accumulated wisdom of an acute mind? In what follows, we examine this precise question.

2

The Office of the Solicitor General: "The Finest Law Firm in the Nation"

During his testimony before the Senate Judiciary Committee to become solicitor general (SG), Paul Clement discussed the virtues and complexities of working in the Office of the Solicitor General (OSG), or what he called "the finest law firm in the Nation" (Clement 2005, 5). The SG, stated Clement, has important responsibilities to each of the three branches of the federal government. An actor with legal and political responsibilities, the SG must advocate for the government but must also be cognizant of the Court's needs and demands:

> The Solicitor General is an executive branch official, and the office defends the policies and practice of the executive branch in the courts when they are challenged. . . . The office quite literally sits at the crossroads of the separation of powers as the primary vehicle through which the Article II branch of Government speaks to Article III. But, of course, the office also owes important responsibilities to the Article I branch, the Congress of the United States. . . . Finally, the office also owes an important responsibility to the Supreme Court of the United States. I have heard reference made to the Solicitor General as the tenth Justice of the Supreme Court. I am quick to add I have never heard that comment made by any of the nine real Justices.

Clement's testimony reflects an important concept. The SG must simultaneously weigh a number of factors when determining whether and how to proceed with cases. Fidelity to the law might mean, at times, rejecting a position of the executive in favor of one in line with the Court's jurisprudence. At other times, it might mean adopting a position of the president, pushing the boundaries of law, and rejecting claims made by Congress or others. And still yet, at other times, the SG may need to strike out and pursue arguments envisioned neither by the administration nor by the Court. Simply put, the SG and the OSG are subject to contextual complexities that push and pull in different directions. If they wish to influence the Court, they must balance their responsibilities and maintain a clear and objective position. But how? And to what end?

These issues define the modern OSG's influence. We will get to them in due time. First, though, we must answer more basic questions such as how was the office created, and what powers did its creators bestow on it? What responsibilities do current SGs have? How do the SG and the OSG use these powers? In short, before we can empirically examine SG influence, we must first ask and answer basic substantive questions about the OSG itself.

As such, this chapter provides an overview of the office and the attorneys who work in it. We begin with a brief overview of the legislation that created the OSG and the reasons Congress created it. We then examine the office today, focusing on the organization of the office and the functions the modern OSG fulfills. We then change our focus a bit and examine SG success before the Supreme Court, analyzing a wide array of descriptive data about OSG participation before the Court. More specifically, we provide descriptive data on how often the OSG succeeds before the Court. This chapter educates readers about why Congress created the OSG, the composition of the office, the functions it performs, and OSG success in the Court.

CREATING THE OFFICE

Before Congress created the OSG, the U.S. Attorney General (AG) was responsible for arguing the government's cases before the Supreme Court. In one of Congress's first acts, it passed the Judiciary Act of 1789, which, among other things, created the Office of the Attorney General.[1] The Act directed the AG to undertake two primary duties: "to prosecute and conduct all suits in the Supreme Court in which the United States shall be concerned" (Cooper, 1990, 677) and to give formal legal advice (via written "opinions," not to be confused with court opinions) to members of the executive branch who so requested (Bloch 1989, 566). As such, the AG's only litigation responsibility to the government was before the U.S. Supreme Court (Bloch 1989, 568).

Whereas the responsibility to appear on behalf of the United States before the Supreme Court fell on the AG, corresponding resources did not. The

---

[1] Enacted on September 24, 1789, the Judiciary Act of 1789 (the "Act") is one of the most important pieces of legislation Congress ever passed. The Act performed three functions. First, it clarified Article III of the U.S. Constitution by creating a hierarchical federal court system. Second, it declared the Supreme Court the final court to decide issues of federal law. Finally, it triggered *Marbury v. Madison*, 5 U.S. 137 (1803), an important case that declared the Court's authority to review the constitutionality of federal legislation. For more information on the history of the OSG, see Waxman (1998), on which much of this discussion is based.

Judiciary Act failed to provide the AG with either an office or a staff. Lacking such resources, the AG had to make do with very little. He went to the Capitol only when needed. He had to draft correspondence personally by hand or hire staff, at his own expense, to do so (Waxman 1998). Not until 1818 did Congress grant the AG a clerk and office space. What is more, the AG received a paltry salary.[2] In fact, Congress did not even make the AG's salary equal to the salaries of other cabinet officers until 1853. And perhaps most important, the AG had no formal control over district attorneys who argued in lower federal courts, a feature that prevented him from systematically coordinating the government's legal strategy (Bloch 1989, 585). The office, put simply, was one that imposed responsibilities on the Attorney General without corresponding assistance, and it was not long until conditions exposed the office's inadequacies.

As the country expanded throughout the mid-nineteenth century, the government's legal demands quickly increased and rendered the statutory scheme impractical. Early on, the AG participated in few cases before the Court. In the forty years between 1790 and 1829, the AG participated in just over 170 Supreme Court cases as a party.[3] Yet, in the thirty years between 1830 and 1859, the office was involved in just over 280 such cases. And while the cases kept coming, so, too, did the requests for legal opinions from members of the executive branch. The AG's dual responsibilities under the Judiciary Act had come to a head. The understaffed AG's office simply could not keep up with the government's growing legal demands. It could not simultaneously provide legal opinions to the executive branch and effectively argue cases in the Supreme Court.

Congress's immediate, and ultimately problematic, response to the AG's growing workload problem was to authorize him to retain private lawyers to argue on behalf of the United States (Fahy 1942). In 1861, Congress authorized the AG to hire private counsel to assist him, stating, "[The AG], whenever in his opinion the public interest may require it, [may] employ and retain (in the name of the United States) such attorneys and counsellors-at-law as he may deem necessary."[4] The AG and various government agencies were quick to employ these private lawyers. As Waxman (1998) put it, the number of privately retained outside counsel soon outnumbered all commissioned U.S. law officers. In short, Congress compounded one problem with a second.

Congress's makeshift maneuver led to three problems. First, allowing the AG to retain private counsel was expensive. To be sure, the retention of

---

[2] Members of Congress envisioned the AG working for the United States on a half-time basis, where he would subsidize his meager salary through private practice.

[3] Search done in LexisNexis using "NAME(United States)."

[4] Act of August 2, 1861, ch. 37, 12 Stat. 285.

outside counsel allowed the AG to spread out its legal work and keep pace with a growing workload, but at backbreaking cost. Between 1864 and 1869, the U.S. government paid $733,208 ($12.1 million in 2010 dollars) for outside legal services, a figure that dwarfed the salary of the AG during the same time period.[5] In a time when total federal outlays were minimal, these costs were titanic. A second problem involved differing incentives between private and U.S. lawyers. The interests of private lawyers did not always coincide with the interests of the United States. Private counsel sometimes pursued short-term victories at the expense of long-term doctrinal goals. Trained as they were to obtain success for their clients, they were often unable – and, indeed, lacked the incentive – to sacrifice immediate victory for long-term goals. Private attorneys even had a financial incentive to delay. As one senator put it, "it seemed as though [the provision allowing the government to hire private counsel] was passed to delay the legal business of the Government."[6] Third, the legislation exacerbated the growing trend among various agencies to litigate independently of one another, without coordinating their legal strategies with the AG. Private attorneys and the government's own attorneys pursued scattershot approaches before federal courts. There simply was not any centralization that would allow the government to speak with one voice in the courts and control the legal "message." The mass of attorneys could not coordinate on a single, unified legal strategy. The government's approach to litigation was, in brief, expensive, occasionally adverse to long-term government goals, and chaotic.

Accordingly, in December 1867, after taking an accounting of the mess before it, Congress asked Attorney General Henry Stanbery to provide a summary of the reforms he thought necessary to improve his office.[7] Congress asked Stanbery to declare the amount paid by the United States for outside counsel, to convey whether the amount of staff he employed was sufficient to his needs, and to certify whether he believed it desirable "to bring all the law officers of the government under one head." Stanbery responded as follows:

> The present force in the office of the Attorney General is not sufficient for the proper business of that office. As to the mere administrative business of the office the present force is sufficient, but as to the proper duties of the Attorney General, especially in the preparation and argument of cases before the Supreme Court... and the preparation of opinions on questions of law

---

[5] Congressional Globe, 41st Congress, 2d Session, 3035, 3038.
[6] Congressional Globe, 41st Congress, 2d Session, 4490.
[7] Ex. Doc. 40-13, p. 1.

referred to him, some provision is absolutely necessary to enable him properly to discharge his duties. After much reflection, it seems to me that this want may best be supplied by the appointment of a solicitor general. With such an assistant, the necessity of employing special counsel in the argument of cases in the Supreme Court of the United States would be in a great measure, if not altogether, dispensed with.

Stated otherwise, Stanbery asserted that he was unable to fulfill his dual responsibilities under the Judiciary Act (arguing cases before the Court and providing legal advice to executive officers) and, consequently, implored Congress to create an Office of the Solicitor General to assist him in presenting cases to the Supreme Court.

Congress granted Stanbery's request. On June 22, 1870, it passed, and President Grant later signed, the Federal Judiciary Act of 1870,[8] which created both the Department of Justice and the OSG, stating, "There shall be in [the] Department of Justice an officer learned in the law, to assist the Attorney-General in the performance of his duties to be called the solicitor-general."[9] The Act also declared that two officers would assist the AG and SG in the performance of their duties. With this Act, Congress fundamentally transformed the government's legal capabilities.

Members of Congress had three goals in mind when they passed the Act. One goal – probably the primary goal – was to save money. When reading the legislative history of the Act, one cannot escape Congress's strong desire to save money by avoiding legal fees charged by private counsel. Indeed, the bill itself came out of the Committee on Retrenchment. Collins English Dictionary (2009) defines retrenchment as "the act of reducing expenditure in order to improve financial stability." Numerous comments from representatives and senators attest to the importance they placed on savings. House Judiciary Committee member William Lawrence (R-OH) stated, "This bill is . . . a measure of economy. It will reduce the expenditures for legal services."[10] Another representative who spearheaded the bill claimed it would address the "great expense the Government have been put to in the conduct of the numerous litigations" in which it was involved.[11] Senator James W. Patterson (R-NH) claimed, "The object of this bill is to cut off that extra and unnecessary expense to the Government."[12] Cost savings, put plainly, were on their minds.

---

[8]   Act of June 22, 1870, ch. 150, 16 Stat. 162 § 2.
[9]   See 5 U.S.C. §293.
[10] *Congressional Globe*, 41st Congress, 2d Session, 3038. Statement of Representative William Lawrence.
[11] *Congressional Globe*, 41st Congress, 2d Session, 3038. Statement of Representative Thomas A. Jenckes (R-RI).
[12] *Congressional Globe*, 41st Congress, 2d Session, 3038. Statement of Senator Patterson.

Congress also sought to centralize control over federal litigation. Prior to the Act, major governmental departments had their own legal officers (Waxman 1998), which meant that the government could not coordinate on one joint legal position. This made the government's position confusing and complicated the president's obligation to execute the laws. As Representative Jenckes stated, the government often observed "one interpretation of the laws of the United States in one Department and another interpretation in another Department."[13] By passing the bill, Congress aimed to "make one symmetrical whole of the law department of [the] Government."[14] The Act would give the AG – and the SG – the power to centralize U.S. appellate strategy. This new unity would also enhance responsibility, as the AG could be held accountable for the government's legal positions. No longer would the government be stuck with divergent legal goals (and diffused responsibility); instead, the Act would coordinate U.S. legal strategy.

Of course, Congress also aspired to fill the new office with a highly qualified and influential SG. Though members devoted surprisingly little attention to the qualifications and skills of future SGs, they did evince a desire to obtain an SG with "such learning, ability and experience, that he [could] be sent . . . into any court wherever the Government has any interest in litigation, and there present the case of the United States as it should be presented" (Chamberlain 1987, 381). This comment suggests not only that Congress intended to fill the post with an intelligent and persuasive SG but also that they believed he would ride circuit and travel anywhere the interests of the United States needed defense. As if to underscore the premium Congress placed on quality, it removed the statutory requirement that the AG be "learned in the law" and placed it on the SG. Congress, in short, wanted someone who could influence judges wherever the United States conducted its appellate business.

Congress achieved its goals. First, it quickly avoided paying fees for outside legal counsel. By December 1872, government attorneys exclusively handled the United States's Supreme Court litigation (Waxman 1998). Second, the SG became the government's appellate fulcrum. As we explain more fully later, appeals on behalf of the United States occur only when permitted by the SG.[15] Third, the SG is one of "the most skilled advocates before the United States Supreme Court" (Scalia and Garner 2008, 33). Put plainly, though they never took up the practice of circuit riding, SGs, and the attorneys who work within their office, live up to the "extravagant expectations" created by the Act (Waxman 1998).

[13] *Congressional Globe*, 41st Congress, 2d Session, 3036. Statement of Representative Jenckes.
[14] *Congressional Globe*, 41st Congress, 2d Session, 3035. Statement of Representative Jenckes.
[15] There are a handful of exceptions to this rule, but for the vast majority of cases, no appeal will be filed unless approved by the SG.

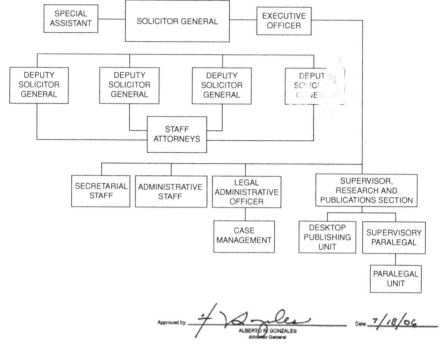

FIGURE 2.1. Hierarchy of the Office of the Solicitor General.

ORGANIZATION OF THE SOLICITOR GENERAL'S OFFICE

Today, the OSG has three tiers. As Figure 2.1 shows, the SG sits atop the office. At the next level sit four deputy SGs. Finally, at the bottom tier are the assistant SGs (staff attorneys), who are responsible for most of the cases coming out of the office.

SGs, sitting atop the office, are both legal and political actors. Most SGs have superlative legal backgrounds, having graduated from top-notch law schools, clerked for Supreme Court justices and prestigious circuit court judges, performed ably in some government attorney capacity, and maybe even won a number of Supreme Court decisions. At the same time, the SG usually has extensive political experience, having worked for one of the political parties, served in a president's administration, or otherwise made his or her name known in political circles. In other words, when it comes time to nominate someone to be SG, presidents will look to individuals with legal qualifications and a shared worldview.

Indeed, a cursory examination of two recent SGs shows the importance of impressive legal and political credentials. Consider former SG Elana Kagan.

Kagan received her law degree from Harvard Law (magna cum laude). She clerked for D.C. circuit judge (and later Clinton adviser) Abner Mikva and went on to clerk for Supreme Court justice Thurgood Marshall. She later was a professor at Chicago Law and went on to become dean of Harvard Law. Her political experience, like her legal capabilities, marked her for upward mobility. In the 1990s, she was President Clinton's associate White House counsel and later went on to serve in similar political capacities for Clinton.

Former SG Kenneth Starr also displayed legal and political credentials. Starr received his law degree from Duke University, clerked for Judge David W. Dyer of the Fifth Circuit Court of Appeals, and went on to clerk for Chief Justice Warren Burger. After working in the private sector for a few years and for the Justice Department, President Reagan appointed him to the D.C. Circuit Court of Appeals, where he confirmed his conservative credentials. President George H. W. Bush nominated him to be SG in 1989. In short, both of these SGs, like their predecessors, had impressive legal qualifications and made important political connections that led them to the office.

As Table 2.1 shows, since Congress created the OSG, forty-six people have served formally as SG, and nearly all served with distinction.[16] Only two SGs appear to have underperformed in any systematic sense. The Supreme Court apparently sent word to President Franklin Roosevelt that Solicitor General James Crawford Biggs was doing a horrible job. After Biggs's first term as SG, the Court notified the president "that Biggs should be forbidden to argue again if the Administration wanted to win any cases before the Court" (Caplan 1987, 13). J. Howard McGrath apparently left his duties "almost completely to his assistants" and never once argued a case before the Court (Caplan 1987, 14). Still, these are the exceptions. The SGs who have represented the government over time have performed ably.

Directly below the SG are four deputy SG's. Of these four, three are career deputies and one is the principal deputy (the principal deputy is often called the "political deputy"; Pacelle 2003, 38). The career deputies are subject matter specialists in legal areas. For example, at the time of this writing, Deputy SG Michael Dreeben is in charge of overseeing the OSG's criminal law cases. Deputy SGs are not attached to the president's broader policy agenda; indeed, they often become career deputies after having served as assistant SGs over numerous presidential administrations, during which time they distinguish themselves as capable legal advocates.

---

[16] A handful of people served as acting SG while the president searched for someone else to nominate formally for the job.

TABLE 2.1. *Name, length of tenure, and appointing presidents of solicitors general of the United States*

Solicitor general	Dates served	Appointing president
Donald B. Verrilli Jr.	June 2011–present	Obama
Neal Katyal[a]	May 2010–June 2011	Obama
Elana Kagan	March 2009–May 2010	Obama
Edwin Kneedler[a]	January–March 2009	Obama
Gregory G. Garre	October 2008–January 2009	W. Bush
Gregory G. Garre[a]	June–October 2008	W. Bush
Paul D. Clement	June 2005–June 2008	W. Bush
Paul D. Clement[a]	June 2004–June 2005	W. Bush
Theodore B. Olson	June 2001–July 2004	W. Bush
Barbara D. Underwood[a]	January–June 2001	W. Bush
Seth P. Waxman	November 1997–January 2001	Clinton
Walter E. Dellinger III[a]	August 1996–October 1997	Clinton
Drew S. Days III	May 1993–July 1996	Clinton
Kenneth Starr	May 1989–January 1993	H. W. Bush
Charles Fried	October 1985–January 1989	Reagan
Rex Lee	August 1981–June 1985	Reagan
Wade H. McCree Jr.	March 1977–August 1981	Carter
Robert H. Bork	June 1973–January 1977	Nixon
Erwin N. Griswold[b]	October 1967–June 1973	L. Johnson[b]
Thurgood Marshall	August 1965–August 1967	L. Johnson
Archibald Cox	January 1961–July 1965	Kennedy
J. Lee Rankin	August 1956–January 1961	Eisenhower
Simon E. Sobeloff	February 1954–July 1956	Eisenhower
Walter J. Cummings Jr.	December 1952–March 1953	Truman
Philip B. Perlman	July 1947–August 1952	Truman
J. Howard McGrath	October 1945–October 1946	Truman
Charles Fahy	November 1941–September 1945	F. Roosevelt
Francis Biddle	January 1940–September 1941	F. Roosevelt
Robert H. Jackson	March 1938–January 1940	F. Roosevelt
Stanley Reed	March 1935–January 1938	F. Roosevelt
James Crawford Biggs	May 1933–March 1935	F. Roosevelt
Thomas D. Thacher	March 1930–May 1933	Hoover
Charles Evans Hughes Jr.	May 1929–April 1930	Hoover
William D. Mitchell	June 1925–March 1929	Coolidge
James M. Beck	June 1921–June 1925	Harding
William L. Frierson	June 1920–June 1921	Wilson
Alexander C. King	November 1918–May 1920	Wilson
John William Davis	August 1913–November 1918	Wilson
William Marshall Bullitt	July 1912–March 1913	Taft
Frederick W. Lehmann	December 1910–July 1912	Taft
Lloyd Wheaton Bowers	April 1909–September 1910	Taft

Solicitor general	Dates served	Appointing president
Henry M. Hoyt	February 1903–March 1909	T. Roosevelt
John K. Richards	July 1897–March 1903	McKinley
Holmes Conrad	February 1895–July 1897	Cleveland
Lawrence Maxwell Jr.	April 1893–January 1895	Cleveland
Charles H. Aldrich	March 1892–May 1893	B. Harrison
William Howard Taft	February 1890–March 1892	B. Harrison
Orlow W. Chapman	May 1889–January 1890	B. Harrison
George A. Jenks	July 1886–May 1889	Cleveland
John Goode	May 1885–August 1886	Cleveland
Samuel F. Phillips	November 1872–May 1885	Grant
Benjamin H. Bristow	October 1870–November 1872	Grant

[a] Denotes acting solicitor general.
[b] Erwin Griswold was nominated by Lyndon Johnson and stayed on through much of the Nixon presidency.

The political deputy, conversely, is selected by the SG to act as an intermediary between himself and the assistant SGs (and even the deputy SGs) while furthering the president's agenda (Pacelle 2003, 42). The political deputy position was created in 1983 to circumvent the awkward situation that arose when the SG was unable to participate in a case, leaving the career deputies responsible for advocating the president's position – a position with which they disagreed. The problem came to a head in *Bob Jones University v. United States* (1983), a case in which the Internal Revenue Service (IRS) sought to strip the university of its tax-exempt status because it engaged in racial discrimination. When Solicitor General Lee had to recuse himself from the case for conflict of interest reasons, Lawrence Wallace, a career deputy, was left in charge of the politically sensitive case. The president opposed the IRS's move and agreed with the university, which argued that its actions were based on religious motivations and were therefore protected. Wallace, however, agreed with the IRS and had, in fact, already made his position clear to the Court in the government's certiorari filing. As such, he was now being asked to change positions midstream. Given that the president was (and, last we checked, still is) constitutionally charged with executing the law, the stalemate led to something of a constitutional crisis within the executive branch. Eventually, Wallace signed the government's brief, which reflected the president's argument, but he included a footnote at the bottom of the brief in which he stated that he personally disagreed with the arguments made within it. The government lost. After the case was over, however, the president and the SG recognized that they needed to ensure that such a dynamic did not occur again. Thus they created the political deputy position as an additional political buffer between the President and SG and the career deputies (Salokar 1992, 61–62).

Below the SG and the deputies are seventeen to twenty assistant SGs (also called staff attorneys; Pacelle 2003, 38), each of whom is served by paralegals and legal secretaries. Unlike the deputies, the assistant SGs are generalists. These professionals have remarkable qualifications and often serve over the course of multiple administrations (Salokar 1992, 57–58). They are highly educated, highly motivated people who have faith in their work and in the office. They litigate on behalf of the United States and do so largely without political bias (Perry 1991). They are, according to numerous sources, consummate professionals (Salokar 1992; Perry 1991). Many assistants have gone on to become Supreme Court justices, federal district and circuit court judges, and attorneys general and to hold other important positions in the private and public sectors.

FUNCTIONS OF THE SOLICITOR GENERAL

Today, the SG serves two primary functions. First, he is a gatekeeper who controls the government's access to the Supreme Court. In this capacity, the OSG centralizes US appellate strategy. Second, SGs and the lawyers in the OSG are lawyers in the normal sense of the word. They provide representation to the government and pursue its interests before the Court.

Centralization

The SG controls the government's access to the Supreme Court, which gives him the power to coordinate US appellate strategy, centralize it, and make it speak with one voice. The SG determines which, among the thousands of cases the government loses in lower courts each year, it will appeal to the Supreme Court. If the government loses a case in a lower court, it cannot appeal that loss to the Supreme Court without the SG's permission. If an agency loses a decision in a circuit court, for example, and believes that decision was wrong, it can only file an appeal with the Supreme Court if the SG permits it to do so and spearheads the appeal.[17]

---

[17] Additionally, according to Michael Dreeben (2010), the OSG will determine whether the United States will appeal a loss from a federal district court to a circuit court of appeals. When, however, the United States wins in the district court and the case is appealed by the losing litigant, the U.S. Attorney argues the appeal without discussions with the OSG.

By choosing the cases and the issues the government will pursue before the Supreme Court, the SG can exercise control over the types of cases appealed by the government to the Court and set the administration's policy. For example, simply by blocking access to appeals, the SG's veto can quash an agency's attempted policy. This power, of course, may be particularly useful for a president who observes poor relations with the agency. But more than that, the SG can use its gatekeeping power to side with one agency over another. When two agencies conflict over the proper policy for the government, the SG, by selecting which will be the official government position, can clarify the government's position for the Court and for the agencies. Former solicitor general Rex Lee summarized the SG's gatekeeping power succinctly:

> If we've got the [FCC] on one side of an issue and the Commerce Department on the other, and I decide that the government's over-all [sic] interest is better served by the F.C.C. . . . That means we'll take the F.C.C.'s position to the Supreme Court and the Commerce Department won't go there at all. (quoted in Jenkins 1983, 737)[18]

The SG also plays the role of gatekeeper to the extent that he is the final arbiter regarding whether the government will file an amicus curiae brief in the Court. An amicus curiae brief is a brief filed by a person or entity, not a party to the dispute but who has an interest in its outcome (Owens and Epstein 2005). If the government is not involved in a case, the SG can inform the Court of its views.[19] The government can file an amicus brief at either the agenda stage or at the merits stage of a case, though, as an empirical matter, the SG files the vast majority of its voluntary amicus briefs at the merits stage.[20] When the government files an amicus brief with the Court, it is able to present

[18] It should be noted that infrequently, the SG will allow independent agencies to argue their own cases and/or pursue appeals without the SG's express permission. Chamberlain, for example, points out that Solicitor General Griswold had an agreement with the National Labor Relations Board that cases dealing with standard administrative law issues would go through the OSG, whereas labor law cases requiring more technical knowledge could be argued by NLRB counsel (Chamberlain 1987, 389). On the whole, however, the SG coordinates all of the government's activities before the Court. Indeed, the Court itself has affirmed its support of the SG's coordination function. See, e.g., *The Gray Jacket*, 72 U.S. 370 (1866); *The Confiscation Cases*, 74 U.S. 454 (1868); *U.S. v. Throckmorton*, 98 U.S. 61 (1878); *U.S. v. San Jacinto Tin Co.*, 125 U.S. 273 (1888); *FEC v. NRA Political Victory Fund*, 513 U.S. 88 (1994). For more on this, see Waxman (1998).

[19] Supreme Court Rule 37 states that the United States can file an amicus curiae brief at its discretion, without satisfying the normal requirement placed on other groups to obtain the permission of the parties. By coordinating the cases in which the government files amicus briefs, the SG gains further leverage over its legal message.

[20] For more on the difference between a voluntary amicus brief and a forced (or "invited") amicus brief, see Chapter 4.

its views on a case, and the broader policy consequences of a decision in the Court, despite the fact that it is not a named party in the suit. In such cases, the government has perhaps more room to roam on policy grounds than when it is a party, as a loss may not engender the same direct, negative consequences.

Representation

The second function the SG – and the OSG – fulfills is to provide quality legal representation on behalf of the United States in the Supreme Court. When deciding whether to appeal a case to the Court, the OSG goes through a fairly extensive process. OSG staff attorneys are in charge of consulting with attorneys from the agencies and divisions of the Department of Justice who were originally involved in the case (Salokar 1992, 63). After discussing the case with those attorneys, the assistant SG makes a recommendation to the deputy solicitor general who specializes in the issue involved in the case.[21] The deputy, in turn, will either write his own memo or annotate the career attorney's memo and present that information to the SG (Chamberlain 1987, 382).[22] The SG then reads the recommendations (and other case material) before determining whether the United States will seek review (Cooper 1990).[23]

When the SG decides to move forward with a case, the office flies into high gear. The assistant SGs prepare the government's petition for certiorari (or jurisdictional statement, if an appeal). The government's certiorari petitions are better, on average, than those filed by all other parties. The SG knows how to frame the petition and what factors (such as lower court conflict, case importance, and policy consequences) matter most to the Court when it determines whether to grant review (Perry 1991; Black and Owens 2009a).

If the Court grants review to the government's petitions – which it typically does – one or two attorneys in the office will be assigned primary responsibility for the case (Salokar 1992). At this point, the assistant SGs will work closely with federal agencies involved in the case to obtain useful technical information, to conduct legal research, and to find other materials that will support the government. Since the assistant SGs are generalists, they serve an effective filtering mechanism. They will take the arguments made by the agencies

---

[21] If the agency or division attorney disagrees with the assistant SG's recommendation, it can appeal to the SG (Salokar 1992).

[22] See also "Confirmation Hearing on the Nomination of Paul D. Clement to Be Solicitor General of the United States," p. 39.

[23] A similar process occurs when the government seeks to file an amicus curiae brief. When the Court invites the SG, he must file a brief in the case but still retains control over what the brief says.

and translate them into more understandable language – language generalist judges can understand. Once the brief is written, it gets passed up to the deputy SG who has responsibility for the issue in the case. The deputy reviews the brief, makes recommendations, and will make sure the SG sees a version. The SG has the final review of the brief. Once the SG approves the brief, the office files it with the Court. The staff attorney who drafts the merits brief often presents the oral argument to the Court. As Salokar (1992) notes, the SG himself generally argues six cases per term, the deputies each about five, and the assistants three.

It is worth pointing out that while the SG exercises gatekeeping powers and represents (along with the OSG) the government before the Court, multiple actors within the OSG and the executive branch provide information and recommendations. Former solicitor general Charles Fried summed up the interactive relationship between agencies and the OSG quite well in a hearing before the House of Representatives:

> We do not sit on the fifth floor of the Department of Justice, scan the legal universe, and then decide what happens. Rather, they, divisions and departments of Government with programmatic responsibilities come to us with recommendations, which we approve, and then proceed, in the Supreme Court, to brief and argue for them. (Salokar 1992, 13)

SOLICITOR GENERAL SUCCESS

Like the Green Bay Packers of the 1960s, the SG rarely loses. The OSG is astonishingly successful throughout the decision-making process. As we show more fully later, at both the agenda stage and the merits termination stage, the OSG usually obtains its preferred outcome. The Court grants review to cases the OSG wants it to review. And when deciding that case, the Court often follows the position advocated by the SG.

At the agenda stage, lawyers in the OSG often persuade the Court to hear the government's cases. The Supreme Court is more likely to grant review to OSG petitions and petitions it supports than to those supported by any other actor (Black and Owens 2009a; Caldeira and Wright 1988; Provine 1980). The OSG's grant rate for cert petitions ranges from 75 to 90 percent, a standard that no other party or law firm comes close to matching (Perry 1991). Caplan (1987) points out that while the Court hears roughly 80 percent of SG cert petitions, it agrees to review a mere 3 percent of those filed by other lawyers (see also Jenkins 1983). And Scigliano (1971) finds that between the 1958 and 1967 terms, the Court accepted 70 percent of the government's cert petitions but only 7 percent of non-OSG cert petitions.

Our own data also reveal that the Court is much more likely to accept OSG recommendations at the agenda stage than the recommendations of other participants. We randomly sampled 756 paid non–death penalty petitions coming out of a federal court of appeals that made the Supreme Court's discuss list during the 1986–1993 terms;[24] that is, when the OSG was a party (either petitioner or respondent) or an amicus curiae supporting one of the parties, how frequently did the Court adopt the SG's recommendation? When the SG was not at all involved in the case (either as a party or amicus participant), the Court granted review to the petition about 26 percent of the time. (This number is larger than the figures we cited in the previous paragraph because those studies examine all petitions filed, while we look here at the grant rate of those cases that already made the Court's discuss list.) When we introduce the SG into the mix, however, things change dramatically.

Consider instances in which the SG was the petitioner and asked the Court to review – and overturn – the lower court decision. As we show in Figure 2.2, the percentage of petitions in which the Court granted review more than doubles to 70 percent. The Court became much more interested in hearing the case when the government was the petitioner. Conversely, when the government was the respondent, and implores the Court to deny review to the case, it granted review less frequently. While the usual grant rate (i.e., when the United States was not involved) is 26 percent, that percentage drops to a hair over 23 percent when the government was the respondent.

The story is similar when we examine the SG's agenda success as an amicus curiae. When the OSG voluntarily took a position in favor of granting review, the Court granted review almost 88 percent of the time. We should point out that when the SG weighed in as an amicus participant and recommended that the Court deny review, the Court actually reviewed the petition more often than the baseline figure. This likely has to do with the signal provided by the SG's amicus brief. As Caldeira and Wright (1988) point out, filing a brief to try to block Court review sends the Court a signal that the case is important. In short, with the exception of the OSG as a pro-respondent amicus – which

---

[24] As we explain more fully in Chapter 4, the discuss list is the first round of cuts through which a case must pass before proceeding to the Court. Prior to each conference during which the Court discusses cert petitions, the chief justice circulates a list with the names of all petitions he thinks the Court should discuss. Other justices can add cases to this list. Once finalized, the chief sends out this list to the full Court. This "discuss list" provides the names of all cases the Court will discuss (and formally vote on whether to review) at its next conference. Cases that do not appear on the discuss list are summarily denied cert by the Court. Roughly one-third of paid petitions end up making it onto the discuss list.

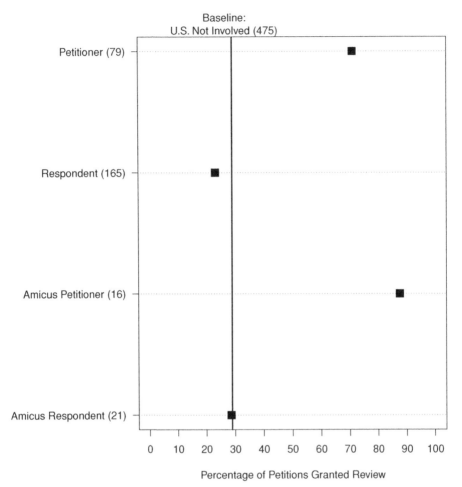

FIGURE 2.2. Success rate of solicitor general during agenda-setting stage. Data collected by the authors.

Caldeira and Wright's signaling argument explains – the Court is quite likely to follow the OSG's recommendation at the agenda stage.

The OSG is also highly successful at the merits stage. As Epstein and her coauthors show, during the Rehnquist Court era, the OSG won over 62 percent of all cases in which the United States was a direct party. During the Burger Court era, the OSG won over 67 percent of cases in which the United States was a party and, during the Warren Court era, it won over 59 percent of such cases (Epstein, Segal, Spaeth and Walker 2007). Indeed, as Figure 2.3 shows, the SG's success at the merits stage is astonishing. The average win rate for the

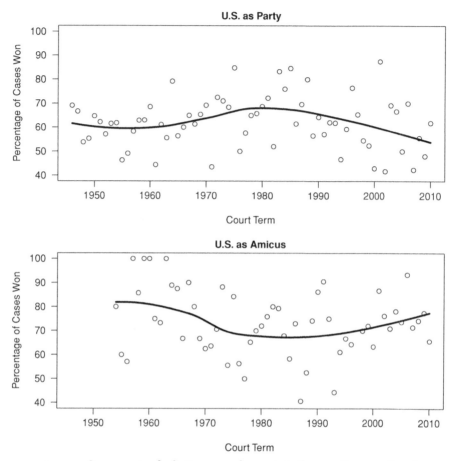

FIGURE 2.3. Success rate of solicitor general as party to the case (top panel) and as amicus (bottom panel) at merits stage. The thick black line is a loess smoothing line, which we estimated using the *loess* function in R. Data from 1946–2004 (party) and 1954–1996 (amicus) come from Epstein, Segal, Spaeth and Walker (2007). Data for 2004–2010 (party) and 1998–2010 (amicus) were collected by the authors from the OSG's Web site. Amicus data for the 1997 term were unavailable.

SG when he participates as a party to a case never dips below 50 percent and nearly always hovers close to 60 percent. The SG's success rate as an amicus participant at the merits stage is even higher than as a direct party. In fact, in some Court terms, the OSG won 100 percent of its cases as amici. To be sure, there are some years in which the SG's office performs better (or worse) than others, a feature that is worthy of study (see, e.g., Wohlfarth 2009), but the general pattern remains fairly consistent over time. The OSG seems to achieve the disposition it wants on the merits of cases.

Of course, there are other ways to measure SG success at the merits stage. These measures tell a similar story. Consider the extent to which the Court incorporates in its opinions arguments made by the SG. Spriggs and Wahlbeck (1997) find that the Court is more likely to employ OSG arguments than arguments made by other amicus curiae participants. The probability that the Court would use an argument made in an amicus brief by an average amicus participant was just 0.26 but skyrocketed to 0.64 when the OSG made the argument. Corley (2008) uses plagiarism software to examine whether the Court's majority opinions "borrow" from the OSG's briefs more than other briefs. They do. Corley finds that when the SG is an appellant in a case, the Court becomes 16 percent more likely to draw from that brief than from the others in the case. And when the brief is written by the SG's office, there is a 49 percent increase in probability that the Court will employ more words from it than from the other party's brief.

Put simply, regardless of the stage of decision making or the measurement used to examine OSG success, the findings are clear. The SG and his or her office are highly successful. Whether success comes in the form of getting the Court to hear a case (or decline to hear it) or to find for the government on the merits, the office's success is beyond all others.

Congress created the OSG to overcome the government's considerable resource constraints, to centralize control over its cases, and to win more often before the Court. Early in the country's history, the AG alone was responsible for the government's litigation before the Court. As the country grew, though, and the caseload increased, the AG was simply unable to perform as strongly in all his capacities as he and Congress wished. To surmount these problems, Congress allowed the AG to contract litigation out to private lawyers. This solution led to even greater problems. Soon, the country was faced with stiff legal bills and divergent appellate strategies; that is, a lack of control. Congress created the OSG to impose order on the government's appellate practices, to save money, and to win cases. And that is exactly what happened. Today, the OSG is more successful than all other law firms.

Just what the OSG's success means, however, is less clear. Does the OSG actually influence justices to rule in ways they otherwise would not prefer to rule? Or is there something less unique going on? And if the OSG does influence the Court, why? Is it because OSG attorneys have more experience than others? That they have more resources? Are their victories tied to the separation of powers and their capacities as executive branch officials? Or is it something else, such as professionalism and quality? Each of these theories deserves our attention. Accordingly, the next chapter addresses them individually. Our hope is to inform the reader of these theories for OSG success and highlight their observable implications so that in our empirical chapters, we can discuss which among them explains OSG influence.

3

Explanations for Solicitor General Success

In 1983 Scott Nelson read a job advertisement in a trade journal for a position as a monitoring systems engineer at King Faisal Specialist Hospital in Riyadh, Saudi Arabia.[1] The Saudi hospital – which was run by the Saudi government – had contracted with a U.S. firm, the Hospital Corporation of America (HCA), to help with its recruiting. Nelson contacted the HCA and expressed his interest in the job. In short order, he received an interview with the Saudi hospital. After he returned home to the United States from his interview, he was offered – and accepted – the job.

Soon after Nelson began his job in Saudi Arabia, he ran into trouble. He discovered a number of safety defects at the hospital and reported them to his superiors. They never fixed the problems. So Nelson informed a Saudi government commission of the defects. Apparently, this was out of bounds. Shortly after contacting the government commission, Nelson was told by his superiors to go to the hospital's security office. There he was arrested (without being told why), beaten, placed in a rat-infested jail, and forced to fight other prisoners for food. Not until days later did Saudi officials inform his wife that he was jailed. And even then, they never told her why he was jailed or when he would be released. All they told her was that they would release him only if she provided them with sexual favors. Finally, at the behest of a U.S. senator – after Nelson had been held for thirty-nine days – the Saudi government freed him. When he returned to the United States, Nelson sued Saudi Arabia and the King Faisal Hospital.

From the start, Nelson's lawsuit faced an imposing obstacle – the Foreign Sovereign Immunities Act of 1976.[2] The law stripped U.S. courts of the

---

[1] The facts of the case can be found in the Supreme Court's opinion in *Saudi Arabia v. Nelson*, 507 U.S. 349 (1993), as well as in the cert pool memo in the case (91-522) (Epstein, Segal, and Spaeth 2007).
[2] 28 U.S.C. §1604.

jurisdiction to hear cases where foreign countries were parties; that is, following centuries of international law holding that nation-states were sovereign within their borders, the law prohibited U.S. citizens from suing other countries or their agents for acts committed in those countries. The law, however, carved out an important exception that Nelson sought to use. It held that a foreign state would not be immune from suit in the United States where the foreign government's action was based on a commercial activity "carried on" in the United States.[3] If Nelson could show that his damages were the result of some commercial activities that took place in the United States by Saudi Arabia, he could invoke the Court's jurisdiction.

First in line, the federal district court that heard the case determined that Nelson's damages were not the result of commercial activity and thus did not meet the law's exception. On appeal, the Circuit Court of Appeals for the 11th Circuit gave the phrase *commercial activity* a much broader interpretation. It held that Nelson's damages were the consequence of commercial activity taking place in the United States. But for the recruitment ad, which occurred in the United States (and Nelson's communication with HCA in the United States), Nelson would not have taken the job and suffered his damages. As such, the injuries were based on commercial activity that took place in America.

On November 18, 1991, the Supreme Court held a conference to determine whether to hear the case. Six justices voted to seek the views of the solicitor general (SG). Perhaps not surprisingly, given Justice White's penchant for granting review (Owens and Simon 2012), he voted to grant review. Justices Blackmun and Stevens believed it was not necessary to grant or to invite the office of the solicitor general (OSG) to participate. Because at least four justices voted to call for the views of the OSG, though, the Court issued an order seeking its views.

The OSG's amicus brief asserted that the Court should grant review to the case and reverse the lower court decision. Unlike the circuit court, the OSG believed that the Saudi government's actions simply were not commercial in nature. The beatings were not directly tied to commerce in the United States. To be sure, the beatings would not have taken place but for the recruitment ad which ran in the United States, but nevertheless, the ad and the beatings were so remote from each other in time and context that they were not part of "commercial activity."

At the Court's next conference vote, every justice who voted to call for the views of the solicitor general (CVSG) now voted to grant. Justice White again voted to grant, while Justice Stevens held tight to his deny vote. Justice

---

[3] 28 U.S.C. §1605(a)(2).

Blackmun, however, despite his earlier preference to deny review, switched his vote to grant. With a cert vote of 8–1, the case would move forward.

After reviewing briefs and hearing oral argument, a Court majority reversed the circuit court and determined that the Foreign Sovereign Immunities Act of 1976 did indeed block the courts from hearing the case. Following the logic of the OSG's position, and taking a restricted view of commercial activity, the majority argued that Nelson's damages were not based on Saudi Arabia's commercial activity. Put plainly, the beatings were too far removed from anything commercial in nature to fall within the purview of the sovereign immunity exception. Justice White, joined by Justice Blackmun, filed a special concurrence (a separate opinion agreeing with the outcome in the case, but on different legal grounds) in which he agreed that the decision should have been reversed, but on different grounds. They argued that Saudi Arabia's actions were commercial in nature (the beatings were disciplinary behavior for Nelson's whistle-blowing) but were not based on commercial activity occurring *in the United States*. In short, according to both the majority and concurrences, Nelson had no judicial recourse in the United States.

Certainly the facts in the *Nelson* case were unique. Most Supreme Court cases do not involve beatings at the hands of despotic foreign governments. Still, *Nelson* highlights dynamics that are similar in nature to many cases that involve the OSG: two parties sought an outcome in the Court and asked the justices to adopt their position, and both parties faced skepticism from the Court. For example, Justice Blackmun quite clearly did not want to grant review to the case. His internal notes to his clerks show that he thought the dispute should have been addressed in diplomatic channels rather than in the judicial arena. Indeed, his first conference vote in the case was to deny review. Yet, after receiving the SG's brief and the arguments contained therein, he reversed his position. What is more, Blackmun adopted some of the SG's arguments. Why did Blackmun switch his vote in the case after receiving the OSG's recommendation? And why did a majority of justices on the Court in *Nelson* adopt the SG's position? Did justices in this case – and others – vote in line with the SG because he influenced them, or for some other reason?

When it comes to explaining the SG's success before the Court, there is no shortage of studies. Scholars have put forth a number of theories that seek to explain OSG success. Though these theories are important, and we examine them in detail in this chapter, they do not explain whether the OSG *influences* the Court. What is needed is a research design and modeling strategy that comes much closer to making the kinds of causal inferences that would allow us to determine if the OSG influences the Court. In the following chapters, we seek to do just that. But for now, we believe it is necessary to explain the existing theories, their limitations, and their observable implications. Once we provide this information, we can, in the following chapters, test the theories and explain which best explain OSG influence.

THEORIES OF SOLICITOR GENERAL SUCCESS

Scholars have dedicated lengthy books (Pacelle 2003; Salokar 1992; Caplan 1987) and numerous articles (Lemos 2009; Thompson and Watchell 2009; Wohlfarth 2009; Nicholson and Collins 2008; Pacelle 2006; Deen, Ignagni, and Meernik 2005; Bailey, Kamoie, and Maltzman 2005; Zorn 2002; Meinhold and Shull 1998; Segal 1988; Segal and Reedy 1988) that seek to explain SG success. Some scholars argue that the OSG succeeds so often because the office is an agent of the Court (an approach that has merit but whose discussion has been corrupted by cliché). Other scholars argue that the OSG wins because it is a repeat player. A related argument holds that the OSG is so successful because it employs, on average, the best attorneys in the country. Additional theories hold that the OSG wins so often for ideological or separation-of-powers reasons. Still others suggest that SG success might be a function of strategic case selection – that the OSG primarily participates in cases its lawyers predict they will win. In what follows, we address each of these theories.

The Solicitor General as Agent of the Court . . . or Consummate Legal Professional?

One view of SG success holds that the OSG wins because the Court trusts the unbiased, objective information OSG lawyers provide it. Attorneys in the OSG present the Court with impartial information and do not make legal arguments or otherwise take action that would impair the integrity of the Court (Caplan 1987). Sometimes called the *Agent of the Court* theory, the essence of the argument is that OSG lawyers succeed because they make balanced, principled arguments before the Court. Lawyers in the office believe that they have an obligation to provide the Court with neutral, unbiased information that reflects the proper (or at least, a proper) interpretation of the law. To be sure, there will be times when solicitors make overly political arguments to the Court (Wohlfarth 2009), but by and large, SGs and the attorneys who work within the office are consummate professionals who believe in the roles they play and in the Court as an institution. As Deputy Solicitor General Michael Dreeben once stated, "the Solicitor General owes a duty of unflinching candor to the Court" (Dreeben 2010).

Evidence of SG professionalism can be found throughout the OSG's interactions with the Court. For example, the OSG screens cases and will refuse to appeal those that turn on twisted legal logic or issues that might significantly impair the Court's legitimacy; that is, OSG lawyers observe a degree of "professionalism and expertise" that is unmatched (Salokar 1992, 175), pursuing only the most certworthy cases (Perry 1991).[4] "By tightly controlling the flow of cases to the Court, the solicitor general becomes a valued ally of the justices in their quest to control the Court's burgeoning caseload" (Jenkins 1983, 735).

Research on the theory that the OSG is composed of consummate legal professionals points to the OSG's practice of "acquiescing." The OSG acquiesces when the government is a respondent (and thus won below) but recognizes that the issue involved in the case is important and thus recommends that justices grant review to the certiorari petition (Salokar 1992). Rather than protecting its victory in the lower court, the OSG is willing to expose it to Supreme Court reversal because of the Court's institutional interest in the case.

The practice of confessing error also supports the professionalism theory. When the United States wins a case in a lower federal court on grounds that the OSG believes have turned out to be erroneous, an OSG lawyer will inform the Supreme Court that the decision should be vacated and remanded for reconsideration, though the government prevailed. The confession of error is a strong signal to the Court that the OSG treats its job seriously and therefore can be trusted. Deputy SG Michael Dreeben put it aptly: "The fact that the Solicitor General will confess error two or three times a year is a way of saying that, look, we're standing behind all of the other judgments that we're defending in this Court. The ones that we're letting go are indications to you, Supreme Court, that we're really looking carefully at this" (Dreeben 2010).

Indeed, Perry's seminal text on agenda setting is replete with comments from justices who assert that the SG aids the Court by acting professionally:

> Every solicitor general . . . has taken this job very seriously . . . not to get us to take things that don't require our attention relative to other things that do. They are very careful in their screening and they exercise veto over what can be brought to the board. (Perry 1991, 132)

Another justice put it similarly:

> He is a policeman himself. We assume that he screens out a lot of junk cases. (Perry 1991, 132)

---

[4] This does not mean that the OSG will pursue only those cases that it believes it will win; rather, it will pursue those cases that the Court ought to decide.

Recent empirical work suggests that OSG success may be tied to its objective and professional behavior. For example, Wohlfarth (2009) finds that when SGs deviate from the boundaries of acceptable legal behavior (by taking political positions as amici curiae), justices become less likely to side with them. Wohlfarth's data suggest that SGs who use the amicus brief in an overly political fashion are less likely to see their favored side prevail and will even find themselves less likely to win later when the U.S. is a party to a case. Specifically, the Court sided with the position taken by politically neutral SGs in roughly 87 percent of cases. Conversely, politically biased SGs observed success in just 60 percent of their cases. What was more, excessive amicus politicization created a spillover effect, with political SGs less likely to win when they were respondents in cases.

While the SG under this theory is the consummate legal professional, he is not a "tenth justice." The common depiction of the SG as a tenth justice is unhelpful for at least two reasons. First, it ignores the political nature of the office. As Fisher (1990) points out, the SG is an executive officer who is nominated by the president and serves at his pleasure. Although the SG is largely objective, there are instances in which the president and SG combine to push the president's agenda. We should not lose sight of these instances through silly monikers. Second, the term *tenth justice* inflates what the SG does. The SG does not decide cases; the SG does not grant review to cases; and the SG does not write Supreme Court opinions. To be sure, the SG is very influential throughout all of these processes, but that does not mean scholars should put the SG on the same level as the justices. Accordingly, it is fatuous to call the SG a tenth justice. The SG is no such thing.

So the theory does not argue that SGs are tenth justices; rather, it argues that SGs and OSG attorneys are professionals who take the law and their relationship to the Court seriously. Put plainly, they know their place, and they fulfill their duties with candor. And in response, justices come to trust and rely on them.

The Solicitor General as Repeat Player

A second theory of SG success argues that lawyers in the OSG succeed so often before the Court because they are repeat players. Repeat players are actors who appear before the Court frequently. As Galanter defines it, a repeat player is a "unit which has had and anticipates repeated litigation, which has low stakes in the outcome of any one case, and which has the resources to pursue its long-run interests" (Galanter 1974, 98); that is, repeat players tend to be actors with the resources to stack the deck in their favor and focus on long-run goals. Indeed, three attributes that come along with repeat player status lead to heightened success: repeat players observe frequent interaction with the Court, bring significant resources to bear in their cases, and present the Court with truthful information.

Repeat Players and Experience before the Court

First, repeat players are experienced before the Court and know the types of information justices desire in cases. Repeat players "know how to construct able written and oral presentations [and understand] which style and substance or argument may be most influential in different circumstances" (Scigliano 1971, 183); that is, over time repeat players acquire important insight into the justices themselves and the types of arguments justices accept, which, in turn, leads them to be more successful. As evidence, McGuire (1995) finds that attorneys who are more experienced than their opposing counsel are more likely to win their cases.

Repeat Players and Resource Advantages

Second, repeat players fare well before the Court because they have the resources to stack the deck in their favor (Songer, Kuersten, and Kaheny 2000, 540). They tend to be better lawyers who conduct extensive research. They can anticipate legal challenges to their actions and inoculate themselves against those challenges by creating "comprehensive litigation strategies" (Songer, Sheehan, and Haire 1999, 812). At the trial level, repeat players engage the services of solid expert witnesses, who thereby create better trial court records (which serves them well on appeal). They take polls and hold mock trials, which allow them to test legal arguments in harmless venues. In sum, repeat players can use their resources to bolster their cases and do what is necessary to win.

Repeat Players and Truthful Information

Third, frequent interaction with the Court presents repeat players with strong incentives to provide justices with credible information.[5] Unlike parties who will appear only one time before the Court, repeat players know that they

---

[5] We should note that while the consummate professional legal actor theory also suggests that attorneys in the OSG will provide credible information, the motivation is different. Under the consummate legal professional theory, SGs provide such information because they believe it is part of their duty; that is, as professionals, it is their responsibility to provide unbiased information. The repeat player theory, conversely, presents the motivation as *instrumental*. Because the attorney wants to win, he or she presents credible information. The observable implications are similar, but the motivation is different.

will need Court support in the future. As such, they must prepare for the future; they must concern themselves with it always; and they must jealously protect their reputations. For justices will surely remember attorneys or parties who deceive them or play fast and loose with the facts or law. If they seek to maintain thriving Supreme Court practices and succeed before the Court, they have strong incentives to provide the Court with credible information – even when it contradicts the goals of their present case. As such, justices come to trust the information provided to them by repeat players. They know that such litigators are reliable. When the attorney for a repeat player makes an argument about the law or about legal policy, justices (who generally need information to pursue their own goals) can rely on such information. The end result is that the Court begins to follow the recommendations of repeat players.

The OSG as a Repeat Player

Many have argued that the SG is the quintessential repeat player. The OSG appears before the Court regularly, provides the Court with credible information, and enjoys significant resources. As Figure 3.1 shows, the SG participates as a party or amicus on average in over forty-seven cases per term. (In fact, one lawyer in the OSG, Lawrence Wallace, appeared before the Court to present 157 oral arguments before he retired in 2003 (Baum 2010).) Our own data, which we show in Figure 3.2, tell a similar story. We examined the number of appearances made by attorneys between the 1979 and 2007 Supreme Court terms. When an attorney hails from the OSG, he or she enjoys much more experience than an attorney outside the OSG. More specifically, the average OSG attorney in our sample made 18.2 previous appearances before the Court. The median number of appearances by OSG attorneys was nine, and the ninetieth percentile was forty-four appearances. Consider, conversely, the attorney who never practiced in the OSG. The mean non-OSG attorney during in sample made 2.5 previous appearances before the Court. The median number of appearances by these attorneys was zero, and the ninetieth percentile was only seven appearances.

Not only does the OSG appear regularly before the Court and have extensive experience litigating there, it also enjoys the third feature of a repeat player: significant resources. Salokar (1992) notes that the government "can afford to – and does – litigate over any question of principle regardless of the amount in controversy" (citing Mutterperl 1982). Without being saddled with the financial limitations that constrain private sector attorneys, the government can take on cases simply to further general points of law. Government lawyers can use all the resources at their disposal to pursue a case. This not only gains them

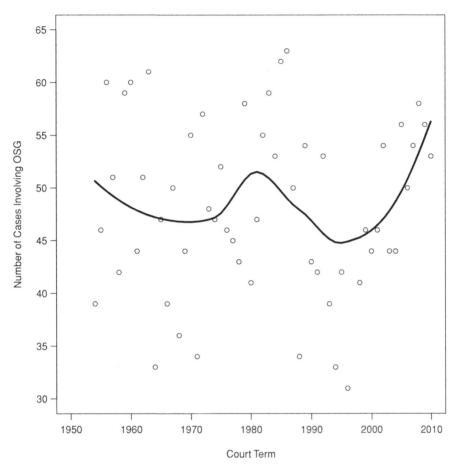

FIGURE 3.1. Number of cases in which the SG participated, 1953–2010 terms. Data for 1953–2004 come from Epstein, Segal, Spaeth, and Walker (2007). Data from 2005–2010 were collected by the authors from the OSG's Web site.

experience before the Court but also allows them to lean on resources that others cannot.

Perhaps the most important resource on which OSG attorneys can rely is their access to the expertise of agencies within the government (Zorn 2002). As we noted earlier, whenever an agency is involved in the Supreme Court, its appellate arm must communicate with the OSG. The result of this constant contact is the sharing of important policy information. OSG lawyers learn substantial amounts of policy information from agency lawyers. And when they do not readily have the answer to policy questions at their fingertips, they can simply discuss it with an agency that has expertise over

Not Affiliated with OSG (N = 5161)

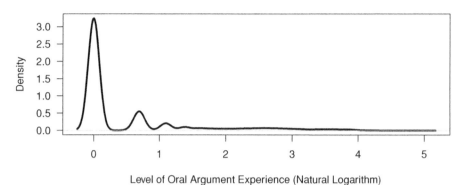

Affiliated with OSG (N = 1543)

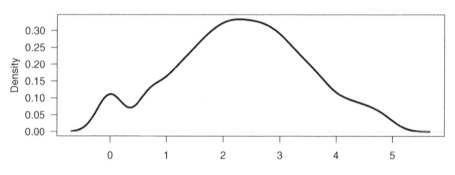

FIGURE 3.2. Kernel density plot of attorney's previous oral argument experience, conditional on affiliation with the OSG. The top panel describes attorneys who were not affiliated with the OSG at the time of argument. The bottom panel shows attorneys who were affiliated with the OSG when they argued before the Court. Note that the values on the *x* axis for both panels are not raw experience counts but rather are equal to the natural logarithm of (1+) an attorney's level of experience (e.g., a value of 1 on the natural log scale is equal to roughly 2.78 appearances, but a natural log value of 5 is equal to approximately 148 appearances).

the matter. This is, of course, a resource that private lawyers largely do not share.

In sum, repeat players know that they must interact with the Court in the future, regularly, and thus will provide credible information. At the same time, having appeared before justices frequently, they can learn what arguments meet with justices' approval and which do not. Because they often enjoy significant resources, they are well positioned to put this information to effective and systematic use. The OSG is a repeat player and enjoys each of these three attributes. As such, the theory goes, it succeeds frequently before the Court.

The Quality of OSG Attorneys

A related theory of SG success holds that lawyers in the OSG win so frequently because they are better advocates than other lawyers. Attorney quality may have less to do with experience or resources, the argument goes, than with innate lawyering ability. The theory suggests that "the quality and intellectual force [of an OSG argument] can persuade judges not only to interpret existing precedents in particular ways but also to develop new legal rules that channel decisionmaking in future cases" (McAtee and McGuire 2007, 261); that is, the attorney quality argument hinges on two components: the ability of quality arguments to persuade justices and OSG attorneys, providing more high-quality arguments than their opposition.

As to the first component, empirical evidence suggests that quality arguments can persuade justices. For example, Johnson, Wahlbeck, and Spriggs (2006) analyze the effect of oral argument quality on a litigant's likelihood of winning and find that attorneys who provide a stronger argument to the Court are more likely to win, even while controlling for justices' policy agreement with the argument proffered by the SG. McAtee and McGuire (2007) further point out that despite the Court's shift to the right in the last two decades, "carefully crafted legal arguments have successfully limited that conservatism" in a host of areas (261). Put plainly, the evidence suggests that there is plenty of room for attorneys to persuade justices with their quality arguments (see also Wahlbeck 1997).

As to the second component, there is reason to believe that OSG lawyers are at least among the best and the brightest lawyers in the country. Salokar (1992, 33) argues that "the members of the solicitor general's office, both the political appointees and the small corps of career civil servants, are some of the best attorneys in our nation." Many of these attorneys once clerked for federal circuit court judges and Supreme Court justices, and most of them graduated from the best law schools in the country. Former SG Charles Fried once explained the qualifications he looked for when hiring attorneys to work in the OSG. The qualifications he sought were unsurprising – attorneys must be very good:

> They have largely to do with very acute analytical and writing abilities, which are demonstrated, first of all, by very high academic records, then, also, by clerkships, appellate court clerkships. And, in many instances, about half

our lawyers are former Supreme Court clerks. And then a certain amount of experience in doing, at a lesser level, I suppose, the kind of work that they would have to do in our office ... altogether we try to get a picture of the person in terms of their analytic and writing abilities. (quoted in Salokar 1992, 58)

Other comments also suggest that the lawyers within the OSG are among the best. Carter Phillips, a former assistant SG, once stated, "The office has great success in getting A-plus lawyers who work hard without an ax to grind" (quoted in Pacelle 2003, 38). Still other scholars refer to them as "smart, highly trained, articulate people who [have] a passion for law" (Caplan 1987, 210).

Because good attorneys are able to persuade the Court to adopt particular legal positions, and because the OSG is full of the best and brightest attorneys in the country, the OSG is more successful than other attorneys and other law firms. Simply put, the cream of the crop can be found in the OSG, and according to the theory the result is a law firm that is astonishingly successful.

The Solicitor General as an Ideological Actor

A very different view of SG success – an ideological theory – holds that the SG succeeds before the Court when he happens to share the same ideological preferences as a majority of justices. This theory argues that the SG is an ideological actor, much like the justices themselves. Solicitors are picked by presidents for ideological reasons, pursue those ideological goals before the Court, and win more often when they are aligned ideologically with a majority of justices. The tenth justice, the partisan theory argues, "is no less political than the other nine" (Bailey, Kamoie, and Maltzman 2005, 226).

Presidents largely select justices and SGs with the same considerations in mind: the pursuit of policy goals. The "selection process is designed to ensure that the solicitor general will share the basic political values of the administration" (Salokar 1992, 3). Presidents employ a vetting process to select SGs who are loyal followers of their broader policy agendas. It is no wonder that Lyndon Johnson selected Thurgood Marshall to be SG, that Jimmy Carter selected Wade McCree, or that George W. Bush selected Theodore Olson. Each of these individuals had a career path that led his appointing president to believe he would be a loyal agent.[6]

---

[6] In fact, this dynamic likely explains why former SGs often discuss how independent they were while serving; they likely did not require much hand-holding from the president or attorney general.

Once selected, SGs often, but not always, follow the president's broad goals. Meinhold and Shull (1998) examine presidential speeches and find that SGs make arguments consistent with the ideological preferences of their supervising presidents. Caplan (1987) and Salokar (1992) argue that SGs often pursue political goals, particularly by filing amicus curiae briefs in agenda cases (i.e., cases in which the government is not a party but about which the adminstration strongly cares). And Fisher (1990) points to historical examples where the SG followed controversial presidential goals. Of course, it is worth pointing out that SGs do not always follow executive preferences. For example, former solicitor general Days recounts that after the federal district court for the District of Columbia struck down the North American Free Trade Agreement and the Mexican stock market plunged, the Clinton administration asked *him* whether he was going to authorize an appeal (Days 1995, 647).

So presidents pick SGs who they predict will loyally follow their goals, and the evidence suggests that SGs often follow those goals. How does this translate into SG success? Empirical evidence shows that justices "condition their support for the solicitor general on the ideological direction of the brief" (Segal 1988, 142). Segal (1988) finds that liberal justices are more likely to support the SG when he files a liberal brief, whereas conservatives are more likely to support him when he files a conservative brief. Deen, Ignagni, and Meernik (2005) agree, arguing that "attitudes and policy preferences among the justices are highly predictive of support for the solicitor general" (76).[7] Wohlfarth (2009) likewise finds that when the Court median becomes more liberal, Democrat-appointed SGs fare better, while Republican SGs fare worse. When the Court becomes more conservative, Republican SGs prevail more often and Democrat SGs less often. Thus, when SGs are ideologically in line with the Court majority, they will be more likely to win.

This all explains why justices who agree ideologically with the SG follow his or her position, but what happens when the Court majority is opposed to the SG ideologically? After all, our earlier descriptive data showed a large winning percentage by the OSG even when facing Court majorities of opposite ideological bents. On this score, the theory is less helpful, though it does suggest that justices pay attention when an SG takes a counterideological position. Ideology can affect the credibility of the signal the SG sends. Bailey, Kamoie, and Maltzman (2005) employed signaling theory to examine the conditions under which justices side with the SG. Their results provided two general

---

[7] Justice Douglas, they find, sided with the SG 42% more when he made a liberal versus a conservative argument. Justice Marshall produced a 25% differential and Justice Fortas a 21% differential. Justice Thomas sided with the SG 21% more when the SG made a conservative claim.

findings. First, they reaffirmed the findings that justices who are ideologically close to the SG (i.e., president) are more likely to support him. Second, they found that if an SG and justice hold competing worldviews, the justice will nevertheless deem the SG's message credible when it is contrary to the SG's general ideological position (see also Calvert 1985). A conservative justice is likely to follow a liberal SG when the SG makes a conservative argument in the case. (Conversely, when the SG and justice are ideological allies but the SG takes a counterideological positions the justice will likely cast a counter-ideological vote.) And even liberal justices will follow the conservative position in the case.

Put together, the theory holds that policy goals largely explain the relationship between the SG and the Court. When a majority of justices and the SG (and, by default, the president) share a worldview, the Court will be more likely to side with the SG. Conversely, when the SG and Court majority disagree, the Court will be less likely to side with the government, unless, of course, the government takes a position that is contrary to its expected ideological position.

The Solicitor General and the Separation of Powers

A further theory of SG success turns on separation-of-powers (SOP) considerations (Epstein and Knight 1998; Johnson 2003). The theory asserts that because justices render decisions in an interdependent environment where Congress and the president must protect, fund, and execute their decisions, justices must hew closely to the legal arguments proffered by the government. Failure to do so could result in political repercussions that not only undo judicial policies but might also damage the Court's legitimacy (Epstein, Knight and Martin 2001).

More specifically, justices care about legislative and executive preferences for the following reasons. Each branch possesses broad powers under the constitution to force justices to do the Washington two-step and engage in a strategic behavior. For example, Congress can initiate and support constitutional amendments to overturn judicial decisions, a power it has used five times. It can alter the Court's composition, which it has done, for political reasons, a number of times. It can reduce the Court's budget, regulate Court procedure, hold judicial salaries constant, and strip the Court of jurisdiction (Owens 2010). It can also impeach and remove justices. While impeachment has only led to the resignation or removal of under a dozen federal judges over time, there is considerable evidence to suggest that a key factor leading to Justice Fortas's resignation was the impeachment charges likely to be leveled against him. Perhaps most important, however, Congress can pass legislation that overrides Supreme Court decisions. Since 1975, each Congress has overridden an average of roughly twelve statutory interpretation decisions, and during the same time period, nearly half of the Court's decisions received some type of congressional hearing (Eskridge 1991; Ignagni and Meernik 1994).

Presidents also have tools they can use against the Court, which might force justices to defer to that branch. Presidents might refuse to enforce the decision, publicly attack it, or otherwise threaten the Court's legitimacy (see, e.g., Staton and Vanberg 2008); that is, they can refuse to enforce the Court's decisions and order cabinet secretaries and other high-ranking officials to ignore them. They can unilaterally create their own executive policies and shift the policy status quo (Moe and Howell 1999; Black et al. 2007), mobilize interest groups to attack and undermine the Court's decisions (Peterson 1992), and use their agenda-setting power to focus public scrutiny on judicial decisions. And of course, they can sign or veto override legislation.

The combination of these powers, the argument goes, will force the Court to anticipate how Congress and the president will respond to its decisions and may even lead justices to adopt positions they would otherwise choose to avoid (Spiller and Gely 1992; Bergara, Richman, and Spiller 2003; Harvey and Friedman 2006; Epstein and Knight 1998). If justices perceive that by voting for their most preferred alternative, they will create policy out of step with the president and key policy makers in Congress (i.e., party medians, committee chairs, chamber medians, filibuster pivots), they will moderate their votes to make policy that is more favorable to them.

Figure 3.3 illustrates. It shows the policy preferences (i.e., ideal points) of each of the relevant pivots in Congress as well as the ideal points of the president and the Court. In the top of Figure 3.3, the Court is inside the legislative equilibrium. The legislative equilibrium is the set of all policies that Congress and the president will not override. If the Court renders a decision that sets policy somewhere within that set, there are no alternative points that make all legislative actors at least as well off (Hettinger and Zorn 2005, 7). So assume that the Court renders a decision at its ideal point. If the House tries to override it with a policy to the left of *J*, the Senate and president will block it, and if the Senate or president tries to override the Court's decision with a policy to the right of *J*, the House will block it. The Court's policy decision, in short, is safe from Congress and the president. In the bottom of Figure 3.3, however, we can see that the Court falls outside the legislative equilibrium. Here, if the Court renders a decision at its ideal point, it might very well observe punishment or an override by Congress and the president. The SOP theory argues, then, that in such cases (when the Court is

Inside Legislative Equilibrium

Outside Legislative Equilibrium

FIGURE 3.3. Separation-of-powers context for judicial decision making. H = ideal point of the relevant pivot in the House of Representatives. S = ideal point of the relevant pivot in the Senate. P = president's ideal point. J = Ideal point of relevant pivot on the Court (i.e., the policy the Court most sincerely would like to adopt). When the Court falls between the leftmost and rightmost legislative pivots, it is unconstrained by the political branches. When the Court falls outside that legislative equilibrium, justices must beware the responses of the political branches and act strategically (i.e., follow SG recommendations).

outside the legislative equilibrium), justices will pay particular attention to – and will follow – the recommendations of the SG. More specifically, because the SG is an agent of the president – at whose pleasure he serves – he can be seen as the mouthpiece of the government.

In other words, when the Court is more conservative or liberal than the president and Congress, justices will need to defer more often to the government. As such, the OSG might observe more victories in such contexts.

Selection Strategy

Finally, some scholars have argued that the SG succeeds so often before the Court because the office participates in Supreme Court cases it believes it will win. The theory looks like prosecutorial discretion. District attorneys (DAs) only proceed with trials when they believe they will get convictions. Thus DAs have very large conviction rates – and they tout them in their reelection advertisements. The same logic applies to the OSG. SGs will only involve the United States with cases in which the government's probability of winning is high. What looks like influence, in short, is just good "strategy."

There are theoretical reasons to believe that SGs strategically select cases for review and thereby drive up their success rates. Previous OSG lawyers suggest that they pay attention to the probabilities of success. Consider the following comment from Kenneth Geller, onetime principal deputy for Solicitor General Rex Lee:

> We are at the base of a funnel ... In an average year we may only appeal 80 cases; that means another 420 won't be appealed. We want the Court to hear those cases that are the most important to the government – and we think we can do a better job of picking the most important ones than the Court can. (quoted in Jenkins 1983, 736)

One might certainly infer from this quotation that the OSG also predicts which cases it is likely to win. Other comments from former SGs concur. According to former SG Erwin Griswold, the last thing the SG wishes to do is "risk an important legal question, on a poor case that has bad facts" (quoted in Chamberlain 1987, 393). The OSG therefore winds up filing cert petitions in very few cases in which it theoretically could seek review, perhaps to get its ducks in a row and make sure that it has a strong chance of victory. Former SG Wade McCree notes that during the 1979 term, he had the opportunity to file 426 cert petitions to challenge lower court rulings but filed a mere 67 (15.5%) (McCree 1981). And former SG Rex Lee noted that he declined to file five out of six agency requests to appeal (Lee 1986). By choosing carefully among various cases, the SG might be able to select those cases he is most likely to win.

WHAT DO THESE THEORIES TELL US ABOUT SOLICITOR GENERAL INFLUENCE?

While these theories offer some well thought out explanations for SG success, they provide little empirical evidence that the OSG influences the Court. Some of them tell us, theoretically, how the SG might influence the Court but provide no empirical verification thereof. Simply put, none of the existing approaches links a strong theory of influence with strong empirical results supporting that inference. Let us consider the approaches in reverse order.

The strategic selection theory is the easiest to explain in the context of OSG influence: there is none, or at least very little. Neither theory nor empirical observation suggests that the OSG influences the Court under this approach. The theory argues that the OSG participates when the SG believes he or she is likely to win. When the SG predicts that five or more justices will likely agree with his or her position, he or she moves forward with the case. If not, the SG refuses to appeal it. This is not influence. Influence, as we define it, occurs when the OSG persuades justices to do something they might not otherwise do. Sitting out the game when you know you will lose is not influence – indeed, it seems to be the opposite of it. What is more, empirically, the strategic selection perspective falls short.

What little evidence there is on the matter suggests that SGs do not file amicus curiae briefs simply because a case looks winnable. Nicholson and Collins (2008, 404) "reject the hypothesis that the SG selects cases based on their perceived winnability." At the same time, comments from former SGs suggest that winning is not always at the heart of their decisions to proceed with a case. For example, Salokar (1992) points out that SGs sometime file briefs even in cases they know they will lose, simply because they want the Court to be exposed to the argument. In *Hobbie v. Unemployment Appeals Commission of Florida* (1987), Solicitor General Fried argued a position he knew he would lose. "But it was a position which deserved to be put in front of the Court, deserved to be attended to and responded to, and there it was. Sometimes, even though you didn't think you were going to win, nevertheless, you did want to have a particular position put before the Court" (Salokar 1992, 137). In short, there is no theoretical or empirical evidence to support the strategic selection argument.

The separation-of-powers theory comes closer to theorizing SG influence, but there is no empirical evidence to support it. Again, the theory argues that if justices do not follow the administration's wishes, the president will try to evade the Court's ruling or punish it. Thus, when justices face possible political sanction, they will moderate their behavior in line with majoritarian preferences. Although the theory is clear, there is only bare empirical reason to believe that such influence exists. Johnson (2003) finds that the Court is more likely to invite the SG to participate in cases when the justices believe they need the executive's support to enforce their decisions. Johnson's data suggest that the Court invites the SG in salient cases, as the percentage of House seats held by the president's party increases and, among other conditions, when the president enjoys high approval ratings. The reason, of course, is to determine how likely the president would be to support a potential decision. Still, these studies merely find that justices are more likely to call for the views of the SG when they need to rely on the president to execute their decisions or protect the Court's decision from a legislative veto override bill. Whether the Court renders different decisions than it otherwise would in the absence of the theoretical separation of powers constraint escapes the research. In sum, while the theory is clear as to why the SG might influence the Court, the empirical evidence has yet to show such a relationship.

The ideological actor theory also does not say much about OSG influence. On a theoretical level, there is little reason to believe that the SG persuades justices to vote in a way they otherwise would not have voted. If justices follow the SG when they agree with him, does that show influence? We think not. That the Court accepts a position with which it already agrees surely cannot be considered influence. And even when the SG takes a counterideological position, the theory still does not necessarily suggest influence. If a conservative SG makes a liberal argument in a case and a liberal justice (who usually opposes the SG) accepts it, does that mean the liberal justice was influenced? Probably not, since he likely just voted the way he would have voted otherwise. If that same conservative SG makes a liberal argument in a case, and a conservative justice follows that recommendation, does that suggest influence? Perhaps, but without knowing for sure whether she would have voted liberally or conservatively in the first place, we cannot be sure.

The attorney quality approach has a clear theory for why the Court would be influenced by the OSG but little data to support it. On the theoretical side of things, the argument suggests that justices are susceptible to sound legal arguments, which can persuade them to vote in ways they otherwise may not have voted; that is, when justices observe a solid legal argument, regardless of the lawyer who makes it, they will be more likely to vote in that direction. As we stated earlier, there is strong evidence to suggest that justices are persuaded by quality legal arguments (Johnson, Wahlbeck, and Spriggs 2006; McAtee and McGuire 2007). This might suggest, then, that the OSG influences justices because of the quality of its lawyers. Still, though, none of these empirical tests has matched quality attorneys against other similar quality attorneys. For example, if a former OSG attorney squares off against a current OSG attorney, who is more likely to win? The OSG attorney? The non-OSG attorney? Neither? Each answer would have considerable implications for the theory. At any rate, without making such comparisons, we cannot know whether attorney quality drives OSG success.

The repeat player theory, too, leaves us wanting when it comes to OSG influence. One part of the theory (attorney experience) argues that the OSG wins because, through frequent interaction with justices, its attorneys learn which arguments justices are most likely to accept and then makes those arguments. To test whether a purported OSG experience gap leads to success (and influence), one must compare the success of experienced attorneys with equally experienced attorneys. If we can compare the probability of victory between OSG lawyers and equally experienced non-OSG lawyers, we might infer whether SG experience leads to success. Because no existing study has used such a research design, we are unable to determine empirically whether

OSG experience leads to OSG influence. And for the same reasons, we know little about whether attorney experience leads to success.

Finally, consider the consummate legal professional theory. Does it allow for influence? Certainly. It theorizes that the credible legal arguments OSG attorneys make can influence justices to take positions they otherwise would not take. Justices, recall, require sound legal and policy arguments, and OSG lawyers typically provide it. Justices will rely on the information presented to them by the OSG, as that office has built up a reputation as a truth-telling law firm. Justices will use such information, when they can, to bolster their positions. And when they must, they will reconsider their positions as a consequence of the OSG's information, as Justice Blackmun apparently did in the *Nelson* case that led off this chapter. Just how to verify the theory empirically, however, is difficult to determine. As such, existing empirical approaches have not isolated such a dynamic. In perhaps the most direct test of the theory, Wohlfarth (2009) shows that in the absence of objectivity, the OSG's success rate decreases, but to our knowledge, no study is able to examine the dynamic systematically and pit it against the other theories.

SUMMARY

Where, then, does this leave us? The OSG represents the government before the Court with distinction, winning the majority of cases it pursues. Yet we still do not know the likely action(s) the Court would take but for the OSG; that is, despite the number of existing theories on OSG success, we still do not know whether the OSG influences the Court and, if so, why. Our goal in this book is to provide such information. We begin our effort to test for influence in Chapter 4, by examining the Court's agenda stage and focusing on whether the OSG influences justices to hear cases they otherwise would prefer not to hear. It is to this task that we now turn.

4

Solicitor General Influence and Agenda Setting

We began this book with a behind-the-scenes story from NOW v. *Scheidler* (1994). The data suggested that Solicitor General Drew Days influenced Justice Sandra Day O'Connor to switch her agenda vote and thereby triggered full Supreme Court review of the case. And in the *Nelson* case in the previous chapter, it appeared that the Office of the Solicitor General's (OSG's) recommendation led Justice Blackmun to switch his vote. Were these isolated incidents? Did the OSG simply get lucky? Did O'Connor and Blackmun switch their votes by happenstance? Likely not.

In this chapter, we examine whether the OSG influences justices' agenda votes. We analyze how justices respond to OSG recommendations to grant or deny review to cases. Using existing research on judicial agenda setting as our guide, we theorize justices' ex ante preferences in each case. Then, to determine whether the OSG has caused justices to change their votes, we compare their actual votes to their theoretically derived expected votes.

We begin by explaining how the Supreme Court's agenda-setting process operates. We then discuss the conditions under which justices set the Court's agenda. We next hypothesize when and how the OSG can influence justices' agenda votes. After we discuss our data and methods, we present our results and discuss our findings.

The Court's agenda-setting process begins when a party loses its case in a lower court, wants the Supreme Court to review that decision, and files a petition for a writ of certiorari (or an appeal) with the Supreme Court clerk.[1]

---

[1] For the purposes of our study, the process begins after a litigant has decided to seek review of his case. Recent work, however, highlights the importance of studying the decision to

These days, parties seek Supreme Court review more than ever before. When Chief Justice Burger took his seat on the Court in 1969, it received just under four thousand requests for review. When Chief Justice Rehnquist took over in 1986, that number had increased to just over five thousand cases. By the time Chief Justice Roberts joined the Court in 2005, it received just under nine thousand requests to review lower court decisions (Epstein, Segal, Spaeth, and Walker 2007). Without question, a hallmark of the modern Court is that it is inundated with requests to review lower court decisions.

As a consequence, the Court has developed procedures for processing these sundry requests. Once the petitioning party files the certiorari request (or jurisdictional statement, if an appeal) and all accompanying information, the Supreme Court clerk's office circulates it to the justices' chambers.[2] Each cert petition is then assigned to a law clerk in the cert pool. The cert pool is a collection of law clerks who have combined to share responsibility for the processing of cert petitions. Rather than each justice's chambers reviewing all the cert petitions the clerks can divide up the work into more manageable numbers (Ward and Weiden 2006). (On the current Roberts Court, every justice but Justice Alito participates in the cert pool.[3] Thus all law clerks, save for the Alito clerks, join together in the pool.) The pool memo writer drafts a report about the petition for the chambers in the cert pool.[4] After the clerk writes and circulates the pool memo – complete with a recommendation for how the Court should treat the petition – to the participating chambers, the clerks in those chambers review and "mark up" the memo for their justice. The justices will use these memos and the markups to determine how to cast their agenda votes.

---

appeal a lower court decision (Hume 2007; Zorn 2002). For a more extensive discussion of the agenda-setting process, see Stern et al. (2002) or Perry (1991).

[2]   While the Court has the discretion to grant or deny certiorari requests, it is theoretically obligated to hear appeals. Appeals can be filed only in a small subset of issues such as apportionment cases.

[3]   Not all justices have joined the pool since its creation. Indeed, when the pool was created in the early 1970s, the liberal justices largely avoided it, thinking that the conservative justices would simply use it to work their will. Over time, however, the practice became institutionalized, and newer justices – liberal and conservative alike – joined in it. Eventually every justice but Stevens took part in the pool. Like Alito, Stevens believed that it was good practice – a check, if you will – to have at least one justice outside the pool to avoid the problems of groupthink and to provide an alternative perspective (Ward and Weiden 2006).

[4]   Each pool memo we examined took the following form: it began with a very brief summary of the dispute; it then provided the facts of the case and the decision rendered in the lower court(s); it then laid out the petitioner's claims and the respondent's claims; next it discussed the legal and policy considerations for granting or denying review to the petition (and, often, the consequences of such a decision); and it concluded with the clerk's recommendation to the Court.

Prior to each Friday conference (except immediately before the start of a new term in October, when agenda conferences are held more frequently), the chief justice circulates a list with the names of all petitions he thinks the Court should discuss. Other justices can add cases to this list, but no one can remove another justice's cases. (A justice can remove a case from the list that she placed on it, but other justices are then free to put the case back on the list.) Once all justices have placed the cases they want on the list, the chief sends out the list to the full Court. Called the "discuss list," it provides the names of all cases the Court will discuss at the next conference; that is, the justices discuss whether the Court should grant cert to each of the cases on the list. Cases that do not appear on the discuss list are summarily denied Court review (i.e., without a formal vote). Figure 4.1 provides an example of a discuss list. It represents the first discuss list of the 1985 Court term. It shows appeals as well as certiorari petitions that the Court discussed.

At the Court's conference, the justice who placed the case on the discuss list – generally the chief justice – begins the discussion, stating why he thinks the Court should grant full review. That justice then casts his or her vote. In order of seniority, the remaining justices then vote. To receive full merits review by the Court, at least four justices must vote to hear the case (Rehnquist 2001). This is called the Rule of Four.

In some cases, like *NOW v. Scheidler*, justices go through a series of votes before they determine whether to grant or deny review to the case. Most important for purposes of this discussion are instances in which they call for the views of the solicitor general (CVSG). When the United States is not a party to the case, the OSG may voluntarily file an amicus brief supporting or opposing review. If the OSG does not file such a brief, the Court can invite (i.e., force) it to do so. When the Court invites the OSG to file a brief, it issues a statement that reads, "The Solicitor General is invited to file a brief in this case expressing the views of the United States." The invitation is, in practice, an order by the Court to appear as an amicus curiae at all stages of the case's progression. It is a command to appear and provide the Court with relevant information.

Take, for example, *Mertens v. Hewitt Associates* (91-1671), represented by Figure 4.2. Justice White placed the docket on the Court's discuss list. Accordingly, he led off the conference discussion about the case and cast his vote first. He voted to call for the views of the OSG. Chief Justice Rehnquist, voting next, cast a vote to deny review. Justices Blackmun, Stevens, and O'Connor, however, then cast their votes to CVSG, triggering OSG participation. (Justices Scalia, Kennedy, Souter, and Thomas all voted to deny.) The OSG suggested

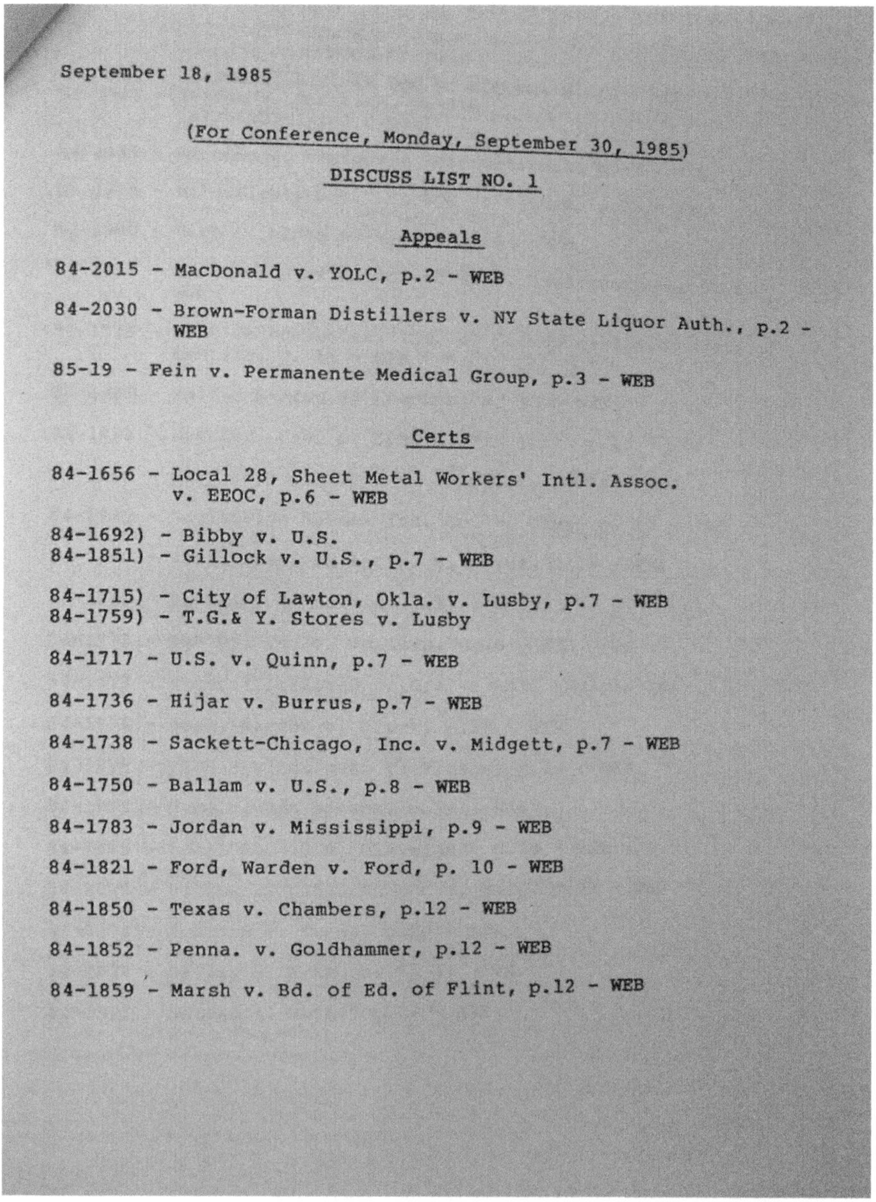

September 18, 1985

(For Conference, Monday, September 30, 1985)

DISCUSS LIST NO. 1

Appeals

84-2015 - MacDonald v. YOLC, p.2 - WEB

84-2030 - Brown-Forman Distillers v. NY State Liquor Auth., p.2 - WEB

85-19 - Fein v. Permanente Medical Group, p.3 - WEB

Certs

84-1656 - Local 28, Sheet Metal Workers' Intl. Assoc. v. EEOC, p.6 - WEB

84-1692) - Bibby v. U.S.
84-1851) - Gillock v. U.S., p.7 - WEB

84-1715) - City of Lawton, Okla. v. Lusby, p.7 - WEB
84-1759) - T.G.& Y. Stores v. Lusby

84-1717 - U.S. v. Quinn, p.7 - WEB

84-1736 - Hijar v. Burrus, p.7 - WEB

84-1738 - Sackett-Chicago, Inc. v. Midgett, p.7 - WEB

84-1750 - Ballam v. U.S., p.8 - WEB

84-1783 - Jordan v. Mississippi, p.9 - WEB

84-1821 - Ford, Warden v. Ford, p. 10 - WEB

84-1850 - Texas v. Chambers, p.12 - WEB

84-1852 - Penna. v. Goldhammer, p.12 - WEB

84-1859 - Marsh v. Bd. of Ed. of Flint, p.12 - WEB

FIGURE 4.1. Discuss list for Court's September 30, 1985, conference. Docket numbers are listed on the left. Initials on the right represent the name of the justice who placed the case on the discuss list.

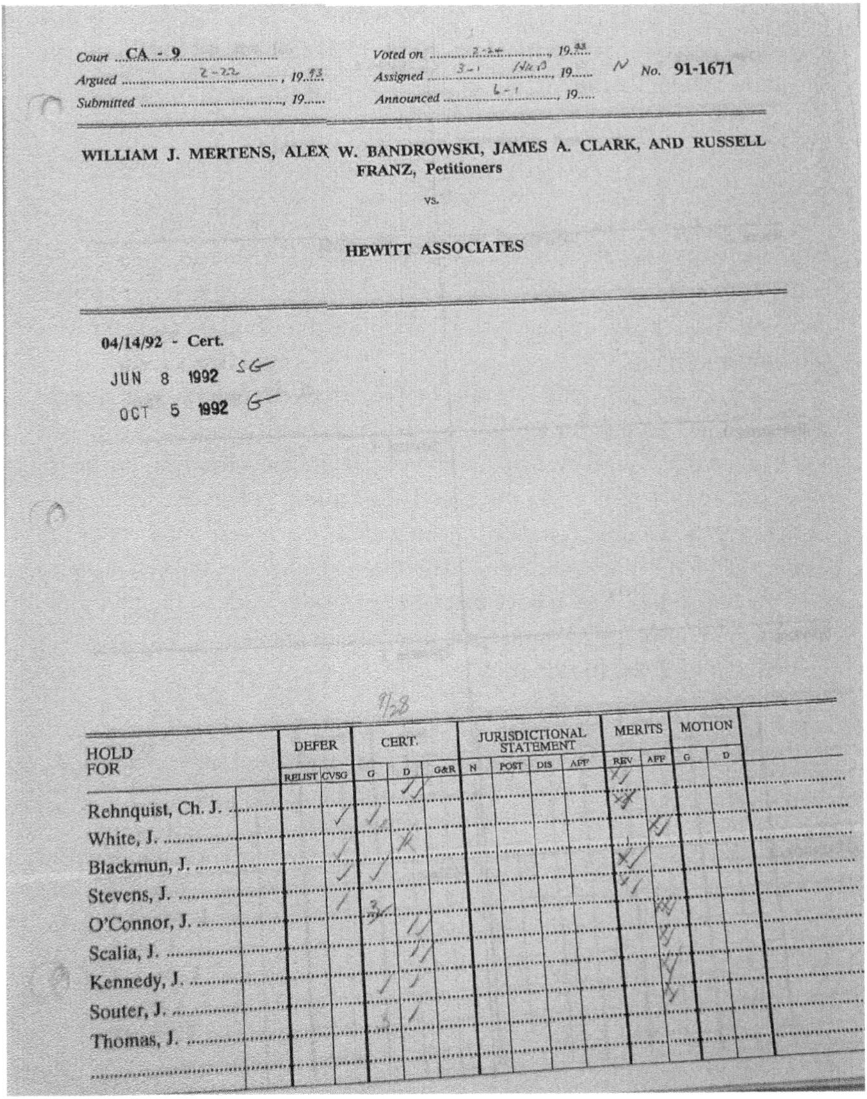
Court CA - 9 Voted on 2-24, 19 93
Argued 2-22, 19 93 Assigned 3-1, 19 No. 91-1671
Submitted , 19 Announced 6-1, 19

WILLIAM J. MERTENS, ALEX W. BANDROWSKI, JAMES A. CLARK, AND RUSSELL FRANZ, Petitioners

vs.

HEWITT ASSOCIATES

04/14/92 - Cert.
JUN 8 1992 SG
OCT 5 1992 G

HOLD FOR | DEFER (RELIST, CVSG) | CERT. (G, D, G&R) | JURISDICTIONAL STATEMENT (N, POST, DIS, AFF) | MERITS (REV, AFF) | MOTION (G, D)

Rehnquist, Ch. J.
White, J.
Blackmun, J.
Stevens, J.
O'Connor, J.
Scalia, J.
Kennedy, J.
Souter, J.
Thomas, J.

FIGURE 4.2. Docket sheet for *Mertens v. Hewitt Associates* (91-1671).

that the Court grant review to the case because of the conflict among the circuits. The lower courts, it pointed out, could not agree on the proper interpretation of the law. At the Court's next conference, a majority of justices voted to grant review, just as the OSG requested. Notably, both Justices Souter and Thomas, who had previously revealed a preference to deny review, now cast their votes to grant.[5] Their votes ultimately led to Supreme Court review and the adoption of law that closed the door on equitable relief for certain violations of fiduciary duties.

THEORY AND HYPOTHESES

Our goal in this chapter is to examine whether the OSG influences justices to cast agenda votes they otherwise would not cast. To do so, we focus on both policy and legal considerations and the role they jointly play in justices' decisions to set the Court's agenda. We examine the Court's agenda stage for two primary reasons.

First, scholars have a strong handle on the conditions under which justices set the Court's agenda. As a result, we can make fairly accurate predictions about how justices would vote in the absence of OSG involvement. We know, for example, that justices set the agenda to achieve policy and legal goals. Justices set the Court's agenda by looking ahead to the expected policy the Court will make if it hears the case to determine whether they prefer that policy over existing policy. Few quotes make the point so clearly as the following, which comes from a Blackmun clerk in the markup to a cert pool memo in *Thornburgh v. Abbott* (no. 87-1344):

> I think it pretty much comes down to whether you want to reverse the judgment below (the likely outcome of a grant). If you are pretty sure you do, you should vote to grant now. Otherwise, it's better to wait.

Systematic empirical studies likewise illustrate the tremendous importance of policy predictions during the agenda-setting stage. For example, Black and Owens (2009a) find that all else equal, justices are more likely to vote to hear cases when the policy they expect the Court to make is better than the status quo. Justices who are closer to the expected policy location of the Court's decision are 75 percent more likely to grant review to a case than justices who prefer the status quo (see also Caldeira, Wright, and Zorn 1999; Boucher and Segal 1995; Benesh, Brenner, and Spaeth 2002). At the same time, there are well-defined and measurable legal variables that can also motivate justices' agenda votes. As such, we can use these known variables to make strong predictions about how justices would vote in the absence of an OSG recommendation.

---

[5] Thomas actually cast a join-3 vote, which as we stated in the introduction has the effect of triggering review when three other justices cast grant votes.

Second, the agenda stage provides a good opportunity to circumvent selection effects that could bias a finding in favor of solicitor general (SG) influence. During the agenda stage, the OSG makes recommendations to the Court as an amicus curiae in one of two ways: voluntarily or at the direction of the Court. If the strategic selection theory is correct and the OSG only (or largely) participates in cases the SG knows he will win, we must look for influence where the advantages from this selection effect are absent. The CVSG minimizes such a threat. As such, we focus primarily on justices' agenda votes in cases where the Court forced the OSG to participate.[6]

We tackle the question of SG influence in four stages. First, we examine the concept of general agreement (i.e., ideological compatibility) between a justice and the SG. Second, we focus on the notion of specific agreement between the SG and the voting justice – whether the two desire the same outcome in the particular case. Third, we examine how legal factors affect votes. Finally, we examine the interaction of general policy agreement, specific policy agreement, and legal agreement.

General Ideological Agreement

Whether a justice follows the OSG's recommendation likely depends, in part, on the ideological distance between the justice and the SG. Empirical findings suggest that justices may take the OSG's general ideological proclivities into account when casting their votes. Bailey, Kamoie, and Maltzman (2005) show that justices follow the recommendation of the SG when they are ideological allies. Wohlfarth (2009) finds that the OSG's success rate is, in part, because of the SG's ideological relationship to the Court median. Accordingly, we hypothesize that as the ideological distance between a justice and the SG decreases (increases), the likelihood a justice will follow the SG's recommendation will increase (decrease).

---

[6] Of the 277 unique cases included in our data, only 19 (roughly 7%) were voluntarily submitted. Owing to data availability issues, we only could examine voluntarily filed briefs submitted by the SG between the 1984 and 1993 terms. We should note that these 19 cases between the 1984 and 1993 terms paled in comparison (10.92%) to the 174 cases the SG filed by invitation between the same years. To ensure that our findings were not the result of the truncated sample of voluntary briefs, we refit our models for just the 1984–1993 terms. Our findings remain unchanged. We should also note that fitting a selection model in this instance is not feasible. There simply are not enough data. Moreover, we have different units of analysis across our two models; that is, in a potential model of the SG's decision to submit a voluntary brief, there will be a single observation per case in the selection equation. In the outcome equation of whether a justice follows the SG's recommendation, however, there will be (usually) nine observations per case. Existing statistical models do not allow for such an imbalance between the selection and outcome equations.

Specific Policy Agreement

Justices are also likely to follow the OSG's recommendation when it accords with their preferred outcome in the specific case at hand. We draw on a host of studies to support this theory. Segal (1988), for example, examined justices' support for the SG's position based on the ideological position taken in his brief. Of the twenty justices in Segal's study, thirteen exhibited significant differences in how they responded to liberal and conservative SG briefs. Indeed, Justice Marshall supported the SG 86 percent of the time when he filed a liberal brief but just under 30 percent of the time when the SG filed a conservative brief. Guided by the logic of these studies, we expect that a justice will be more likely to follow the OSG's recommendation when it supports the justice's desired outcome in a case; that is, if a justice is predicted to want to grant review to a case and the OSG recommends a grant, we would observe what we call specific agreement. Conversely, if the OSG recommends a denial in that case, we would observe specific disagreement. Justices who are expected to grant review to a case should be more likely to follow a grant recommendation made by the SG. Conversely, justices who wish to deny review to a case to preserve the status quo should be less likely to follow a grant recommendation made by the SG.

Legal Agreement

Of course, policy preferences do not fully explain the behavior of justices (Songer and Lindquist 1996). Research documents the role played by legal factors at various stages of the Court's decision-making process (Knight and Epstein 1996; Black and Owens 2009a; Hansford and Spriggs 2006; Richards and Kritzer 2002). We argue that legal factors are likely to affect how justices respond to OSG recommendations. After all, "politics *and* the law are at the intersection of the Solicitor General's responsibilities" (Pacelle 2003, 10; emphasis added).

What are these legal factors? To determine the operative legal factors at the agenda stage, we turned to Perry (1991) and Stern et al. (2002), who suggest that legal conflict and legal importance apply, as do the exercise of judicial review in the court below and justiciability concerns.

One critical duty of the Supreme Court is to resolve conflict among the lower federal courts, which occurs when two or more lower courts diverge over the interpretation or application of the law. Supreme Court Rule 10 (as well as statements made by the justices) highlights that part of the Court's role is to resolve such conflict: "I would say that there are certain cases that

I would vote for . . . if there was a clear split in circuits, *I would vote for cert. without even looking at the merits"* (Perry 1991, 269; emphasis added). Legal conflict, then, is a legal factor that counsels toward granting review and might influence whether justices follow the OSG's recommendation.

Legal importance is a second factor that motivates justices during the agenda stage. Perry (1991) explains that justices believe themselves obligated to grant review to some cases that are legally important and to deny review to cases that are legally unimportant. Surely importance turns on a number of factors; yet whether the lower court published its decision must be among them. Courts of appeals judges are allowed to dispose of easy or mundane cases through a brief opinion (usually no more than a few sentences) that they declare to be unpublished. Justices are hesitant to review such decisions because of their nonprecedential nature. In *Calderon v. United States* (no. 91-6685), for example, the pool memo writer argued that the Court should deny review to the petition because the case was legally unimportant, as the lower court decision was unpublished: "I recommend denial [because the lower court's] decision is unpublished and therefore no 'rule' was created by the case."[7] Accordingly, an unpublished lower court decision is a legal factor that would, on average, counsel against granting review and might influence a justice's decision whether to follow the OSG recommendation.

The use of judicial review in the lower court is a third legal factor that is likely to affect agenda behavior and whether a justice follows the OSG's recommendation. When a lower court strikes down a federal law as unconstitutional, legal norms compel the Supreme Court to grant review to the case (Stern et al. 2002, 244). As one justice stated:

> If a single district judge rules that a federal statute is unconstitutional, I think we owe it to Congress to review the case and see if, in fact, the statute they've passed is unconstitutional. (Perry 1991, 269)

Thus we expect that judicial review exercised below is a legal factor justices consider when voting and might affect whether they follow OSG recommendations.

Finally, justiciability concerns constitute legal issues that make granting review less likely when present.[8] When the Court faces a petition that suffers

---

[7] While we do not suggest that every unpublished decision is irrelevant or somehow unworthy of attention, we feel confident making the assumption that on average, unpublished decisions are less important than those the circuits elect to publish.

[8] Justiciability refers to whether a case is "appropriate or suitable for a federal tribunal to hear or to solve" (Epstein and Walker 2005, 74). If a case is nonjusticiable (e.g., is moot or involves a political question), then the Court should be less likely to review it.

from justiciability problems (e.g., the dispute is not ripe or it is moot), it is supposed to deny review unless compelling reasons direct otherwise.

In sum, when legal considerations support the granting of review and the OSG recommends a grant (i.e., we observe "legal agreement" between the law and the OSG recommendation), a justice should be more likely to follow the OSG recommendation. Conversely, when the OSG's recommendation clashes with the outcome predicted by those legal factors (i.e., we observe "legal disagreement"), a justice should be less likely to follow the OSG recommendation.

The Conditional Relationship among General, Specific, and Legal Agreement

It is likely that general and specific policy agreement and legal agreement are conditionally related to one another and that to examine OSG influence, one must examine them jointly. The reason, again, for so doing is that to infer OSG influence, one must examine whether the OSG succeeds in persuading justices to vote differently than they would like. This standard, of course, requires that we make inferences based on the behavior of justices who lack both general and specific agreement with the OSG in cases where the OSG makes recommendations that contradict the legal cues in the case. Since we would expect justices to follow OSG recommendations when they all agree, we could not falsify the claim of influence. To overcome this limitation, we must examine justices under conditions in which they are least likely to follow OSG recommendations.

MEASURES AND DATA

To examine whether the OSG influences justices' agenda votes, we analyze every case coming from a federal Court of Appeals in which the OSG filed an amicus curiae brief at the agenda stage between the 1970 and 1993 terms ($N = 277$). We sample from Court of Appeals cases so that we may use the Judicial Common Space (JCS) to place a legal status quo on the same scale as the policy preferences of justices and the SG. (No similarly scaled preference estimates exist for state courts.) As stated earlier, we examine cases in which the Court forced the OSG to participate at the agenda stage as well as the much smaller number of cases in which the SG voluntarily elected to participate at that stage.

Before we proceed, we address one question: does the OSG's failure to participate voluntarily in cases suggest that those cases are unimportant or that the OSG does not care about them? The data say no. We examined a variety of sources to make sure that invited (i.e., CVSGed) cases are just as important as noninvited cases. Establishing the importance of invited cases is necessary because we are testing whether the OSG can influence justices to move from their preferred positions. If, conversely, invited cases are unimportant and neither justices nor the SG care significantly about them, our finding of OSG influence would be empty – the result of a flawed assumption. A wide array of empirical and archival evidence (which we include in the appendix to this chapter) shows strongly that invited cases are just as important as noninvited cases. For example, we find that justices CVSG in cases with significant interest group involvement, that future Supreme Courts are just as likely to rely upon opinions rendered in invited cases as opinions in uninvited cases, and that the *New York Times* reports on invited cases to the same degree as uninvited cases.

Our dependent variable is whether a justice cast a vote consistent with the OSG's recommendation. If the justice voted in the manner recommended by the OSG, the dependant variable equals 1, and 0 otherwise. To make this determination, we examined the docket sheets and cert pool memos of former justice Harry A. Blackmun.[9] We reviewed the docket sheet in each case to determine how each justice voted in every successive round of voting at the agenda stage. The cert pool memos provided information on the OSG's recommendations. We examined only those cases in which the SG recommended a clear outcome such as recommendations to grant or deny review, note probable jurisdiction, or affirm or dismiss the appeal. We could not include other types of recommendations, such as hold or grant, vacate the lower court decision, and remand (GVR), because they do not provide the Court with clear policy guidance. The data we use for our dependent variable account for 91 percent of the OSG's agenda recommendations made in our sample between 1970 and 1993.

General Agreement

To tap into the general policy agreement between a justice and the SG, we created a variable called *Justice-SG Distance*, which is simply the

[9] We personally gathered all data for the 1970–1985 terms from the Library of Congress. The raw docket sheets and memos for the 1986–1993 terms come from Epstein, Segal, and Spaeth (2007). We note that the Blackmun papers are highly reliable sources of data (Black and Owens 2009b). What is more, to make sure that the pool memo writer's summary of the OSG's recommendation accurately represented the OSG's recommendation, we conducted a reliability analysis using data available on the Office of the Solicitor General's Web site. Among the briefs that were available on the OSG's Web site, we found perfect agreement between the clerk's coding and the OSG's actual brief.

ideological distance between the justice and the SG. Coding this variable required three steps. First, we employed the JCS (Epstein et al. 2007) to estimate the preferences of each Supreme Court justice. Second, to estimate the ideological preferences of the SG, we followed common practice (e.g., Bailey, Kamoie, and Maltzman 2005; Nicholson and Collins 2008) and assumed that the SG's preferences reflect those of his or her appointing president, which we measure as the first dimension of a president's Poole and Rosenthal Common Space Score.[10] Finally, we calculated the absolute value of the difference between a justice's JCS score and the SG's score.[11]

Specific Agreement

To measure specific policy agreement between a justice and the OSG, we created a variable called *Policy Agreement*, which examines whether the OSG and the justice agreed on how to treat the petition. We undertook five steps to create this variable. First, to measure each justice's revealed preferences, we again relied on the JCS. Second, we estimated the predicted policy location of the Court's merits decision – that is, the policy the justice would expect the Court to make if it were to hear the case. We believe that justices will predict the Court's policy outcomes by looking back at the majority coalitions in the Court's recent cases in the same general area. To determine this, we read the cert pool memo written in each petition to determine the topic at issue in a petition. We then looked backward at the Court's previous rulings in the same areas, following the coding scheme for the *value* variable, as defined by Spaeth (2006). To place these previous rulings in ideological space, we followed Carrubba et al. (2007) and used the JCS score of the

[10] Beyond the frequency with which this approach is used, there is empirical evidence to suggest that on average, SGs track the preferences of their presidents (Segal 1988; Fraley 1996; Meinhold and Shull 1998). Nevertheless, as a robustness check of this assumption, we also multiplied the SG's (i.e., the president's) ideal point with the polarization measure adopted by Wohlfarth (2009), who analyzed the percentage of partisan positions adopted by every recent SG in his amicus filings. High values of this percentage correspond to, for example, a Republican-appointed SG taking a high percentage of conservative stances in his or her briefs. Conversely, low values would imply that, for example, a Democrat-appointed SG was taking a higher proportion of conservative positions in his briefs. In short, this approach would account for any observed disconnect between a president and his SG. Our results remained consistent when employing the alternative approach.

[11] During the time period of our analysis, two SGs served under presidents from different political parties. Fifteen of our 277 cases involved President Johnson's SG, Erwin Griswold (a moderate Republican), serving under President Nixon. Five additional cases involved President Carter's SG, Wade McCree, serving under President Reagan. We used Nixon's and Reagan's Common Space scores for these observations, respectively. Our results remain unchanged if we estimate our model excluding these twenty cases.

median member of the majority coalition. (Our results remain unchanged if we simply expect the Court's merits outcome to reflect the ideal point of the median justice on the Court.) That is, we assumed that the policy location of a decision could be represented by the JCS score of the median member of the majority coalition in a case. We then took the median of those medians to determine the expected policy outcome.

We were agnostic as to how many previous cases the justices would look back to in order to determine the Court's likely outcome. We opted to follow a broad approach and measured the expected policy of the Court as the median of the majority coalition medians using the Court's previous two cases all the way back to its previous twenty-five cases. The results we present here assume that justices look back to the previous ten cases decided by the Court in the issue area, though our results remain the same whether we looked at any case window of two to twenty-five years.

Third, following Black and Owens (2009a), we estimated the status quo; that is, we examined the JCS scores of the judges who sat on the circuit court that heard the case. In the typical unanimous three-judge circuit court panel decision, the status quo is the JCS score of the median judge on the panel. In cases with a dissent or a special concurrence, where only two circuit judges constituted the winning coalition, we coded the status quo as the midpoint between those two judges in the majority. If the lower court decision was en banc, we coded the status quo as the median judge in the en banc majority. When district court judges sat by designation on the circuit panel, or when the appeal was from a three-judge district court panel, we followed Giles, Hettinger, and Peppers (2001).

Fourth, we computed spatial distances between the justice and the status quo as well as between the justice and the expected merits outcome. If a justice was ideologically closer to the expected merits outcome than to the status quo, we expected her to vote to grant review. If the justice was closer to the status quo than to the expected merits vote, we expected her to vote to deny review.

Finally, we compared the justice's expected vote to the OSG's actual recommendation: if a justice was expected to grant (deny) review to a petition and the SG recommended a grant (deny), *Policy Consistent* equals 1, and 0 otherwise. So, to summarize, we did the following: (1) Located each justice's JCS score; (2) Located the predicted policy of the merits decision; (3) Located the status quo; (4) Determined whether the justice was closer ideologically to the status quo or the expected merits decision; and (5) Determined whether the OSG recommended the same outcome as the justice was predicted to prefer.

Legal Considerations

To tap into the various legal considerations that might influence whether justices follow OSG recommendations, we constructed measures for legal conflict, legal importance, judicial review, and justiciability. We code *Weak Legal Conflict* as 1 if the law clerk writing the pool memo – while acknowledging a split – suggests that it is shallow and tolerable, and 0 otherwise. We also include *Strong Legal Conflict*, which is coded as 1 when the pool memo writer notes the existence of conflict that is neither shallow nor tolerable.[12]

To determine whether the lower court decision was published, we again examined the cert pool memo in the case. If the pool writer notes that the case was published, *Published Opinion Below* equals 1. If the case was unpublished, the variable takes on a value of 0. If the pool memo writer notes that the lower court struck down a federal legal provision as unconstitutional, *Judicial Review Below* takes on a value of 1, and 0 otherwise. If the pool writer notes problems with justiciability, *Justiciability Concerns* takes on a value of 1, and 0 otherwise.

We were then in the position to measure whether the OSG recommendation contradicted or accorded with any of these four legal factors. To measure *Legal Agreement*, we examined the OSG recommendation in the case. If there were one or more legal reasons to grant (e.g., strong conflict or judicial review exercised below) and the OSG recommended granting the petition, we coded *Legal Agreement* as 1. For the same reasons, if there were one or more legal grounds on which to deny the petition (e.g., no conflict, an unpublished lower court decision) and the OSG recommended denial, we coded *Legal Agreement* as 1. *Legal Agreement* equals 1 for 30 percent of the petitions in our data. Conversely, when the SG's recommendation ran contrary to the legal cues embedded in the petition, we coded *Legal Agreement* as −1.[13] For

---

[12] The coding of strong and weak conflict in the clerk's discussion required, on occasion, some judgment on the part of the coders. Accordingly, we conducted an intercoder reliability study for a subset of the petitions in our sample. Our weak conflict measure had 86.7% agreement ($\kappa = 0.640$), and our strong conflict measure had 93.3% agreement ($\kappa = 0.814$). Both values of Kappa are statistically significant ($p < 0.001$) and correspond to "substantial" and "near-perfect" agreement through a commonly used metric (Landis and Koch 1977, 165). As Black and Owens (2009a, 1069–70) point out, there is little to fear from systematic clerk bias in the pool memos. Clerks know that their colleagues will review each memo they draft and will punish (or at least recommend punishment) for ideological transgressions. What is more, the randomization of the cert pool will largely mitigate against any ideological basis.

[13] A possible alternative measure for law might combine the reasons to grant (or deny) into a scale of legal support; that is, if there were three reasons to grant a petition, the law might be considered clearer (and thus more compelling) than a petition with only one legal reason to

example, if there was strong legal conflict but the OSG recommended denial, *Legal Agreement* would equal −1. Of the petitions in our data, 18 percent are coded with *Legal Agreement* as −1. Finally, we identified and categorized as legally neutral those petitions that possessed no explicit legal reasons to grant or deny review as well as the small number of petitions (11 out of 277) in which there are legal reasons both to grant and deny the petition.[14] We code *Legal Agreement* as 0 when petitions are legally neutral. Fifty-two percent of the petitions in our data are coded this way.

We then interacted legal agreement with general and specific policy agreement. We created six exhaustive and mutually exclusive dummy variables that correspond to each of the possible combinations of specific policy and legal agreement. We then interacted each of these dummy variables with our *Justice-SG Distance* variable.

Controls

We also control for a host of additional factors. Perhaps most important, because we expect justices who initially sought the views of the OSG to be more likely to follow its recommendation, we code *Justice Voted to CVSG* as 1 if a justice voted to CVSG (and 0 if she did not). Similarly, if the justice originally voted to support the position ultimately recommended by the OSG, we code *Initial Agreement with SG* as 1, and 0 otherwise. We control for the *Political Salience* of the case by counting the number of amicus curiae briefs filed when the Court decides to grant, deny, or CVSG. We next control for whether the voting justice was a freshman. We code *Freshman Justice* as 1 if the voting justice was in her first two full terms of service on the Court when casting an agenda vote, and 0 otherwise. To examine *Case Complexity*, we code the proportion of the cert pool memo devoted to a discussion of the case's procedural history.[15] We further control for whether the OSG's

---

grant. Unfortunately, our sample contains no petitions with multiple legal reasons to grant. Furthermore, out of the 2,151 observations, only 129 have two legal reasons to deny, and only 17 have three reasons to deny. In short, while scaling the legal variable might help us to determine whether legal influence is stronger when "stacked," we do not have the data to test that proposition.

[14] E.g., a case may have genuine conflict but justiciability concerns. We note that separating them out into a fourth category (i.e., legally ambiguous) does not appreciably alter our results.

[15] Each pool memo in the time period we studied followed the same format. It began with a summary of the case, moved to the facts and decisions below, and then to petitioners' contentions, respondents' contentions, a discussion, and a recommendation. In complex cases, the clerk must spend more time explaining the facts and decisions below to the Court. Thus our measure accounts for how much explaining the clerk had to do when it came to the facts and procedural history.

submission was voluntary or invited. If the brief was voluntary, *Voluntary SG Recommendation* takes on a value of 1, and 0 otherwise. *SG Experience* is the natural logarithm of the number of oral argument appearances by the SG or OSG lawyer. We also control for several separation-of-powers variables that Johnson (2003) found related to the Court's decision to CVSG. *Presidential Honeymoon* takes on a value of 1 if the president was in the first year of his first term when the cert vote took place, and 0 otherwise. We next control for whether the Court was theoretically constrained by Congress during the term in question. When the median justice on the Court is more liberal or conservative than pivotal actors in the House and Senate (and the president), the Court may be more likely to defer to the government to avoid political rebuke and possible punitive legislation (Epstein and Knight 1998; Harvey and Friedman 2006). Following standard spatial separation-of-powers models (see, e.g., Owens 2010), we code *Constrained Court* as 1 if the median justice on the Court is more liberal or conservative than all pivotal members of Congress and the president.[16]

METHODS AND RESULTS

As our dependent variable is dichotomous, we estimate a logistic regression model. We cluster our standard errors on each of the unique cases in our data. The model correctly predicts approximately 76 percent of the observations, which translates into an 8 percent reduction in error over guessing the modal category (agreement between the justice vote and OSG recommendation).[17] Owing to the interactive specification of our model,[18] we present a full summary of parameter estimates in the chapter's appendix (see Figure A1) and jump directly into visual presentations of the results.

We start first with describing the performance of our controls. These variables perform largely as expected. We summarize their marginal effects in

[16] We present results using the filibuster and veto override pivots in Congress (Krehbiel 1998). Because scholars of congressional decision making have not settled on one model of congressional decision making, we refit our results in the appendix using other models that accord with these other legislative models. As we show in the appendix, our results are robust regardless of the legislative model employed.

[17] Using the same simulations typically deployed for quantifying uncertainty around a predicted probability, we can also easily express uncertainty in our description of the model's predictive power. The 95% simulation intervals for our prediction and our error reduction rate are [74%, 77%] and [2%, 12%], respectively.

[18] Both the statistical significance and the sign of an interactive term can change across a variable's range (Ai and Norton 2003; Kam and Franzese 2007; Berry et al. 2010). Thus others, such as King, Tomz, and Wittenberg (2000) and Brambor, Clark, and Golder (2006), advise using figures to check for statistical and substantive significance.

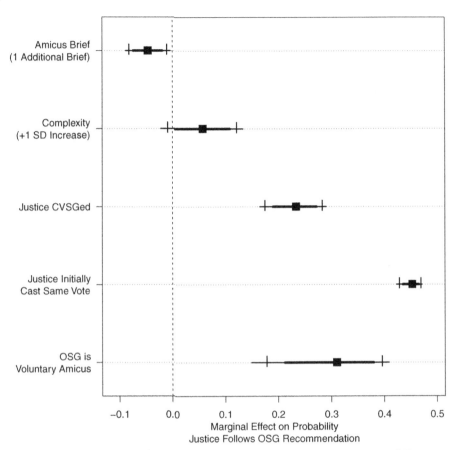

FIGURE 4.3. Marginal effect of control variables on the probability a justice follows the OSG's agenda setting recommendation. Squares represent point estimates. Thin horizontal lines, vertical tick marks, and thicker horizontal lines denote 95, 90, and 80 percent confidence intervals (two-tailed), respectively. These values were obtained through stochastic simulations using model parameter estimates reported in the chapter's appendix.

Figure 4.3. Consider, first, case salience, which we measured by the presence of amicus curiae briefs. As the top line in Figure 4.3 shows, a growing number of amicus briefs tends to decrease the likelihood that a justice will follow the OSG's recommendation. We estimate that a one-brief increase yields a 0.05 decrease in the probability that a justice will follow the OSG. This result accords with existing scholarship, which finds that justices are more likely to stick to their policy preferences in salient cases (see, e.g., Maltzman, Spriggs, and Wahlbeck 2000). Although there is some evidence to suggest that justices are more likely to follow the OSG in complex cases, these results are not statistically significant under commonly employed thresholds of significance ($p = 0.15$). Unsurprisingly, justices who voted to call for the OSG's views in the case are much more likely ($+0.23$) to vote consistently with its recommendation. Similarly, justices who, in the initial round of voting, cast the same vote as the OSG ultimately recommended were more likely to follow the OSG's recommendation ($+0.45$); that is, when the justice reveals a preference in the first round of voting (i.e., his colleagues voted to CVSG in round 1, whereas he cast a grant or deny vote) and that vote happens to be the same as the OSG's recommendation, the justice, not surprisingly, sticks with his vote. We also find that justices are more likely to follow the OSG recommendation when it voluntarily submits a brief at the agenda-setting stage ($+0.31$). We find no results to suggest that justices follow increasingly experienced OSG attorneys, nor do we find support for the proposition that justices are more responsive when constrained by Congress. Finally, justices are no more likely to follow OSG recommendations in their initial versus later years on the bench.

We now turn to our covariates of interest. We argued that the interaction of general, specific, and legal agreement would explain whether justices follow OSG recommendations. More specifically, an exacting test of influence comes from examining whether justices follow OSG recommendations when they are ideologically distant, when they disagree on policy grounds, and when the recommendation contravenes the legal factors in the case. In short, in such instances, the only thing weighing in favor of the OSG is that the recommendation came from the OSG. Figure 4.4 speaks to this specific scenario and shows considerable evidence of OSG influence.

Figure 4.4 examines the voting behavior of justices who disagree with the OSG's specific recommendation (i.e., no specific agreement) when that recommendation also clashes with the legal cues in the case. On the y axis, we present the probability that a justice will follow the OSG's recommendation. The x axis presents the level of general agreement, as measured by the ideological distance between the SG and a justice. Justices on the left of the x axis are ideologically close to the SG, whereas those on the right are ideologically distant from the OSG.

Figure 4.4 shows that justices of all ideological stripes heed OSG recommendations. The estimated likelihood of agreement – holding all other variables at their mean or modal values – is quite high. Regardless of a justice's level of general ideological agreement with the OSG, we find a 0.36 probability that the justice ultimately follows the OSG's recommendation, even when she lacks specific agreement with the OSG and the OSG makes a recommendation that conflicts with legal considerations in the case.

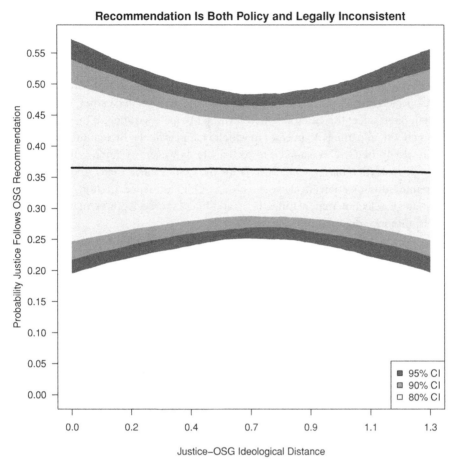

Recommendation Is Both Policy and Legally Inconsistent

FIGURE 4.4. Effect of general ideological agreement on OSG influence when the OSG's recommendation conflicts with both policy and legal expectations in a case (i.e., no specific agreement, no legal agreement). Light, medium, and dark shading denotes two-tailed 80, 90, and 95 percent confidence intervals, respectively.

While it would be unsurprising to find that justices who generally agree with the SG are likely to follow his recommendations, a better indicator of influence comes from the fact that the most ideologically distant justices follow OSG recommendations in such an unfavorable combination of policy and legal disagreement. And Figure 4.4 shows that such justices *do* follow OSG recommendations in these inhospitable situations. Put in more personal terms, Justice William Brennan, a staunch liberal, was just as likely to follow a recommendation made by President Reagan's SG Rex Lee as then associate justice William H. Rehnquist, an ardent conservative. Again, we emphasize that this is the predicted agreement level in cases in which the OSG's recommendation clashes with both a justice's specific policy goals (e.g., deny instead of grant) and the legal considerations in the petition. That such justices follow OSG recommendations speaks volumes of OSG influence.

What do these findings tell us about existing theories of OSG influence? Consider, first, the strategic selection argument. As we noted earlier, the OSG can often select the cases in which it will participate. As such, it may be able to choose to participate in cases in which victory is likely. By examining cases in which the OSG was forced to participate, however, we remove the threat of this selection bias potentially inflating the OSG's success rate. And after we remove this selection effect, we still observe OSG influence. In short, although strategic selection may, at times, be an additional source of power for the OSG, its influence does not hinge on it.

We also believe that the results cast doubt on the separation-of-powers argument. Drawing from the logic of strategic separation-of-powers arguments, we examined whether justices were more likely to follow OSG recommendations when the Court is theoretically constrained by the political branches. Contrary to the theory, we observed justices following OSG recommendations just as often when the Court was unconstrained by Congress and the president as when it was theoretically constrained by them.

Also suspect is the claim that the OSG succeeds so often before the Court because it largely shares justices' preferences or when the OSG takes a counter-ideological position. As we noted earlier, Bailey, Kamoie, and Maltzman (2005) argue that SGs are most likely to win under two conditions: when justices agree with the SG ideologically and when a SG beefs up the credibility of his message by taking a counterideological position. To test these theories, we examined cases in which the law provided no clear answer or shortcut for a voting justice; that is, we examined those instances in which there are no legal cues on which justices can rely to determine whether to grant or deny review. In these cases, we would expect that justices can focus primarily on policy. The two panels of Figure 4.5 present these results. Starting with the top panel, we plot the predicted likelihood that a justice will follow an SG recommendation, conditional on the level of general ideological agreement (x axis) and whether the OSG's specific recommendation is consistent with a justice's policy goals. The solid line represents when the OSG's recommendation agrees with a justice's preferred policy outcome (i.e., when there is specific agreement). The dashed line represents when the OSG's recommendation does not agree with the justice's preferred policy outcome (i.e., there is no specific agreement). Consider, first, the far left side of the plot, which examines a justice who is ideologically close to the SG. When the OSG recommendation is consistent

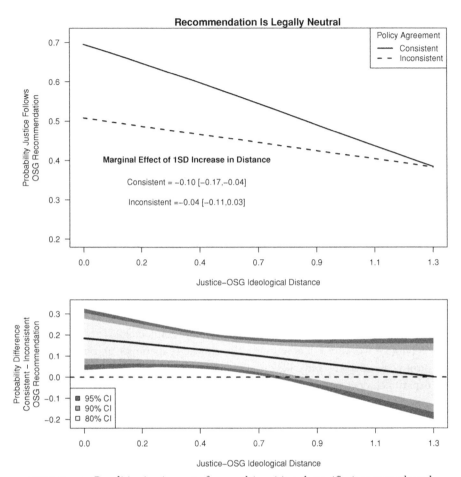

FIGURE 4.5. Conditioning impact of general (*x* axis) and specific (separate plotted lines) policy agreements on OSG influence. Marginal effects – with 95 percent confidence intervals around those estimates – in the top panel were computed at the mean value of our distance variable. The bottom panel shows the *difference* between the policy-consistent and policy-inconsistent lines. The difference between the dashed and solid lines is statistically significant for 67, 64, and 63 percent of the observations in our data at the 80, 90, and 95 percent confidence levels, respectively.

with that justice's specific policy goals in the case, we estimate roughly a 70 percent chance that the justice will vote consistently with that recommendation. Conversely, still looking at that justice who is ideologically close to the SG, when the SG recommendation runs contrary to the justice's specific policy goals in the case, the probability that the justice will follow the OSG recommendation drops to a coin toss. Looking down to the bottom panel of Figure 4.5, we plot the magnitude of the difference – and its confidence interval – for the comparison between these two lines. For high levels of general agreement, the difference is statistically significant; that is, the presence of specific policy agreement strongly enhances the likelihood that justices with high levels of general agreement with the SG will follow his recommendation in a case.

Yet, as the level of general ideological agreement between a justice and the SG decreases, the effect of specific agreement diminishes. Consider, again, Figure 4.5, which shows that as general agreement decreases (i.e., a justice becomes increasingly ideologically distant from the SG), the gap between the consistent and inconsistent lines decreases. Indeed, for justices and SGs who are maximally distant from each other (the right side of the plot), we find no increase in the likelihood that a justice who generally disagrees with the SG – but agrees specifically with him in a case – will follow the SG recommendation. This runs contrary to existing findings, which suggest that OSG influence will be highest when it adopts such an outlier-type position (Bailey, Kamoie, and Maltzman 2005). In short, ideological symmetry matters but does not explain OSG influence more broadly, nor does the counterideological argument.

Though we were not able to test the attorney experience argument as rigorously as we would have liked, our results nevertheless suggest that attorney experience does not drive OSG success. To examine fully whether attorney experience explains OSG success, we would want to examine OSG and non-OSG attorneys (which is what we do in our remaining chapters). Still, though, we were able to examine whether justices are more likely to side with experienced OSG attorneys. They were not. If experience, independent of OSG status, explained SG success, one would think that more experienced OSG attorneys would fare better than less experienced OSG attorneys. That they did not casts doubt on the attorney experience theory. But stay tuned for more on this in remaining chapters.

DISCUSSION

This chapter analyzed whether the OSG influences Supreme Court justices' agenda-setting votes. Our results show that the OSG wields significant influence over the Court. We examined the agenda-setting votes of justices who could be expected to follow the OSG's recommendations as well as those who would be unlikely to follow those recommendations. Drawing on archival materials and using a research design that allows us to overcome selection effects, we discovered that justices who are least likely to follow the OSG still do so 36 percent of the time. Justices who agree with the OSG follow its recommendations but, more important, so do those who largely disagree with them. This, we argue, is strong evidence of OSG influence.[19]

What explains this influence? Although our results do not come down conclusively on one side, they do challenge a number of existing theories. The strategic selection theory, attorney experience theory, and separation-of-powers theory all seem to come up short. So, too, does the theory about ideological agreement – to be sure, justices and SGs who are ideologically sympatico join together more often, but even ideological foes follow the OSG. What is left? One theory that remains is that the OSG is so successful – and can influence justices – because OSG lawyers are consummate legal professionals whose information justices can trust. Also remaining are the attorney quality and attorney resources theories. Future chapters will directly examine those theories.

So the OSG influences justices at the agenda-setting stage, persuading them to hear cases they otherwise would prefer not to hear. What happens once the Court agrees to hear a case that involves the OSG? Do similar results hold across other contexts? Does the OSG continue to influence the Court, or does OSG influence end at the agenda stage? In the following chapters, we examine these questions.

---

[19] We should point out that in a similar study, Black and Owens (forthcoming) find that the SG's influence over the Court, while strong, is also bounded to some extent by legal considerations; that is, justices sometimes discount OSG recommendations that seem to conflict with legal considerations involved with a petition.

5

Solicitor General Influence and Merits Outcomes

On May 31, 2011, the Supreme Court determined that the attorney general could not be sued for damages when he allegedly misused the material witness statute to detain criminal suspects without probable cause.[1] At issue in the case was Attorney General Ashcroft's "material arrest" warrants in the aftermath of September 11. The federal material witness statute allowed judges to authorize the arrest of individuals whose testimony was necessary in a criminal proceeding but who might flee or otherwise be absent during the trial. Ashcroft used the material witness arrest power to arrest and hold a number of individuals, including Abdullah al-Kidd, whom FBI agents arrested as he checked in for a flight to Saudi Arabia. Yet, over a fourteen-month period of jail and supervised release, Kidd was never called by the government to testify. Kidd claimed that Ashcroft simply used the material witness statute to arrest and detain him because the government had no probable cause to believe he had ever committed a crime.

The government, of course, had a different take. The Office of the Solicitor General (OSG) argued that Kidd's position was "inconsistent with repeated decisions of this Court establishing that the Fourth Amendment prescribes an objective inquiry under which an officer's subjective purpose is irrelevant." Ashcroft's subjective intent did not matter. What mattered, said the OSG, was whether the arrest was objectively justified. The Court agreed.

The Supreme Court held that the detention was objectively reasonable, given the facts. Therefore, held the Court, Ashcroft was entitled to qualified immunity. The objectivity standard exists, said the Court, to give government officials the freedom to take action without fear of liability. "Qualified immunity gives government officials breathing room to make reasonable but mistaken judgments about open legal questions. . . . [such actions] cannot be

[1] *Ashcroft v. al-Kidd*, 131 S. Ct. 2074 (2011).

challenged as unconstitutional on the basis of allegations that the arresting authority has an improper motive."[2] Because the facts objectively supported Ashcroft's decision, he was entitled to qualified immunity.

The Court's decision was significant in many ways. For starters, the decision arguably restricted the public's interest in securing executive compliance with the Constitution. While the rule relieved officials of liability, except in the rarest of cases, it had the additional effect of limiting judicial control over the executive. Equally profound, the decision quashed future controversial cases before they even started. If the Court had ruled that judges could look into the subjective intent of federal officials, courts might have been flooded with suits requiring judges to interpret the latent intent of government officials.

Still, one aspect of this otherwise profound case was routine. Like it often does, the Court sided with the OSG. The government wanted the Court to apply immunity, and the Court obliged. But we are left wondering whether the OSG's recommendation caused the Court's decision. Did the Court rule in favor of the government because of the OSG's recommendation, or would it have done so even in its absence? To ask the question is to ask whether the OSG influences the Court, and why. Conceptually, that is, we seek to examine a "but for" question: but for the presence of the OSG in a case, would the outcome of interest be the same?

In this chapter, we examine whether the OSG influences the Court's merits decisions. We take advantage of cutting-edge matching software that allows researchers to compare treatment and control groups to make stronger inferences about causation. More specifically, it allows us to compare cases that are nearly identical in terms of context and ideology, with the exception being that the OSG argues for a position in one case while a non-OSG lawyer argues that the same position in the other case. By comparing otherwise identical cases, we can isolate the treatment effect (whether the OSG participated) and answer the kind of "but for" questions raised earlier.

COARSENED EXACT MATCHING: A PRIMER

Though we have tried, thus far, to keep the book free of methodological jargon, we must discuss how matching works. It is, after all, what we use throughout the remaining chapters to investigate OSG influence. We make every effort here to keep the discussion tolerable for those less interested in methods and models.

[2] *Ashcroft v. al-Kidd*, 131 S. Ct. 2085 (2011).

Our goal in this chapter is to examine whether the OSG influences the Court's decision in a case. We examine OSG influence by determining whether, in the absence of the OSG, the Court's decision would look the same as its decision when the OSG participates. Of course, in a world without constraints on resources (or ethics), we would simply execute an experiment. We would take a random batch of cases and randomly separate them into two groups. One group would receive the treatment (an OSG attorney would represent it), while the other would not (a non-OSG lawyer would represent it). So long as our sample was sufficiently large, the powers of randomization would neutralize the potential impact of all known (and unknown) confounding variables. Any difference in wins we observed would solely be a function of the presence (or absence) of the treatment variable.

Unfortunately, such a design is impossible to implement on such a grand scale.[3] As a result, social scientists have typically turned to parametric models (e.g., linear or logistic regression) with control variables. Such models, however, do not permit causal inferences, unless one assumes that nature has randomly assigned individuals to the treatment and control groups and that the two groups are otherwise similar in all relevant respects; that is, one must assume that the data are balanced. For a large percentage of applied research questions, this assumption is dubious.

To overcome the problems associated with fitting standard parametric models to imbalanced data, researchers have increasingly turned to matching methods. Boyd, Epstein, and Martin (2010), for example, apply matching methods to investigate whether a judge's sex causes different outcomes in the U.S. Courts of Appeals. After matching circuit court panels and cases on as many relevant dimensions as possible, the authors look to determine if an otherwise identical circuit court panel rules differently in a case simply because a woman serves on it. They find that, with the exception of sex discrimination suits, there are no differences. Similarly, Epstein et al. (2005) employ matching methods to examine whether the presence of war causes justices to restrict civil liberties. They find that it does, but not in the way commonly expected. These studies illustrate that matching methods allow scholars to overcome research design limitations stemming from imbalanced data. As Epstein and her colleagues note:

> While we may not be able to rerun history to see if the Court would decide the same case differently [given the presence or absence of the treatment] . . . , we can match cases that are as similar as possible on all relevant dimensions . . . to make that same causal assessment. (Epstein et al. 2005, 65)

---

[3] But see Greiner and Pattanayak (2011) for a fascinating analysis of the impact of legal representation programs.

TABLE 5.1. *Example of matching*

Treatment	Matches	Control
(OSG attorney)	= experience = = resources = = net amici = = petitioner status = = ideological distance from Court =	(Non-OSG attorney)

We take these studies as our methodological starting points but capitalize on recent innovations that make matching even more accessible and user-friendly. In particular, for this chapter and the remaining empirical chapters, we use a method called coarsened exact matching (CEM) to preprocess our data (Iacus et al. 2011b).

On a broad level, the logic of matching is simple.[4] The analyst takes the data she has collected on the topic of interest and then matches observations such that the values of covariates in the treatment group and control group are as close as possible to each other. Observations that do not match across groups are discarded. The goal is to retain data such that the treatment group is identical to the control group, with the only difference between the two being the presence of the treatment. Using matches, treatment groups, and control groups that we apply subsequently, Table 5.1 provides a tabular image of how matching works.

The most intuitive matching technique is exact matching, in which the analyst "matches a treated unit to all of the control units with the same covariate values" (Blackwell et al. 2010, 2); that is, the analyst identifies the treatment and then seeks out exact matches among the control group. An example illustrates. If we wanted to examine OSG influence over Court decisions while controlling (only) for the effect of attorney experience, we could simply locate OSG lawyers with x previous oral arguments before the Court and then compare their successes in the Court with non-OSG lawyers who made (only) x previous oral arguments before the Court. If we were to observe differences

[4] Our discussion of CEM intentionally focuses on the conceptual underpinnings of the method, as opposed to a technically motivated exposition, which can be found in Iacus et al. (2011a) and, to a slightly lesser extent, Iacus et al. (2011b). Easy-to-use software for CEM is available both for Stata (Blackwell et al. 2009, 2010) and R (Iacus, King, and Porro 2009, 2010). It is important to point out that matching is not a statistical model in any sense. It is, instead, simply a way for researchers to "prune" their data from imbalance that can lead to inappropriate inferences after model fitting or difference-of-means comparisons (Iacus et al. 2011b).

between the two groups, we could infer that those differences were the result of the attorney's status as an OSG attorney.[5]

The approach with exact matching is simple enough, until one must match on multiple covariates. At that point, multidimensionality makes exact matching intractable. To return to our example, if we wanted to examine the causal effect of attorney OSG status while simultaneously controlling for attorney experience, party resources, and organized interest involvement, we would quickly reduce the number of exact matches between the treatment and control groups. Indeed, it is unlikely that we would observe any exact matches.

To circumvent the limitations with exact matching (while still retaining the general logic of matching), scholars have employed two types of approaches: propensity score matching and the more recent CEM. For a number of reasons, we employ CEM rather than propensity score matching.[6] The benefits of CEM appear on the front and back ends of the approach. At the front end, the approach is useful because it allows the analyst to define the level of imbalance that is acceptable between the treatment and control groups. The software then evaluates how many matched units remain, given that level of balance. In other words, the CEM approach allows the analyst to define acceptable balance not just in some overall sense but for each individual pretreatment variable of interest. This approach is important because for continuous variables, exact matching is often unnecessary. Return to our preceding example, in which we sought to examine the causal effect of OSG status while controlling for attorney experience and other covariates. The problem with exact matching was that we would be unlikely to retain any matches between the treatment and control groups. To be sure, there are certain instances in which we might want one-to-one matches, particularly among the inexperienced attorneys, but once our attorneys gain experience, the marginal value of each additional appearance surely diminishes. To wit, the difference between attorneys who argued, say, eleven cases versus fifteen cases will be negligible. And therein lies the value of the CEM method. Under the CEM approach,

---

[5] Note the assumption that there is no omitted variable bias (Blackwell et al. 2010).

[6] Propensity scores estimate the likelihood that an observation in one's data received the treatment (i.e., its propensity to be treated), conditional on a series of pretreatment covariates. Matching then occurs based on a particular algorithm based on these propensity scores (e.g., "nearest neighbor"). The analyst then reassesses balance within the newly matched data. This method, though tractable, is demanding to the extent that it requires supervision and revisions to ensure covariate balance. It is also potentially problematic. As Iacus et al. (2011b) note, propensity scores are somewhat "backward" in that balance is not guaranteed. As the ultimate promise of matching is to reduce imbalance in a set of covariates between the treatment and control groups, this presents a potential shortcoming of existing methods. Thus Iacus and his colleagues recommend CEM.

we can specify the level of coarsening that is acceptable. We can match on clusters or groupings of covariates to achieve balance, while still maintaining enough observations to execute the study. Thus we can treat attorneys with eleven and fifteen previous cases as being equivalent (or as exact matches, if you will), while still forcing exact matches on attorneys with, say, zero cases or one previous case under their belts.[7]

At the back end, once the data are balanced (or less imbalanced), the analyst can then simply fit a standard parametric model to the data. If the data are exactly matched, parametric models are not needed to make inferences. The analyst can simply perform a difference-of-means test to infer causation. Where, as here, one deals with approximately balanced data, parametric models are appropriate to make such inferences. Approximately balanced data lead to stronger statistical estimates and less model dependence. Even after using matching to reduce pretreatment variable imbalance, some will always exist in the data. Using traditional parametric methods (e.g., logistic regression) on a matched data set can account for any remaining imbalance without being overly dependent on the functional form imposed on the data (Ho et al. 2006). "The only inferences necessary [after approximately balancing the data] are those relatively close to the data, leading to less model dependence and reduced statistical bias than without matching" (Blackwell et al. 2009, 526). In short, the analyst can preprocess the data with CEM and then make causal inferences, something that is infeasible to do with imbalanced data.

DATA, MEASUREMENT, AND MATCHING

To determine whether OSG attorneys influence the Court's disposition of cases, we collected all orally argued Supreme Court cases decided between the Court's 1979 and 2007 terms ($N = 2,837$). We downloaded the oral argument transcript in each case from LexisNexis and identified each attorney who appeared at oral argument. Across the 2,837 cases, we observed 6,704 attorney appearances distributed over approximately 3,900 unique attorneys. Because our focus is on whether OSG attorneys influence the Court, our unit of analysis is each attorney in each case. Therefore we started with 6,704 potential observations and began to match the data, seeking to ensure that our treatment cases were as similar as possible to our control cases.

---

7 Though the user has the option of defining any and all coarsening that takes place, automated algorithms exist as well. These approaches are analogous to the binning process used in constructing a histogram. In working with the data in this and our subsequent chapters, we have generally found that an automated approach often produces a more significant reduction in imbalance than values we define.

We matched cases on a host of characteristics that likely influence litigant success but are nonrandomly distributed between members of the OSG and other attorneys. In particular, we examined attorney experience, net resource advantage, net number of supporting amicus briefs, petitioner status, and the attorney's ideological distance from the Court median. Most of these features are associated in one way or another with an existing theory that seeks to explain OSG success.

Attorney Experience

We matched on the amount of previous experience each attorney enjoyed when arguing before the Court; that is, we sought to ensure that our treatment attorneys had just as much experience before the Court as our control attorneys. We did so to address head-on the argument that attorney experience drives OSG success. To measure attorney experience, we calculated the number of total prior cases each attorney in our sample orally argued before the Supreme Court prior to the case at issue.[8] Our measure, then, is dynamic, looking backward from each case to the totality of the lawyer's previous oral argument experience. As we note earlier, although CEM allows the user to specify a set of values to pool, in working with these data, we have generally found that the automated binning executed by the software results in a great reduction of imbalance. This also allows the coarsening to be sensitive to unique characteristics of a specific treatment or control data set. For example, the initial level of imbalance between an OSG attorney and a non-OSG attorney is significantly greater than when we compare the OSG's participation as a party versus its participation as amicus curiae. Accordingly, because our overriding goal is to maximize balance across the treatment and control groups, we allow the CEM software to construct the bins for this and all other variables described later. In any event, our substantive effects are consistent if we manually coarsen the data (but with the caveat that we retain greater imbalance in the data).

We measure two different variations of experience. First, we start by including the amount of experience for the attorney who is arguing before the Court. To this value, we also add the experience of any additional attorneys who

[8] We examined each attorney's oral argument experience rather than his presence on a brief or status as counsel of record for two reasons. First, oral argument experience has already been established as a reasonable measure of attorney experience (Johnson, Wahlbeck, and Spriggs 2006). Second, as McGuire (1998) points out, the *United States Reports* do not consistently record which attorneys were on the briefs in a case but do consistently record the identity of the attorney who orally argued the case.

appear at oral argument as amicus participants. We take this step to control for the possibility that while a specific attorney might be an oral argument novice, the presence of a veteran advocate as amicus who supports the novice's side could help tip the scales toward victory in a case.[9] Second, because the argument process is an adversarial one, we also include the cumulative amount of experience possessed by attorneys on the opposing side. The basic intuition here is that the likelihood of a seasoned veteran winning in a case should be higher when he is squaring off against a side represented by first timers as opposed to frequent Supreme Court litigators.

Net Resource Advantage

We also match attorneys on resource advantage to avoid inferring a special OSG advantage that might simply be a function of its resource advantages when compared to other attorneys. To match on litigant resources, we follow the trend among scholars (e.g., Black et al. 2011; Black and Boyd 2012; Collins 2004, 2007; Songer, Sheehan, and Haire 1999; Sheehan, Mishler, and Songer 1992; Songer and Sheehan 1992) and rank order litigants along a sliding continuum. We follow the approach of Collins (2004, 2008b) and assign each petitioner and respondent to one of ten potential categories, which we present in ascending order of resources: poor individuals, minorities, non-minority individuals, unions or interest groups, small businesses, businesses, corporations, local governments, state governments, and the U.S. government. The weakest category, poor individuals, is coded as 1, whereas the strongest category, the U.S. government, is coded as 10. We then subtract the ranking for the opposing side from the ranking for the side being supported by a specific attorney, which identifies the relative differential between the two sides.[10] Positive (negative) scores reflect cases in which the attorney's side (opposing side) was advantaged.

Net Number of Supporting Amicus Briefs

A host of studies suggest that amicus curiae briefs influence the choices justices make (Collins 2004, 2008b; McGuire 1995; Vose 1959). Collins (2004)

---

[9] Our results are substantively unchanged if we treat these two initial quantities separately. This is likely due to the high correlation between the measures ($r = 0.81$, $p < 0.001$).

[10] An alternative approach would involve matching on the rank of the attorney's side and the opposing side. We opted to match on the differential for two reasons. First, we believe the difference in resources is more important than the actual identity of the parties. Second, when we try to match on the identity of the parties, we are unable to retrieve enough matches to make meaningful inferences.

shows that after holding all else constant, the petitioner's probability of victory increases roughly 6 percent simply because of the presence of a few supportive amicus briefs (see also Collins 2008b). Spriggs and Wahlbeck (1997) show that the Court often adopts language of amicus curiae briefs in its opinions. Wahlbeck (1997) shows that amicus support often influences legal change. As such, we believed it important to control for their presence. Using data provided by Collins (2008a) – which we updated for the 2002–2007 terms – we created a variable that measured the net number of amicus briefs supporting a particular attorney's side, which we then used in the CEM algorithm. For example, if a case observed five briefs for the petitioner and two briefs for the respondent, then our amicus variable would take on a value of $+3$ for any attorney supporting the petitioner; similarly, the variable would take on a value of -3 for any and all attorneys arguing on behalf of the respondent.

Petitioner Status

We also matched cases based on whether the attorney – including each attorney who appeared as amicus curiae – represented (or supported) the petitioner or the respondent. We did so to control for the Court's trend to reverse cases it reviews (Perry 1991; Palmer 1982). Indeed, between the 1977 and 2008 terms, the Court reversed 63 percent of all cases it heard. Accordingly, as there is a built-in bias toward reversing lower court decisions, we thought it empirically prudent to level the playing field by matching petitioner attorneys against other petitioner attorneys and respondent attorneys against other respondent attorneys.

Ideological Congruence with the Court

A large portion of judicial decision making turns on the ideological preferences of justices (Segal and Spaeth 2002). Johnson, Wahlbeck, and Spriggs (2006) find that justices are more likely to reverse a lower court decision when they are ideologically closer to the petitioner than to the respondent. Collins (2004) finds that petitioners aligned ideologically with the Court enjoy a 10 percent increase in the probability of winning, and both Bailey, Kamoie, and Maltzman (2005) and Wohlfarth (2009) find that justices are more likely to adopt the position of the solicitor general when they agree ideologically with it. As such, we determined for each attorney in each case in our sample his ideological distance from the Court median, following the same procedure as Johnson, Wahlbeck, and Spriggs (2006).[11]

---

[11] We determined, first, the ideological direction of the lower court decision as reported in the Supreme Court Database. If that decision were liberal (conservative), we coded the petitioner

METHODS AND RESULTS

Our dependent variable takes on a value of 1 if the side an attorney represents wins, and 0 if it loses. Our key independent variable of interest is a binary indicator for whether an observation was assigned to the treatment versus control group. In what follows, we describe and present results for a series of treatment–control pairings. For each pairing that is presented, we preprocessed our data using CEM and then estimated a logistic regression model on the matched data. Following the recommendation of Ho et al. (2006), we include each pretreatment variable as a regressor in our models to further reduce any remaining imbalance in the data. Using these parameter estimates, which we report in the chapter's appendix, we then conducted simulations to generate predicted probabilities (and confidence intervals) for each treatment effect.

We begin the presentation of our results with the three panels contained in Figure 5.1. As we will use an identical presentation format for subsequent chapters, a few additional words of explanation are in order here. The top panel of the figure displays the treatment effect for, in this specific figure, three treatment–control counterfactual pairings. These counterfactuals are identified by the labels on the *y* axis. Within a single label, the first value will always refer to the treatment group, while the second value will refer to the control group. Thus the top line of Figure 5.1 takes an attorney from the OSG and pits him against another attorney who is similar on all the pretreatment covariates; the only relevant difference between them is that one makes the argument on behalf of the OSG, while the other does not (and never worked in the OSG). The values plotted in this top panel show the treatment effect for each counterfactual, which we present as the marginal effect of being in the treatment group on the likelihood that an attorney will win. Sticking with our top line example, we estimate that the benefit of being from the OSG translates into a 0.14 boost in one's probability of winning, even after matching observations on experience and the myriad other variables we describe earlier. We'll have much more to say about this panel's contents in a minute, but first consider the other two panels in the second row of the figure.

The lower left panel of the figure speaks to the level of imbalance in the data, both before and after preprocessing. Again, each line in the plot corresponds to a separate treatment–control pairing. The triangle points provide the pre-CEM level of imbalance, and the circles denote the post-CEM level of imbalance. The specific values plotted are multivariate $\mathcal{L}_1$ values, which take into account

as making a conservative (liberal) argument. If the petitioner's argument were conservative, we coded Ideological Distance as the Court median's ideal point, as estimated by Martin and Quinn (2002). If the argument were liberal, we coded Ideological Distance by multiplying the Court median's Martin–Quinn score by −1.

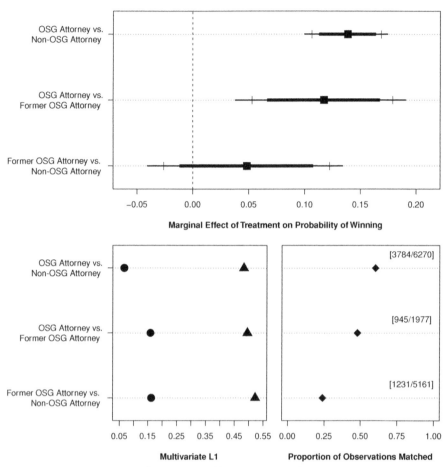

FIGURE 5.1. Dot plots of treatment effects and model diagnostic information. Each line in the top panel corresponds to a separate regression and effect estimate, which are denoted by the labels on the y axis. The first value listed in the y label comparison indicates the treatment group, and the second value in the comparison is the control. Plotted values indicate how much more likely a treatment attorney is to win a case than a control attorney. Squares represent point estimates. Thin horizontal lines, vertical tick marks, and thicker horizontal lines denote 95, 90, and 80 percent confidence intervals (two-tailed), respectively. These values were obtained through stochastic simulations using model parameter estimates reported in the chapter's appendix. The lower left panel presents the multivariate value of $\mathcal{L}_1$ for the unmatched (triangle point) and matched (circle point). Note 12 provides additional details on the calculation of these values. The lower right panel presents the proportion of observations retained by our matching solution for each treatment–control pairing. The numbers in square brackets provide the raw values for the matched and unmatched data, respectively.

not just univariate balance between two variables (say, the difference in means in attorney experience between OSG and non-OSG attorneys) but also the multivariate combinations across all of the pretreatment variables; that is, rather than looking at the overlap between two single distributions – treatment and control – for a specific variable, the multivariate $\mathcal{L}_1$ summarizes the degree of overlap between two multivariate distributions (again, treatment and control).

This imbalance measure, initially developed by Iacus et al. (2011a), provides an easy-to-interpret index of the degree of imbalance in a data set. Zero, which is the minimum possible value taken by $\mathcal{L}_1$, corresponds to perfect overlap between the treatment and control groups in a data set, whereas $\mathcal{L}_1$'s theoretical maximum, 1, indicates that no overlap exists between the two groups. Hence a useful matching solution exists when the overall level of imbalance – that is, the multivariate value of $\mathcal{L}_1$ – is smaller in the matched data than it is in the unmatched data.[12]

Looking first at our initial batch of results, we observe large reductions between our pre- and post-CEM values of $\mathcal{L}_1$. While our initial imbalance level in the OSG versus non-OSG attorney comparison is 0.48, for example, it plummets by just over 85 percent to a value of only 0.07 in the matched data that we use to estimate our treatment effects. This result – and the others presented beneath it – suggest that our use of CEM goes a long way toward reducing the harmful imbalance initially present in the data.

The last component of our figures, contained in the lower right panel of the figure, provides a visual summary of the degree of data loss experienced from matching. The diamond-shaped point presents the proportion of original observations that remain in the matched data set. The numbers in the square brackets located just above the dotted line give the specific number of obser-vations in the matched and original data sets, respectively. Although some of these proportions might seem on the small side, it is important to bear in mind that the observations pruned from our initial data set are those that would ultimately do more harm than good; that is, their inclusion would increase the level of imbalance in our data and thereby undermine our ability to make quality inferences. As Boyd, Epstein, and Martin (2010, 398 n25) counsel,

---

[12] The calculation of $\mathcal{L}_1$ is analogous to the construction of a univariate histogram in the sense that the number of bins an analyst uses will alter the shape of the result figure. So, too, is the case in the calculation of $\mathcal{L}_1$, where the cut points used will affect the degree of overlap calculated. To ensure that an arbitrary set of cut points is not driving our apparent reduction in imbalance, we follow Iacus et al. (2011a) by taking five hundred draws from the $\mathcal{L}_1$ profile. The value we report in this and all subsequent figures is the median from this vector of five hundred draws.

"While it may seem counterintuitive, balanced data that are comparable – even if smaller in number – are preferable to a complete sample for the purpose of estimating causal effects."

Now, turning back to the substance of Figure 5.1, we consider an initial set of three basic – yet highly informative – counterfactual pairings. First, as we already noted, we paired OSG attorneys against non-OSG attorneys who represented the same side (i.e., both argued as or for the petitioner, or both argued as or for the respondent), observed the same amicus brief (dis)advantages over their opponents, had the same resource advantages, presented arguments of similar ideological appeal to the Court, and enjoyed similar levels of experience before the Court. Presented with an equal playing field – but for the difference that one attorney is from the OSG and one is not – the data clearly show a sizable OSG advantage. The Court is 14 percent more likely to rule in favor of the OSG than a nearly identical non-OSG litigant, and this, again, is when controlling for a host of conventional explanations for OSG success. More specifically, the OSG wins on top of the experience and resource advantages it normally enjoys.

The middle and bottom lines of the figure provide additional details. The second line retains the main character of the story – our OSG attorney – but now we pit the OSG attorney against someone who previously served in the OSG but now appears in a private (and likely far more lucrative) capacity. This additional nuance is important, as it can capture the fact that experience accrued while working for the OSG is likely more valuable than just appearing before the Court. Short of some alternative universe in which the OSG is forced to argue against itself (see, i.e., Figure 5.2 and Figure 5.3), this is likely to be the most difficult opponent an OSG attorney could face. As the plotted value makes clear, however, we still observe a statistically and substantively meaningful OSG advantage. In particular, we estimate that an OSG attorney enjoys a 0.12 higher probability of winning than a former, but otherwise identical, OSG lawyer.[13]

Rounding out this panel, the counterfactual in the third line takes a former OSG attorney as the treatment group and uses an otherwise equal attorney who has never been associated with the OSG. Substantively, then, the counterfactual seeks to assess whether the halo of being with the OSG follows an attorney after he or she leaves the office. Contrary to the conjectures of some

---

[13] A careful reader might observe that our estimated treatment effect appears to be larger for the OSG–non-OSG pairing than for the OSG–former OSG pairing (i.e., 0.14 > 0.12). We should note, however, that these two values are derived from different data sets and, as a result, are not directly comparable.

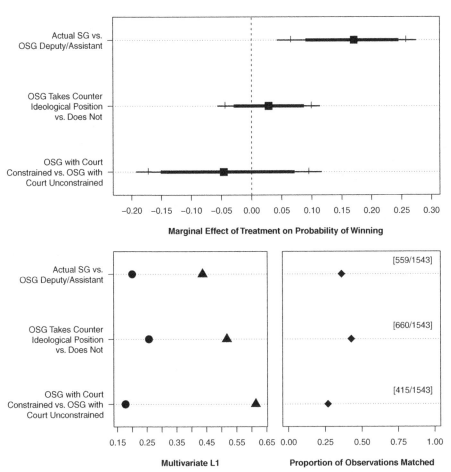

FIGURE 5.2. Dot plots of treatment effects and model diagnostic information. The first value in the *y* axis label denotes the treatment group. The second value (i.e., after the "vs.") denotes the control group. See the caption to Figure 5.1 for additional information.

(e.g., Sundquist 2010) and the wage premiums paid to former OSG lawyers,[14] the data say that the former OSG lawyer enjoys no heightened probability of winning. Once we match attorneys on the set of confounding variables likely to affect success, we fail to recover a statistically significant advantage for our

---

[14] Sundquist (2010, 71) cites an anonymous member of the Supreme Court bar who states that "a [former SG] heading an appellate practice can earn *five to six million* dollars per year" (emphasis added, along with a healthy dose of jealousy).

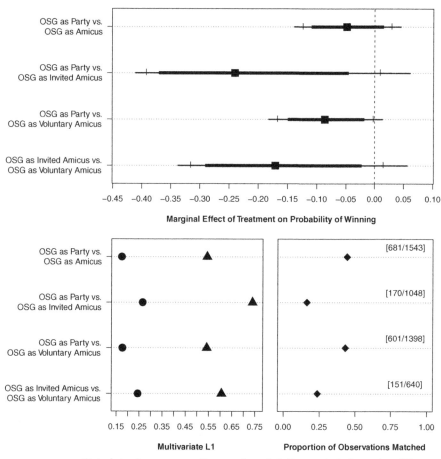

Dot plots of treatment effects and model diagnostic information. The first value in the *y* axis label denotes the treatment group. The second value (i.e., after the "vs.") denotes the control group. Marginal effects in the top panel denote increase in probability of positive treatment. See the caption to Figure 5.1 for additional information.

former OSG attorneys. In short, there is something inherently unique about arguing as part of the OSG that leads its attorneys to heightened success.

Having demonstrated an important and stable level of OSG influence, we next turn to creating a series of alternative universes in which we probe the additional complexities of OSG influence. We begin this endeavor by examining counterfactuals where the OSG appears in both the treatment and the control group. Across this set of treatment–control pairings, the key "but for" aspect relates to a specific aspect of the OSG's argument or mode in which it participates.

Starting with the top line of Figure 5.2, we follow insights from previous research – not to mention statements from former SGs – that suggest a differential depending on whether the actual SG appears before the Court as opposed to a deputy SG or assistant SG. After all, as Salokar (1992, 66) states, "solicitors general feel that their presence tells the justices that the issue before them is significant to the administration and the development of law." In an interview with Charles Fried, the former SG himself stated, "The case is obviously so important that if you don't argue it, it would send a message that you are disassociating yourself" (66).[15]

Clearly the SG is unable to argue each of the dozens of cases involving the United States each term, but does the Court notice when the actual SG shows up? Yes. Having matched attorneys on all relevant dimensions but for the presence of the actual or acting SG (our treatment group) versus a deputy or assistant SG (our control group), we estimate a fairly substantial 0.17 increase in the probability that the OSG will win. It is worth reiterating that by controlling for ideological congruence and opposing attorney experience – among several other variables – we largely eliminate potential concerns that the real SG might simply be cherry-picking cases he has a better chance of winning.

The second line of the same figure examines the practice by which the OSG takes what the literature has called an outlier or counterideological position. This occurs when the OSG supports a case disposition that clashes with its presumed ideological preferences, such as when former SG Kagan supported a conservative case outcome. In an expansive study of the OSG's filings during the Court's 1953–2002 terms, Bailey, Kamoie, and Maltzman (2005) find that a justice is roughly 22 percent more likely to side with an OSG recommendation when it takes an unexpected position. We compare when the OSG takes a counterideological position (the treatment) versus when it does not (the control). Contrary to earlier findings, we fail to find a statistically significant effect; that is, our data suggests that once we match on other confounding influences, the Court as a whole does not reward the OSG for breaking step with its assumed ideological preferences.[16]

---

[15] Empirical evidence also suggests that SGs might personally fare better before the Court than deputies or assistants. Consider Johnson, Wahlbeck, and Spriggs (2006), who discovered that Justice Blackmun was more impressed with arguments made by SGs than by assistant SGs (though it is unclear whether the Assistants' lower success rate is tied to less experience before the Court; see also Johnson, Spriggs, and Wahlbeck 2007).

[16] In terms of reconciling these discrepant findings, we note that owing to data availability and limitations in oral argument transcripts, we must left censor our time period at the 1979 term.

Our third line in Figure 5.2 entertains another possible explanation for OSG success: the separation of powers. As we note in Chapter 3, some scholars argue that the Court defers to the OSG out of separation-of-powers concerns; that is, justices accept the OSG's position for fear of the political ramifications of ruling otherwise. If that theory is true, we should observe heightened OSG success under one key condition. When the Court is constrained by the political branches and falls outside the legislative equilibrium (i.e., the median justice is more liberal or conservative than the president, House, and Senate), it will be more likely to defer to the OSG. Conversely, when the Court is unconstrained by the political branches and falls within the legislative equilibrium in a case (i.e., the median justice is ideologically between the key pivots in the House and Senate and the president), it will be less likely to defer to the OSG. Following standard spatial separation-of-powers models (see, e.g., Owens 2010), we coded as a treatment group those cases in which the OSG appears before the Court and is constrained by the elected branches. Our control group, conversely, occurs in cases in which the OSG appears before the Court and is theoretically unconstrained.[17] As the point estimate and its confidence interval make clear, however, we fail to uncover a significant separation-of-powers effect. An OSG attorney is no more (or less) likely to win when the Court is constrained by the separation of powers than when it is not.

Finally, our last set of counterfactuals, which we present in Figure 5.3, explores differences in OSG influence that come from the mode in which it appears before the Court. While our initial results tell us that the OSG is, in general, quite influential, is that influence conditioned on whether it appears as a party or a friend of the court? The general answer is no, with a caveat. Starting with the top line of the figure, we take the OSG as a party and match it against the OSG as amicus curiae. Pooling across both voluntary and invited (i.e., instances where the Court CVSGs) amicus participation, we fail to uncover a significant difference. When we disaggregate the OSG's amicus participation and compare it with participation as a party, we uncover some minor differences, but they do not rise to conventional levels of statistical significance. When the OSG appears as an invited amicus, it appears to do better than when it appears as a party. These results, however, are not statistically significant ($p = 0.11$; but see Gelman and Stern 2006).

Of course, this also means that we can control for attorney experience, whereas Bailey, Kamoie, and Maltzman (2005) did not.

[17] Congressional scholars are sharply divided over which of several competing models best explains legislative decision making. This chapter's appendix provides additional details on the approach we take for estimating treatment effects.

We find a small substantive bump – a 0.09 increase in the OSG's probability of winning ($p = 0.09$) – afforded to the OSG when it appears as a voluntary amicus versus when it appears as a direct party. Last, in the fourth line of the figure, we compare voluntary and invited amicus participation. Once again, we have some reason to believe that the OSG is more influential (0.17 more likely to win) when it is invited to participate versus when it jumps in on its own accord. Yet this result, too, does not reach conventional levels of significance ($p = 0.13$). The compilation of these three figures, then, suggests that not only is the OSG quite influential but its influence applies across the cases in which it participates.

DISCUSSION

Our data showed clear evidence of OSG influence over the Court. When compared to other attorneys with similar experience who enjoyed similar backgrounds and contextual advantages, the OSG still was much more likely to win its cases. After matching on characteristics most likely to lead to OSG success, attorneys in the OSG still are significantly more likely to succeed. These numbers are remarkable and attest to the importance of the OSG.

What do these results tell us about the existing theories of OSG success? Consider, first, the attorney experience argument. We matched the data such that OSG attorneys, non-OSG attorneys, and former OSG attorneys all enjoyed the same levels of experience. If experience explained OSG success, we would have observed no statistically significant difference between the probability of an OSG victory and a non-OSG victory or former OSG victory, but we did observe such differences. The attorney experience argument, simply put, does not explain OSG success.

A related argument is that the OSG wins so often because it hires the best lawyers in America. This argument is not based on experience but rather on attorney quality. Yet, like the attorney experience argument, our results reject the claim. Attorney quality would travel with the attorney after she left employment at the OSG, and our comparison of current OSG attorneys against former OSG attorneys would reveal no differences. Yet we do observe differences. Moreover, if the attorney quality argument were true, the comparison of former OSG attorneys against attorneys who never worked in the office would reveal a significant difference between them. The Court would be more likely to rule in favor of the former OSG than the non-OSG attorney, but there is no difference between these two. This finding suggests that the influence an attorney enjoys while working in the OSG vanishes once she leaves the office. It also provides insight about how litigants might invest (or not invest) their resources. To the extent that hiring former OSG attorneys costs more than retaining equally experienced attorneys who never worked in the OSG, our data suggest that strictly in terms of enhancing the odds of winning, taking on the additional expense of a former OSG attorney would be irrational.

Next, consider the resource advantage argument. Does the OSG win more often because of its resource advantages? Our results suggest no. We matched on each party's relative resource advantage so that our models compared OSG attorneys with equally resource-advantaged non-OSG attorneys. If OSG success comes from having more resources than most other litigants, we would have observed no statistically significant difference between the probability of an OSG victory and a non-OSG victory. Our matching analysis, however, still revealed an OSG winning advantage.

We also examined the separation-of-powers theory. Recall that an alternative explanation for OSG success turns on the political actors' potential responses to the Court's decisions. Congress can pass override and punitive legislation that undoes judicial decisions and damages the Court's legitimacy. Presidents can sign or veto override legislation, refuse to enforce the Court's decisions, mobilize interest groups to attack and undermine Court decisions, and use the bully pulpit to focus public scrutiny on judicial decisions. As such, the theory goes, justices may side with the OSG when it is constrained by these political actors (see, generally, Johnson, 2003). Again, however, the data do not support this alternative theory. The Court is no more likely to rule for the government when theoretically constrained by Congress and the president than when it is not.

One theory that we were unable to examine directly here was the strategic selection theory. As we stated earlier, it is possible that the OSG wins so many of its cases because it elects to participate in cases it is likely to win, thus driving up its success rate. If this were the case, the OSG would not enjoy any influence over the Court but instead would just get involved when the time was right. While we cannot speak directly to this dynamic, our data in Figure 5.3 nevertheless cast doubt on it. Consider the comparison between the OSG as voluntary amicus versus OSG as invited amicus. The selection theory would suggest that the OSG would be much more likely to win when voluntarily participating than when forced by the Court's invitation, yet we observe no difference between the two. The Court is just as likely to side with the OSG when it is forced to participate as when it chooses to do so. Indeed, while the prediction barely escapes conventional levels of significance, it shows a much lower probability by the Court to follow the OSG as voluntary amicus. These results largely accord with the results we obtain in later chapters and cast doubt on the strategic selection argument.

What, then, *does* explain OSG success? Our data, to be sure, cannot speak to this precise issue, but we believe they suggest that OSG success arises from the OSG's relationship with the Court, and perhaps more important, from the professionals it employs. By placing professionals in key positions – with the ability to take a long-term perspective – policy makers make a credible commitment to broader goals of justice and efficiency; that is, professionals may be able to limit the power of shortsighted and often power-hungry political actors who are otherwise governed by their own underdeveloped sense of self-restraint.[18] If so, the Court has ample reason to trust the information provided by OSG lawyers. We discuss this possibility more in the book's conclusion.

But that is not the end of our discussion about influence and its causes. Yes, we have discovered that the OSG influences the Court, and we have provided some ruminations for why that might be the case. In what follows, we add to these discussions. We seek to examine further data to decide whether the OSG influences the Court, and if so, why. In the next two chapters, we take the argument a step further and investigate the SG's ability to influence the content of Supreme Court opinions as well as doctrinal change.

---

[18] Of course, it is worth pointing out that the Constitution charges these elected actors to do just that.

6

Solicitor General Influence and Briefs

It is hard to overstate the importance of the brief on an appeal.... [It] speaks from the time it is filed and continues through oral argument, conference, and opinion writing. Sometimes a brief will be read and reread, no one knows how many times.

– Judge Herbert F. Goodrich of the Third Circuit Court of Appeals

In Chapter 5, we observed that the office of the Solicitor General (OSG) enjoys a significant advantage in terms of victories over non-OSG attorneys. Even when attorneys outside the OSG have as much experience (and other relevant similarities) as OSG attorneys, the OSG is still more likely to prevail before the Supreme Court. Simply being affiliated with the OSG, the data showed, makes these attorneys more likely to win. Combined with our earlier findings in Chapter 4 that the OSG can influence justices to review cases they otherwise would not review, the findings in favor of OSG influence are beginning to stack up.

We cannot end there though, for the Court's role in crafting legal policy extends well beyond whether it reviews a case or whether a party wins or loses that case. To be sure, these are important considerations. Yet it is rather the content of the Supreme Court's opinions and the doctrine those opinions set that ultimately guide social behavior; that is, the Court's opinions generate legal policy, define its institutional legitimacy, and generate its power. As Spriggs and Hansford (2001, 1092) tell us, "Supreme Court opinions set up referents for behavior by providing actors with information necessary to anticipate the consequences of their actions." Actors within society look to the language of those opinions to determine whether they can engage in particular behaviors. Governments, economic actors, and public citizens all look to the language of the law. Put plainly, the language of opinions creates reliance interests.

Therefore, to understand whether the Solicitor General's (SG's) influence extends to the aspects of judicial decision making that are perhaps most important, we focus our attention on the SG's reach into Court opinions and legal doctrine. Does the OSG write briefs that influence the language of Court opinions? Does the OSG influence how justices interpret and treat legal doctrine?

In this and the next chapter, we examine Court opinions and legal doctrine. In Chapter 7, we explore whether the OSG influences the Court's treatment of existing doctrine. By examining whether the OSG can persuade the Court to treat precedent positively or negatively, we can make inferences about the office's influence over the evolution of legal doctrine. In this chapter, we analyze whether the OSG influences the language of Court opinions. We do so by focusing on the extent to which Court majority opinions borrow from OSG and non-OSG briefs. More specifically, we examine the following question: do Court majority opinions borrow from the language found in OSG briefs more than from the language found in non-OSG briefs? Our goal, once again, is to determine whether the OSG is uniquely influential, and we do so here by examining how much Court opinions draw from the language of OSG briefs.

Because we focus, in part, on the effects of legal briefs on Court opinions, our first order of business in this chapter is to provide a short history of briefs. Once we have done that, we explain the importance of briefs to the contemporary Supreme Court. After highlighting the importance of briefs, we explain our approach to determining whether the SG enjoys a unique advantage when compared to non-OSG attorneys. We then discuss our data and methods, present our results, and conclude the chapter with a discussion of what our findings mean more broadly. So that there is no confusion about our results, we find that the Court's majority opinions borrow more language from OSG briefs than from non-OSG briefs, even when they observe the same relevant background characteristics. In other words, even after we examine two briefs that are identical in all respects but for the fact that one is filed by the OSG and the other is not, the Court is more likely to incorporate into its opinion language from the OSG brief.

A SHORT HISTORY OF SUPREME COURT BRIEFS

Today, briefs are the primary tools lawyers use to communicate with and persuade Supreme Court justices. This was not always the case, however. Throughout most of the Court's early history, briefs played a minimal or nonexistent role. The young Supreme Court followed English custom and relied primarily on oral argument to obtain information from lawyers in cases (Johnson 2004; Stern 1989).[1] Indeed, the early Court imposed no systematic rules on the amount of time over which parties could present oral argument. As a result, arguments often lasted days. Oral arguments in *Gibbons v. Ogden* (1824), for example, took roughly twenty hours over five days (Rehnquist 2001, 242), and in *McCulloch v. Maryland* (1819), they took nine days (Ehrenberg 2004, 1179).

As the country – and the Court's docket – grew, such a heavy reliance on oral argument became untenable. Fortunately, at the same time, technology made circulation of the written word less onerous. Methods of duplication and transcription improved. Commercial printers made written communication more feasible in all walks of life, particularly as a means of political and governmental communication (Ehrenberg 2004, 1180). Consequently, briefs began to appear more frequently (Cozine 1994), just as lengthy oral arguments became difficult to sustain.

Briefs soon became a preferred method of communication with the Court. Its own rules highlight this evolution. In 1833, the Court adopted a rule stating that one or both parties in a case could "submit causes upon printed argument" (Cozine 1994, 487). Four years later, the Court clarified that such written briefs would "stand on the same footing" as oral argument presentations. As docket pressures grew (Swisher 1974), the Court in 1849 adopted a rule limiting oral arguments to two hours per side. (The time was reduced again in 1925 to one hour per party. During the 1970 term, the Court amended Rule 28 and further limited the time for oral arguments to thirty minutes per side (Hoffer, Hoffer, and Hull 2007).) Attorneys, now forced to compensate for the loss of oral argument time, began to file written briefs on a frequent basis. By the time the Court adopted a rule in 1884 requiring written briefs, most attorneys had already begun to rely heavily on the practice (Cozine 1994, 488).

For the contemporary Court, the brief is "the central feature of modern appellate practice" (Martineau et al. 2005, 770). Before Supreme Court justices

---

[1] English custom today remains oral. Not until 1989 were barristers in the Court of Appeal required to file any written argument with the court, and even this requirement is simply a "skeleton argument" akin to summary bullet points (Ehrenberg 2004, 1168). Scholars believe that the English emphasis on oral communication derives, in large part, from centuries of illiteracy among the Crown's subjects. Colonial history, conversely, observed a much higher rate of literacy, which explains in part why early Americans were much less reticent to switch to a writing-based system. Additionally, as Ehrenberg (2004) points out, early American lawyers did not have the training that English barristers enjoyed (largely because earlier colonial laws placed limits on what lawyers could do), giving them little reason to protect a legal status quo that did not necessarily support their capabilities (1179–80).

attend oral arguments in a case or hold a merits conference to discuss it, they first read the merits briefs (Rehnquist 2001, 240).[2] To be sure, before they read the briefs, some justices have their clerks prepare bench memos to summarize them, while others first read the lower court opinion (Rehnquist 2001). Regardless of the sequence, however, one fact seems to be settled: justices read the briefs before oral argument and before their private merits conferences. The brief is thus critical for every Supreme Court justice.

Because briefs stand to offer justices important information at such a crucial time, they may be considerably influential. Indeed, comments from judges and justices have made clear the importance of briefs in the modern appellate process. Judge Frank M. Coffin once stated:

> I know of no other field of human endeavor where a limited number of pages of written and structured argument can be so decisive as in appellate decision-making. The heavy artillery of appellate practice *is* the brief. (Coffin 1994, 107, emphasis original)

In like manner, Judge Charles E. Clark of the Second Circuit Court of Appeals declared, "A brief is a necessity" (Pittoni 1991, viii).

Briefs are uniquely important for at least four reasons. First, they help justices overcome information constraints. Justices have preferences over law and policy but encounter substantial constraints when trying to achieve their goals (Epstein and Knight 1999). Perhaps chief among the constraints they must overcome is a lack of information – information about the policy consequences of their decisions, the law involved in the case, the preferences of actors with whom they must interact, and at times, their own preferences. Put plainly, information is the lifeblood of the U.S. Supreme Court (Epstein and Knight 1998; Spriggs and Wahlbeck 1997; Johnson 2004). The Court's effectiveness derives primarily from its acquisition, interpretation, and application of information. Justices therefore need information to forecast how their votes will translate into real-world policy outcomes. Decisions made without adequate information can be devastating. Briefs can provide such information.[3]

---

[2] We should pause to point out that parties file two categories of briefs. First, they file briefs supporting or opposing the request for certiorari. These briefs discuss some portion of the merits of cases but largely focus on threshold issues such as jurisdiction, legal conflict, and other issues that are necessary for the Court's determination whether to hear the case. Once the case is granted, the parties then discuss the merits of the case more extensively.

[3] Justices also may acquire information from the media, personal experience, and oral arguments. There are tremendous problems with using the media and personal experience as sources of information, however. The media usually cannot provide the type of particularized information justices need to predict outcomes in specific cases. Similarly, justices may hesitate

Second, the briefs in a case go a long way toward defining the issues the Court will address in its ruling. The Court's norm against issue creation (the *sua sponte* norm) constrains justices from rendering decisions on issues outside the record of cases (Epstein, Segal, and Johnson 1996);[4] that is, the norm limits justices to deciding cases based on issues that have been briefed or presented at oral argument. This means, of course, that along with the records from the lower court decisions, the arguments attorneys present in their briefs can set the boundaries of the issues the Court will address. A poorly crafted brief can fail to address (or barely address) issues that might be important to the Court's determination. Like a highway with many exits, however, a well-crafted brief that addresses all issues that justices might consider is one that can open up avenues toward victory.

Third, and similarly, because a justice's initial exposure to the merits of a case often comes when reading the briefs filed in it, those briefs can frame her perception of it. Many judges will formulate lasting impressions of a case from the briefs alone. As Justice Scalia once stated, "Many advocates fail to appreciate that the outcome of a case rests on what the court understands to be the issue the case presents" (Scalia and Garner 2008, 83). Indeed, Judge Paul R. Michel of the Federal Circuit once declared that he is able to reach a decision in roughly 80 percent of cases just from reading the briefs (Michel 1998, 21; quoted in Corley 2008, 468). Recent empirical work suggests that brief writers are quite aware of their framing powers. Wedeking (2010) shows that brief writers will employ certain frames, depending on context and lower court opinions. He also finds that strategic framing can lead to a heightened probability of success before the Supreme Court: "how litigants frame a case does affect the likelihood of receiving a favorable ideological decision even after accounting for other potential explanations" (Wedeking 2010, 627; see also Teply 1990; Sokol 1967).

Finally, briefs are important because they are the only opportunity attorneys have to present justices with an organized, coherent story. During oral arguments (the only other time during the merits stage when attorneys can speak to the Court), justices frequently interrupt attorneys with questions that derail the coherence of their presentations. For example, in one particular case, *Chandler v. Miller*, 520 U.S. 305 (1997), justices waited a mere thirty seconds into an attorney's opening statement before they interrupted and "[tore] him to shreds"

to tap their colleagues' personal experiences because of ideological differences and the fact that complex areas of law evolve so rapidly as to diminish expertise gained in the past. While oral argument clearly provides information, Johnson (2004) observes that 60% of the issues discussed during conference were exclusively found in parties' briefs.

4   For a discussion – and debate – surrounding the *sua sponte* norm, see Epstein, Segal, and Johnson (1996) and McGuire and Palmer (1995, 1996).

(Totenberg 2009, 112). The brief, however, is not subject to such interruptions. Briefs can begin with the attorney's strongest point, minimize the weakest, and attack the opponent's weaknesses, all at the attorney's own pace.[5] As Stern (1989, 227) declares, "seldom will counsel be able to lay out his argument in full with the supporting authorities. That can be done only in the brief."

In short, briefs help justices overcome information constraints; they can define the issues involved in a case, frame justices' perceptions of cases, and offer attorneys freedom to present the arguments they desire in a comprehensive and organized manner. For at least all four of these reasons, briefs are critical to the Court's decision-making process.

Yet, despite the importance of briefs, scholars know very little about them and whether the information contained in them can translate into litigant influence. A small handful of studies have recently been published that address briefs in a more aggregate sense. As discussed earlier, Wedeking (2010) examines how litigants select issue frames and whether that selection is correlated with success. Epstein and Kobylka (1992) analyze the arguments parties and amici made in two case types (abortion and death penalty) to determine whether their arguments led to success. Corley (2008) uses plagiarism software to determine whether Supreme Court opinions rely on the language found in party briefs. All these studies are useful, have advanced our nascent but growing knowledge about briefs, and are worthy reads. Nevertheless, none of them directly examines SG influence, the question we confront in this book.

Thus we are left with the following questions: if the OSG and a non-OSG litigant presented the Supreme Court with the same brief, would the Court draw more from the OSG brief? Or is the OSG's heightened success attributable to nothing other than the fact that it employs more experienced attorneys or strategically selects the cases it pursues? If the answer to the first question is yes, we will have further evidence of OSG influence. Conversely, if the answer to the second question is yes, we will have uncovered a much less consequential role for the OSG. The answers will allow us to make inferences about OSG influence. We must therefore devise a strategy that will allow us to answer each question independently, without the problem of observational equivalence. To do so, we return to the logic of matching.

DATA, MEASUREMENT, AND MATCHING

To examine whether OSG briefs uniquely influence Supreme Court opinions, we return to coursened exact matching (CEM), the same type of matching employed in our previous chapter. We seek to address whether the Court

---

[5] Of course, although parties face page limitations when writing briefs, they are free within those limits to emphasize the points of their choosing.

relies more on OSG briefs than on those submitted by other parties who are not affiliated with the OSG. In other words, we examine whether the Court borrows more language from OSG briefs than from otherwise identical non-OSG briefs.

To collect the data necessary to undertake this examination, we began by using LexisNexis to collect every majority opinion in every orally argued case decided during the Court's 1984–2007 terms that resulted in a nonmixed dispositional outcome; that is, we exclude dispositions that were affirmed or reversed "in-part."[6] Then, using Westlaw, we obtain every merits brief submitted in those cases. In total, we collected 12,533 briefs filed across 1,984 unique cases.[7]

Our dependent variable is the percentage of words the Court's majority opinion borrows from a written brief in a case. We follow the method employed by Corley (2008) and Corley et al. (2011) and use WCopyfind, a free, Windows-based software program that allows users to assess the amount of overlap (think plagiarism) between two or more documents (Bloomfield 2009).[8]

We adopted several treatment variables that allow us to investigate OSG influence under a variety of conditions. First, we coded the identity of the litigant who submitted each brief; that is, we coded whether the OSG filed the brief or whether someone other than the OSG filed it (i.e., OSG, non-OSG). This, of course, was necessary to determine whether the Court treated OSG briefs differently than non-OSG briefs. Determining who filed the brief was typically easy, as the title page of the brief references the name of the party or actor filing it.

Second, we broke down those two categories into two more: whether the brief "won" or "lost" at the merits stage. To do this, we began by determining the disposition sought by the brief, which simply called for us to examine the title of each brief. We treated petitioners as seeking reversal and respondents as seeking affirmance. (For the small number of briefs in which the title

---

[6] In some cases, the Supreme Court will reverse only portions of a lower court decision and leave remaining portions intact. We exclude these types of cases.

[7] We needed to exclude just under 300 of 2,278 eligible cases (about 13%) from our analysis because they had missing briefs or briefs with missing or illegible pages. Though the earlier terms of our data are disproportionately affected by these problems, results from a host of auxiliary analyses give us very little concern about systemic patterns of "missingness" across other variables of interest such as issue area, case complexity, or case salience.

[8] There are a variety of user-programmable options that can be modified in WCopyfind. We left all values at the default values recommended by the software's author (e.g., minimum string length of one hundred characters, zero imperfections allowed within a string). While the very large number of documents in our data set make it impractical to regenerate our data using other settings, we take comfort in the Corley et al. (2011, 37n7) finding that setting modifications did not affect the substance of their results.

TABLE 6.1. *Summary of treatment categories, based on identity, case outcome, and mode of participation – the columns denote the brief writer's mode of participation; the rows show whether the side the brief supported won or lost, and the cell halves indicate whether the OSG or a non-OSG actor wrote and submitted the brief.*

Case outcome	Mode of participation	
	Party	Amicus
Side brief supports wins	OSG / Non-OSG	OSG / Non-OSG
Side brief supports loses	OSG / Non-OSG	OSG / Non-OSG

did not provide us information as to the disposition sought, we read through the content of the brief.) Then, we examined whether the disposition supported by the brief (e.g., affirm or reverse the lower court decision) prevailed at the merits stage. To make this determination, we examined the *caseDisposition* variable in the Supreme Court Database.[9] That database provides a host of information on nearly every Supreme Court decision handed down in the last seventy years. Critical for us here, the database provides information on whether the Supreme Court reversed, affirmed, or otherwise disposed of the lower court decision under review. At the end of this second step, then, each brief fell into one of four categories: OSG win, OSG loss, non-OSG win, non-OSG loss.

Third, we determined the mode of participation for each brief, that is, whether the brief was submitted by a party to the case or by an amicus curiae who had an interest in the case. Ultimately, as Table 6.1 shows, our scheme sorts each brief into one of eight categories.

Breaking down the treatments into these eight categories allows us to examine a host of relevant comparisons between the OSG and non-OSG actors, which, we believe, gives us leverage to determine whether the OSG uniquely influences the Court's opinions. For example, we can examine straightforward treatments, such as a winning OSG party brief versus a winning non-OSG party brief, to determine if the Court borrows more from the OSG than from non-OSG briefs. Further investigation of such a comparison can also allow us to analyze whether the *impact* of winning is higher for the OSG than for non-OSG litigants (i.e., does the OSG win "bigger" than other parties?). We can also examine more complex comparisons such as whether the Court borrows more from a winning non-OSG brief than from a losing OSG brief. We will

---

[9] To access the Supreme Court Database, go to http://scdb.wustl.edu/.

get to the results of these and other comparisons shortly. Right now, though, we discuss the rationale for our broader matching approach.

As we note in Chapter 5, the reason to preprocess data through matching is to reduce the amount of imbalance across treatment categories so that our statistical inferences are more causal in theory. When comparing, for example, the influence of an OSG brief to a non-OSG brief, we want to know that any difference we observe *is solely attributable to the fact that the former brief is from the OSG, whereas the latter is not.* To that end, we cannot simply code our treatments and then proceed to compare them. We must first control for (i.e., match on) other characteristics that are likely to differ among briefs. In other words, there might be key differences between OSG briefs and non-OSG briefs that could, quite apart from OSG influence, drive up OSG success. As an example, we have reason to believe that greater experience generates more influential briefs (Corley 2008). If attorneys drafting OSG briefs have more experience than non-OSG brief writers, and attorney experience correlates with success, we must control for experience to make inferences about OSG influence.

Just what are these additional variables on which we must match that might drive OSG success? Stated differently, which factors might be tied to OSG success and the Court's tendency to borrow language from party briefs? In particular, we match on the following characteristics: the clarity of each brief, attorney experience, case salience, and information quantity. Because brief clarity is something we did not need to discuss in the last chapter, we spend slightly more time discussing it here than we do our other matched covariates.

Brief Clarity

The first feature on which we match is brief clarity – the readability of each brief. Most legal scholars argue that brief clarity is a critical component of a party's success before the Court. Indeed, history, anecdotal evidence, and systematic empirical evidence all point in this direction. Consider one historical example. In 1596, an English chancellor, annoyed with the unnecessary length and lack of quality in a legal document filed before him, made three orders. First, he ordered that a hole be cut into the lengthy document; second, he directed that the author's head be stuck through it; and third, he ordered that the author be paraded throughout the streets, wearing the hollowed-out document around his neck as an example of what would happen to writers who submitted such legal prose (Brand 1979, 292; *citing Mylward v. Welden*, ch. 1596). Apparently, judges of old valued clarity.

Although today's judges are not likely to respond so vigorously (though perhaps appropriately!) to poor-quality briefs, the clarity of the brief still matters. Scores of justices, judges, and legal scholars argue that clarity is among the most important characteristics of a quality brief (Tate 1978; Martineau et al. 2005; Scalia and Garner 2008; Michel 1998; Stern et al. 2002). After all, Supreme Court justices are generalists who lack the time to dig through briefs to find the brief writer's points. What is more, justices face severe limitations on their time.[10] As such, parties must make their points succinctly so that justices can digest them and quickly move on to their next tasks (vanR. Springer 1984). As Deputy Solicitor General Michael Dreeben once stated, "briefs should also be as clear as possible and as short as possible. Appellate judges have a lot to do. They are not interested in reading any more words than they have to" (Dreeben 2010).

Empirical evidence likewise suggests that brief clarity might lead to litigant success. For example, Benson and Kessler (1987) conducted an experiment to investigate whether briefs that employed common language persuaded respondents more than briefs that employed so-called legalese. The respondents found the plain language more persuasive than the legalese. In fact, they found the legalese unconvincing, believing that briefs employing it were filed by bad attorneys from bad law firms. In a similar study, Charrow and Charrow (1979) found that jurors were less able to understand jury instructions written in legalese than those written in plain language. Studies on judicial compliance agree. Spriggs (1996), for example, found that unclear Supreme Court opinions produced major policy change among executive agencies in a mere 3.4 percent of cases, whereas clear opinions secured major policy change in 95.5 percent of cases.

In short, if we believe – as many do – that "the most persuasively written argument components are those written with the precision of a neurosurgeon" (Hamilton 1999, 587), we might believe that a party's success before the Court is a function of his or her brief-writing skills. And if the OSG writes higher-quality briefs than non-OSG litigants, its success might be tied to that feature and not to something more inherent to the office. Accordingly, we opted to match on the clarity of each brief to ensure that brief quality was not an unexamined causal factor leading to OSG success. By matching an OSG brief with an equally clear non-OSG brief, we were able to account for the effects of brief quality and isolate the treatment – OSG status.

To code brief clarity, we determined the Coleman–Liau Index for each brief (Coleman and Liau 1975). This index is a composite of the length of

---

[10] Hart (1959, 91) found that during the Court's 1958 term, justices could devote only about two hours to read the parties' briefs in a case. The remainder of justices' time was dedicated to setting the Court's agenda, listening to oral argument, writing opinions, and attending conference. Today's Court surely faces similar time limitations.

words (measured by the number of characters) and the number of sentences within a text. The key advantage it enjoys over, for example, the Flesch–Kincaid measure (another commonly used readability test) is its nonreliance on the number of syllables in a word. Basic computer script can easily count characters. Yet, because scholars cannot agree on the definition of a syllable, computers have a difficult time systematically counting the number of syllables (Jurafsky and Martin 2008, 372). The formula for the Coleman–Liau index, then, is $0.0588L - 0.296S - 15.8$, where L is the average number of letters per one hundred words and S is the average number of sentences per one hundred words. High values on the index suggest a less readable text, whereas low values suggest a more readable text.[11]

Attorney Experience

Corley (2008) shows that the Court borrows more language from briefs submitted by experienced attorneys. To tap into this influence, we identified the attorney who appeared at oral argument for a particular brief and then counted the number of previous appearances she made to the Court. This approach follows the tack used by Corley (2008) in focusing on a single attorney (as opposed to, say, all attorneys whose names are on the brief) but deviates slightly from Corley's approach in that our variable is measured as the actual count of appearances. Because our overriding goal is to generate the most balanced data possible with regard to our treatment variable, we allowed the CEM software to select the optimal cut point values.

Case Salience

Existing empirical accounts of briefs also suggest that the salience of the case may affect whether the Court adopts language from a brief. In politically salient cases, justices have more at stake ideologically and thus are likely to invest themselves extensively in the opinion (Maltzman, Spriggs, and Wahlbeck 2000); that is, "in salient cases, justices might expend more time and energy shaping the content of the majority opinion than in relatively trivial disputes" (Corley et al. 2011, 39). This intuition has also been formalized by Lax and Cameron (2007), who show that high case salience makes opinion authors more willing to invest the time and energy involved in authoring the opinions. If this is the case, we must be careful that we do not make inferences about our treatment effects when comparing, for example, an OSG brief in a nonsalient case to a non-OSG brief in a salient case. Such an approach would likely

---

[11] As we document in this chapter's appendix, the results we report are robust if we use alternative readability measures.

drive up the Court's propensity to take from the OSG brief and drive down its propensity to take from the non-OSG brief – and not because of the brief's author! Put plainly, we need to make sure that we compare briefs – and examine our treatment effects – in equally salient cases. To measure the salience of a case, then, we follow Corley et al. (2011) and Black and Johnson (2008) and operationalize case salience as the total number of questions asked by the justices during oral argument. Cases of higher salience provoke the justices to ask more questions than cases of lower salience.

Information Quantity

As we noted previously, a key role of briefs is their ability to provide information and arguments for the Court's opinion authors. The Court's propensity to borrow from an individual brief may be different in cases where there are many briefs versus those in which there are fewer briefs. To this end, we use data provided by Collins (2008a, which we updated for the 2002-2007 terms) and match on the total number of amicus briefs submitted in a case.

Before we proceed to our methods and results section, we should point out one further important consideration. By parameterizing the brief space into the eight bins described in Table 6.1, we have already controlled for a feature we would presume is among the most important factors that determine brief influence – whether the Court finds the argument persuasive. We control for this feature by determining whether the brief's supported case disposition ultimately won. As a result (and in contrast to our previous chapter), we no longer need to control for either ideological compatibility or the level of resources possessed by the opposing side as both of these factors are ultimately subsumed by whether the disposition supported by a side wins or loses.

METHODS AND RESULTS

Having matched our data to ensure that they are as similar as possible – save for the treatment effects – we proceed to estimate the connection between those treatment effects and the amount of language the Court borrows from briefs. Because our dependent variable is the percentage of the Court's majority opinion that is borrowed from each brief, we estimate a series of linear regression models on our matched data sets. All regression models contain, in addition to a specific treatment variable of interest, the full set of pretreatment covariates described in the previous section. We take this additional step to reduce further any lingering imbalance that might remain even after matching (Ho et al. 2006). Using the parameter estimates from our statistical models (which we present in the chapter's appendix), we then generated simulations to quantify the impact our treatment variable had on the Court's borrowing habits. We present these results visually in Figures 6.1, 6.2, and 6.3.

In each of our figures, the x axis of the top panel reflects our treatment effects; that is, it represents the estimated additional influence, measured in terms of percentage of the opinion being borrowed, afforded to a brief in the treatment group over a brief in the control group. Positive values mean that the Court adopts more content in its opinion from the treatment brief than from the control brief, whereas negative values mean that the Court adopts more from the control group brief than from the treatment brief. The y axis of each figure identifies the treatment–control pairings for which we estimate treatment effects. Within each pairing label, the first value is the treatment group and the second is the control group. Thus, in the "Any OSG vs. Any Non-OSG" comparison, we compare any (merits) brief filed by the OSG in a case (the treatment) versus any (merits) brief filed by a non-OSG lawyer (the control group).

As in the previous chapter, the bottom row of panels in each figure presents additional diagnostic information concerning our matching solutions. The left panels illustrates the reduction in imbalance observed for each treatment–control pairing. The circles show the postmatched level of imbalance, and the triangles illustrate the prematched imbalance value. These are the same $\mathcal{L}_1$ values used in our previous chapter (see footnote 12 in Chapter 5 for specifics on how we calculated these values). The right panels show the proportion of observations from the original data that were retained in the matched data set as well as the raw numbers of retained observations.

To aid the discussion of our findings, we discuss our results in three groups: author identity and Court borrowing (Figure 6.1); the brief's winning (or losing) status and Court borrowing (Figure 6.1 and Figure 6.2); and author identity, winning status, and Court borrowing (Figure 6.3).

Author Identity and Language Borrowing

Consider, first, the most basic comparison of the Court's borrowing tendencies, found in the top line of Figure 6.1, which illustrates how much the Court borrows from any OSG brief versus any non-OSG brief. Immediately, the OSG has jumped out to a lead. We estimate, with such a comparison, that the Court will borrow 1.4 percent more content in its majority opinion from an OSG brief than from a non-OSG brief. While this is a broad comparison, as it does not account for winning or mode of participation, it does give us an initial and general finding as to the OSG's influence, and it shows clearly that the Court draws more from an OSG brief than from a similar non-OSG brief.

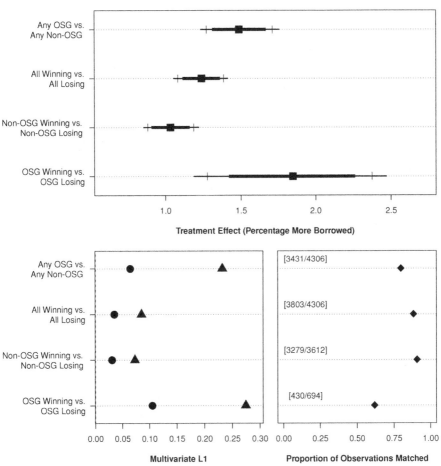

FIGURE 6.1. Dot plots of treatment effects and model diagnostic information. Each line in the top panel corresponds to a separate regression and effect estimate, which are denoted by the labels on the *y* axis. The first value listed in the *y* label comparison indicates the treatment group, and the second value in the comparison is the control. Plotted values indicate how much more the Court will borrow from the treatment brief than from the control brief. Squares represent point estimates. Thin horizontal lines, vertical tick marks, and thicker horizontal lines denote 95, 90, and 80 percent confidence intervals (two-tailed), respectively. These values were obtained through stochastic simulations using model parameter estimates reported in the chapter's appendix. The lower left panel presents the multivariate value of $\mathcal{L}_1$ for the unmatched (triangle point) and matched (circle point). Note 12 in Chapter 5 provides additional details on the calculation of these values. The lower right panel presents the proportion of observations retained by our matching solution for each treatment–control pairing. The numbers in square brackets provide the raw values for the matched and unmatched data, respectively.

To put the finding in slightly more concrete terms, consider the Supreme Court's decision in *Baze v. Rees*, 553 U.S. 35 (2008). In *Baze*, the Court faced the question whether state-sponsored lethal injections violated the Eighth Amendment's prohibition on cruel and unusual punishment. The United States voluntarily joined the case as an amicus curiae participant and supported Kentucky's position that the form of death penalty was constitutional. The Court found, in a somewhat fractious opinion, that lethal injections did not violate the Eighth Amendment. Perhaps more important for us, our estimates reveal that the judgment in the case was roughly 114 words longer than it would have been had the OSG not participated in the case; that is, the opinion was 114 words longer because of the Court's borrowing from the OSG's brief. What this means is that, given the spacing and margins of published Court opinions, *Baze* was almost a full page longer simply because of the OSG's brief.

Winning Status and Language Borrowing

Our next area of attention is whether winning status influences the amount of Court borrowing. Does the Court draw more from briefs that win than from those that lose, and does this dynamic, if it occurs, also apply to the Court's borrowing from OSG briefs? Put simply, the answer to these questions is yes. Consider the effects of winning on every brief filer (OSG and non-OSG attorneys). Across the board, the Court draws more from winning than from losing briefs. The second line of Figure 6.1 shows that the Court opinion draws 1.3 percent more from winning briefs than from losing briefs.

When we look separately at non-OSG filers and OSG filers, we see the dynamic play out more specifically. Line 3 of the same figure shows that non-OSG litigants receive a 1 percent boost in borrowing when they author a winning brief. Line 4 demonstrates that the Court borrows roughly 1.8 percent more content from OSG briefs when they are winning versus losing. While the OSG's slightly larger value might suggest that it is rewarded more for winning, we must caution that since the underlying data and models are different for these two estimates, it is not appropriate to compare these two values directly. Nevertheless, the data show that winning matters across all litigants before the Court.

Author Identity, Winning Status, and Language Borrowing

Thus far, we have discovered that the Court, on average, adopts more language from OSG briefs than from non-OSG briefs and that it borrows more from

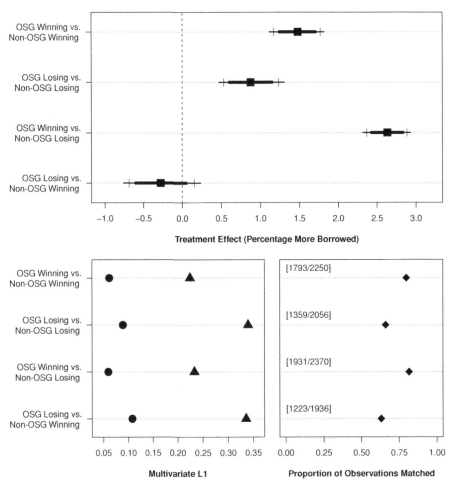

FIGURE 6.2. Dot plots of treatment effects and model diagnostic information. See the caption to Figure 6.1 for additional information.

winning briefs than from losing briefs. We now examine the interactive effects of author identity and winning status. If the Court borrows more from all OSG briefs than from all non-OSG briefs, and if it borrows more from winning briefs than from losing briefs, surely the interaction of these two components should matter.

Figure 6.2 plots our next four comparisons, which examine how author identity and winning status affect the Court's borrowing practices. The results, once again, provide strong evidence of OSG influence. The first line of Figure 6.2 examines the effect of author identity and winning on the Court's borrowing practices. More specifically, we restrict our comparison to winning briefs and ask whether an OSG brief observes an increase in borrowing over non-OSG briefs. As the point estimate and confidence interval make clear, the answer to this question is yes. We estimate that the Court will borrow roughly 1.5 percent more content from a winning OSG brief than from an otherwise identical winning non-OSG brief. While this is not overwhelming in an absolute sense, it is worth noting that the baseline rate of borrowing, which we provide in the chapter's appendix, is only 2 percent. Thus the relative increase is around 75 percent more language. Briefs from the OSG, in short, win bigger than similar briefs from non-OSG litigants.

To put these results in more concrete terms once again, we return to a recent Court opinion. In *District of Columbia v. Heller*, 554 U.S. 570 (2008), the Court declared that the second amendment provided a personal constitutional right to own a firearm. In so doing, it adopted the same principle advocated by the SG, who, in a voluntarily filed amicus curiae brief, argued that "the Second Amendment, no less than other provisions of the Bill of Rights, secures an individual right." Considering again the length and spacing of published Supreme Court opinions, our results suggest that the Court included 352 additional words in its opinion – or roughly two and a half additional pages of material – that it otherwise would not have included had the OSG not filed its amicus brief in the case.

We also find, as documented in the second line of the figure, that losing briefs filed by the OSG are ultimately penalized less than their non-OSG counterparts, at least in terms of the language borrowed from the brief by the Court; that is, if we examine the pool of all losing briefs and look at the unique impact of having a brief filed by the OSG, we estimate that the OSG's presence is good for a 0.9 percent increase in how much the Court will end up borrowing over non-OSG briefs. Again, though number is not overwhelming in an absolute sense, the relative increase is around 45 percent more language in the Court's opinion, attributed solely to the presence of the OSG brief.

The next counterfactual examines the relatively easy comparison of a winning OSG brief and a losing non-OSG brief. We expect big gains here for the OSG, and that is precisely what we observe. The Court's opinion contains 2.8 percent more from winning OSG briefs than from losing non-OSG briefs – a relative increase of 140 percent more language.

More interesting, though, is the comparison of borrowing in cases in which the OSG loses but the non-OSG litigant wins. This is a strong test of influence. After all, because we have found (1) that the Court borrows much more from winning briefs than from losing briefs and (2) that this dynamic applies to all brief filers, including the OSG, one might expect the Court to borrow more from the winning non-OSG brief than from the losing OSG brief. That result, however, does not occur. Instead, the Court will draw equally from losing OSG briefs and winning non-OSG briefs. *Even when the OSG loses, the Court borrows just as much language from its brief as from the brief filed by a non-OSG winner.* Simply put, the OSG is able to offset its losses, in part because of its unique status before the Court.

Author Identity, Winning (or Losing) Status, Mode of Participation, and Language Borrowing

So far, we have analyzed whether author identity and winning party status affect the amount of Court borrowing. The results from all these previous treatments show that the Court borrows more from OSG briefs than from non-OSG briefs. OSG briefs win bigger than non-OSG briefs, and they lose less than non-OSG briefs. Our next aim is to determine whether the OSG's mode of participation matters; that is, we examine when the OSG participates in the case as a party or as an amicus curiae and whether that mode of participation affects the Court's borrowing practices.

We find that the mode of participation matters little. As Figure 6.3 shows, when the OSG files a brief as a party to the case, the Court is roughly 1.1 percent more likely to borrow from that brief than when the OSG files a nearly identical brief in a nearly identical case in which the OSG is an amicus curiae participant. What these differences between the OSG as amicus and OSG as party mean we cannot be sure, but our strong hunch is that politics has something to do with it. Previous work has suggested that presidents pursue political goals more often when filing amicus briefs than when the United States appears as a party (Pacelle 2003). If justices discount OSG arguments more frequently in such cases – and Wohlfarth (2009) suggests that they do – the Court's different borrowing practices could be an artifact of what happens when the OSG as amicus curiae pushes partisan arguments too far.

The second line of the figure considers whether the Court borrows more from the OSG when the office voluntarily files an amicus curiae brief than when the Court has invited it to do so. Some scholars have argued that the Court will treat invited OSG amicus briefs differently than voluntarily submitted briefs (Pacelle 2006). There are, of course, differences between the two types of cases, but are those differences meaningful in a systematic sense? Perhaps not. In comparing the amount the Court borrows from OSG invited briefs to the amount it borrows from OSG voluntary amicus briefs, we find that the Court treats the two the same; that is, the Court is not statistically any more likely to borrow language from one type of brief than the other.

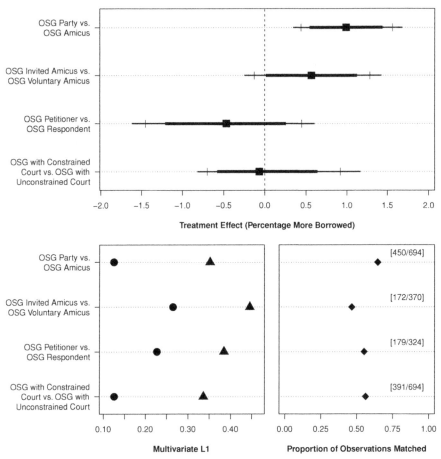

FIGURE 6.3. Dot plots of treatment effects and model diagnostic information. See the caption to Figure 6.1 for additional information.

We retrieve similar results when comparing the OSG as petitioner versus respondent. The Court draws equally from OSG petitioner and respondent briefs. The importance of this finding becomes clearer later, when we discuss how our results fit into the existing theories of OSG success. Suffice it to say, however, that the result casts doubt on the strategic selection theory.

Finally, and consistent with our previous chapter, we also considered the separation-of-powers context that existed during the case. More specifically, we matched OSG briefs written when the Court was theoretically constrained (treatment) with OSG briefs written when the Court was not constrained. If, as some scholars argue, the Court must defer to the government – or otherwise take steps to mollify it – when it is more liberal (conservative) than the most liberal (conservative) legislative pivots, we might expect the Court's borrowing practices to fluctuate in response to its relation to pivotal legislators; that is, the Court might strategically borrow more from OSG briefs to protect its opinions when it worries about congressional reaction. If so, we would observe more borrowing when the Court is constrained by Congress than when it is unconstrained and thus can rule sincerely, without fear of a congressional rebuke. However, we fail to recover a significant difference in the Court's borrowing tendencies from the OSG when it is constrained versus when it is not.[12]

DISCUSSION

We examined whether the United States Solicitor General influences legal doctrine. We did so by analyzing the percentage of words the Court's majority opinion borrowed from merits briefs between the Court's 1984 and 2007 terms. When we compare winning OSG briefs with winning non-OSG briefs, the Court still borrows more from the OSG brief. The same dynamic holds when both briefs are on the losing end. When the OSG wins and the non-OSG in a similar case with a similar brief loses, the Court borrows more from the OSG. And in comparisons in which the OSG loses but a non-OSG party wins, the Court borrows just as much from the OSG brief as from the winning non-OSG brief. All this, we believe, points to considerable SG influence over Supreme Court opinions.

What is more, the results of our models cast doubt on nearly every existing theory of OSG success and thereby raise up one in particular. Consider the attorney experience theory (McGuire 1998). If the OSG were so successful before the Court because its attorneys have more experience than non-OSG attorneys, we would have observed the Court borrowing the same amount of language from OSG briefs and non-OSG briefs when matching on attorney experience. This was hardly the case. After matching treated and untreated cases based on similar levels of attorney experience, the Court still borrowed a larger percentage of words from OSG briefs than from non-OSG briefs.

Consider, next, the separation-of-powers argument. If the OSG were so successful before the Court because of some underlying separation-of-powers considerations, its heightened success would evaporate when the separation-of-powers constraint disappeared. The Court would have borrowed equally from OSG briefs and non-OSG briefs when they were filed in the same separation-of-powers context. That we still observed an OSG advantage, however, casts doubt on the separation-of-powers theory.

---

[12] We follow the same procedure described in the appendix to Chapter 4 to obtain these estimates.

What about the strategic selection argument? We observe little support for this theory as well. Ultimately, three factors challenge it. First, as Figure 6.3 showed, when the OSG participates as a party, which it often *must* do, the Court borrows more of its language than when the OSG participates as an amicus. This would suggest that the OSG is not picking amicus cases more strategically than party cases. Second, our comparison of the Court's borrowing practices relating to the OSG as petitioner and the OSG as respondent revealed no differences. If the OSG strategically petitions for review, one would expect the Court to borrow more when the OSG is petitioner than when it is respondent. Indeed, while the statistical effect is null, the coefficient on petitioner status is actually signed in the negative direction. Finally, it is worth noting that even when the OSG ostensibly calculates wrongly – and *loses* – the Court still borrows from its brief just as much as from a winning non-OSG brief. Put plainly, if the OSG were picking cases strategically that it knew it would win, we would not retrieve the results our models produced.

What this leaves us with is the conjecture that the Court borrows more from OSG briefs because it trusts the professional judgment of the lawyers within that office. We are left, again, with the belief that the OSG consists of highly respected legal professionals who influence the law because of the objective and skilled arguments they make. In short, the data seem to suggest two things: first, that the OSG is indeed influential before the Court – and not just successful – and second, that this influence is most likely tied to the objectivity and overall neutrality of the office.

In the beginning of this chapter, we discussed the importance of legal opinions and legal doctrine. We argued that the language of the law is perhaps the most important aspect of judicial decision making to study. This chapter examined one portion of that dynamic. While we have shown here that OSG briefs influence the content of Supreme Court opinions, we have not yet examined whether the OSG can influence the Court's treatment of precedent. Does the Court treat existing precedent positively or negatively based on the recommmendation of the OSG? Is the Court more likely to overrule precedent when so advised by the OSG? These and other questions must be examined before we can finally claim that the OSG influences legal doctrine. Accordingly, our next chapter examines OSG influence over the Court's treatment of precedent.

7

Solicitor General Influence and Legal Doctrine

In 2002, the U.S. Supreme Court ruled on whether state and local governments must constitutionally provide compensation to landowners for moratoria that impose temporary restrictions on property development.[1] The ruling pulled back from what appeared to have been a significant change in regulatory takings doctrine. Just ten years earlier, in *Lucas v. South Carolina Coastal Council*, 505 U.S. 1003 (1992), a 6–2 Court majority indicated that justices would take a strict stand on local land use regulations that placed restrictions on property development.[2] The question in *Tahoe-Sierra* was just how wedded the Court was to the recently decided *Lucas* ruling.

The facts of the *Tahoe-Sierra* case were similar to those in many regulatory takings cases, including *Lucas*. The water in Lake Tahoe historically was pure and clear – today, a person can look seventy feet into the water[3] – and the area homeowners wanted to keep it that way. During the 1960s, however, those homeowners observed the water becoming dirty. They attributed the pollution to recent property expansion near the lakeshore. Dirt and other runoff from home building seeped into the water, created algae, and started a process that could have permanently muddied the lake. The homeowners turned to the law to place restrictions on growth and its accompanying pollution.

More specifically, the homeowners empowered the Tahoe Regional Planning Agency to conserve the area's natural resources. The agency imposed two moratoria that halted all property development in the area. The purpose of the moratoria was to pause development while the agency could research and

---

[1] *Tahoe-Sierra Preservation Council v. Tahoe Regional Planning Agency*, 535 U.S. 302 (2002).
[2] Chief Justice Rehnquist and Justices Scalia, White, O'Connor, Thomas, and Kennedy were in the majority. (Justice Kennedy filed a regular concurrence.) Justices Blackmun and Stevens dissented. Justice Souter voted to dismiss the case as improvidently granted.
[3] See http://www.trpa.org/default.aspx?tabindex=5&tabid=95.

adopt new building standards and a regional growth plan. Once the moratoria were lifted, development could hit the ground running in an environmentally friendly manner.

Of course, while all this was happening, landowners were prohibited from developing their property. They had no idea just how "temporary" the temporary moratoria would be. And to add to their frustration, many had purchased their property with the specific intent to build on it. While the moratoria were in place, however, they were deprived of all economically beneficial or productive use of their land. As a result, they argued that the government should compensate them for the diminished value of their land – even though the restrictions turned out to be temporary.

The United States, participating as an amicus curiae, supported the moratoria. The Court's *Lucas* precedent, argued the office of the Solicitor General (OSG), was easily distinguishable from the case at hand. *Lucas* held that a taking occurred when a property holder lost all economically beneficial uses of land. Temporary moratoria, however, did not strip them of all uses. Instead, the brief halt on development was done with the understanding that development could occur again at some point in the future. Indeed, the OSG stated that the per se rule described in *Lucas* would apply only when "regulation precluded all economically viable use of property during the period it was in effect" (see Brief for United States, 2000 U.S. Briefs 1167, 28). Thus, in the absence of a more permanent taking, the state and local governments were well within their legal rights to zone land. On policy grounds, the OSG argued further that requiring governmental units to pay landowners for temporary development delays would generate rushed and poorly thought out land use regulations. The OSG pointed out that "government hardly could go on if it were required to pay for every diminution in value caused" by such regulations (14). Local governments would avoid paying compensatory costs that would grow with the length of the development delay. Dollar signs would add up each additional day a moratorium was in place, imposing significant and ultimately backbreaking costs to conduct research for thorough land use plans.

Writing for a 6–3 majority, Justice Stevens agreed with the OSG. He and the rest of the majority made an about-face, distinguished *Lucas*, and adopted a narrow view of regulatory takings. Indeed, Stevens essentially relegated *Lucas* to a set of facts that was unlikely ever to happen again. *Lucas* merely declared that a regulatory taking occurred whenever a landholder was permanently denied of all economically viable land use. The landowners here were only temporarily denied some economic use of the land. The value of the property would recover once the moratoria were lifted. There was, in short, no "obliteration of value" (*Tahoe-Sierra Preservation Council*, 535 U.S. at 330–331).[4] By interpreting *Lucas* in such narrow terms, the *Tahoe-Sierra* decision gutted it. Put plainly, just ten years after *Lucas*, the Court halted what had once looked like a major change in regulatory takings doctrine.

What explains the Court's shift away from *Lucas*? Which factors led justices to side with landowners in *Lucas* but against them in *Tahoe-Sierra*? To be sure, the facts of the case were not identical, but they were similar enough in principle that a contraction from *Lucas* based purely on the facts seemed like a stretch. What about a change in Court composition? Might the law have changed because of new justices opposed to *Lucas*? This does not appear to explain the shift either. Only two justices departed the Court between the cases. Justice Blackmun, who was in the minority in *Lucas*, was replaced by Justice Breyer, a member of the majority in *Tahoe-Sierra*, so there was no change in position there. Conversely, Justice White, who was in the majority in *Lucas*, was replaced by Justice Ginsburg, a member of the majority in *Tahoe-Sierra*. Still, in theory, this switch alone would have merely changed the *Tahoe-Sierra* majority from 6–3 to 5–4 in favor of the landowners. Someone else needed to switch. As it turns out, two justices who were part of the *Lucas* majority switched positions: Justices O'Connor and Kennedy. What led to their switch and to the Court's change in doctrine?

Our hypothesis is that the OSG influenced legal doctrine in this case – and in many others like it. As we have seen throughout this book, the OSG has the power to influence the Court throughout its decision-making process. We observed in Chapter 4 that the OSG can influence justices to grant review to cases they otherwise would not wish to review. Chapter 5 showed us that the OSG is significantly more likely to win its cases than a nearly identical party in a nearly identical case. And Chapter 6 illustrated that the Court adopts more language from OSG briefs than from identical non-OSG briefs. All three of these chapters suggest that the OSG enjoys some unique and influential status before the Court. This chapter follows suit and examines whether the OSG, as it arguably did in *Tahoe-Sierra*, influences the Court's treatment of precedent. To do so, we examine the legal arguments made by the OSG in its written merits briefs filed during the Court's 1984–2004 terms. In particular, we focus on how the OSG suggests the Court should

---

[4] The Court also followed the OSG's recommendation regarding another precedent, *First English Evangelical Lutheran Church of Glendale v. County of Los Angeles*, 482 U.S. 304 (1987). According to the OSG, *First English* did not help the Court determine whether a taking occurred; it only addressed the question of what kind of compensation was required when a regulatory taking was already found to have occurred. The Court's majority agreed with this recommendation and thus distinguished *First English*.

interpret – either positively or negatively – its previous decisions. We then examine how these recommendations influence the Court's decision to treat previous precedent.

Because this chapter focuses on stare decisis and precedent, we begin by reviewing existing research on how precedent evolves over time. We then explain how we examine OSG influence in the context of doctrinal development. Afterward, we present our data and methods, examine our results, and discuss what they mean for the evolution of law and SG influence on the Court.

STARE DECISIS AND THE EVOLUTION OF LEGAL DOCTRINE

Among the oldest questions in judicial politics literature is how law changes. Scholars have largely come down into one of two major camps. One camp argues that law changes simply as a function of Court composition and judicial preferences. In this vein, the law is no independent constraint on justices; rather, justices are single-minded seekers of policy, and the law is merely a cloak for their policy desires. Law changes and becomes more conservative or liberal when justices are conservative or liberal. Another camp has emerged in recent years, however, which argues that though policy factors are important, they are not exclusive. Law evolves as a function of policy-seeking behavior conditioned by a host of contextual and other features. Court outcomes are a function of the policy justices want effectuated but conditioned on what is permissible for them to accomplish. And law can sometimes, even if broadly, define what is permissible. In this section, we examine each of these arguments.

Doctrinal Development and Justices' Preferences

One group of scholars argues that law changes merely as a function of policy preferences on the Court. When the Court is composed of conservative justices, its precedents become more conservative, and when it is composed of liberal justices, its doctrine becomes more liberal. The strongest articulation of this argument comes from Segal and Spaeth (2002), who explicate what has come to be known as the attitudinal model. In it, the authors argue that "precedent as a legal model provides no guide to the justices' decisions" (54). Instead, the best indicator of a justice's vote is his or her underlying ideology: "Rehnquist vote[d] the way he [did] because he [was] extremely conservative; Marshall voted the way he did because he was extremely liberal" (Segal and Spaeth 2002, 86). Legal doctrine becomes increasingly conservative with more Rehnquists on the Court and increasingly liberal with more Marshalls on the Court. Law plays no independent role in influencing justices' votes.

This view of legal change emerged among political scientists largely in the 1930s (though legal realists had made the argument sooner) and gained a strong foothold among social scientists shortly thereafter. During that time, behavioralists employed observational data to study judicial behavior. What they observed cut at the fabric of conventional understandings of the Court. If precedent drove decisions, they asked, why did justices arrive at different conclusions when they interpreted the same law (Pritchett 1948)? The answer was clear. As C. Herman Pritchett (1948, 20) put it, "any examination of the present-day Court must accept the fact that its decisions inevitably have a political character, and the real question is not whether, but how well, its justices perform political functions."

The notion that justices were merely policy seekers who used the law to cloak their extralegal goals soon took hold among judicial politics scholars – and the data seemed to support the argument (Segal and Spaeth 2002; Brenner and Spaeth 1995; Segal and Spaeth 1996). Spaeth made the point clearly in his early analysis of Justice Frankfurter's supposed judicial restraint:

> Judicial restraint is thoroughly subordinated to the attitudes of the justices toward business and labor. The concept serves only to cloak the political character of the judicial process and thereby helps to preserve the traditional view that judges merely find and do not make law. Not only for Frankfurter, but for all the Warren Court justices, the concept of judicial restraint is an effective means of rationalizing response to policy-oriented values. (Spaeth 1964, 38)

Segal and Spaeth (1999) tested these claims more directly, examining whether justices who lost in one case later switched their positions in future, similar cases and adopted the original majority position. The authors examined a set of Supreme Court decisions in which at least one justice dissented. They then examined all progeny cases tied to that original decision to determine whether the dissenting justices followed their original dissenting positions or switched to the original majority's position. If a justice stuck to her original position, the authors coded the vote as preference based; if a justice switched to the original majority's position, they coded the vote as precedent based. A key contribution of this research design was that the authors were able to overcome observational equivalence. The only way to falsify the legal or policy theory was to examine instances in which they generated divergent expectations. By using each justice's revealed preferences from the original case, Segal and Spaeth were then able to disentangle the expectations from the two theories, and the results suggested that justices overwhelmingly stuck to their original votes. Under 12 percent of justices' votes were based on precedent, and not a single justice voted for precedent more than two-thirds of the time. Though some justices moderately followed precedent, they largely did so only in ordinary (i.e., not salient) cases. In short, using the definitions adopted by the authors in the study, justices rarely followed precedent but instead followed their own policy goals. Legal change, then, came on the heels of changing Court composition and judicial preferences.[5]

Doctrinal Development, Preferences, and External Constraints

Of course, the notion that policy alone motivates justices contradicts much of what lawyers are taught and what many legal academics believe about the Court. As Friedman (2006, 266) stated, the attitudinal approach declares that "what lawyers, judges, and legal academics spend years learning, practicing, and theorizing about is meaningless." Certainly there are strong theoretical reasons to believe, contrary to the attitudinal approach, that law influences justices' choices. The Court's decisions are couched in the law. Lawyers' briefs focus extensively on legal considerations (Gillman 2001), and justices discuss precedent privately (Knight and Epstein 1996). These broad features alone made at least some contemporary scholars hesitant to accept the full-throated attitudinalist argument.

Indeed, justices' private conference notes suggest that precedent may influence their votes. Knight and Epstein (1996) examined Justice Brennan's conference notes to determine, among other things, the extent to which justices referenced precedent in their private conferences. The authors' belief was that if precedent were merely a tool justices used to cloak their policy goals, justices would not need to reference it in their private discussions, away from public consumption – but they did. In fact, justices frequently discussed how precedent controlled the outcomes of cases. Why, the authors wondered, would justices cite precedent to each other if it had no controlling effect on them? The answer, they believed, was clear. Precedent played an influential role. Justices may be driven by their policy goals, but they are constrained from acting exclusively on those goals by the preferences and expectations of other actors with whom they must interact. Most important, the public and legal community believe in what one set of scholars has called the "myth of legality" (Scheb and Lyons 2000): the belief that justices rule according to law. If they failed to do so, the Court would lose legitimacy. Thus justices may wish

---

[5] It is worth pointing out, however, that an earlier version of the study (Segal and Spaeth 1996) encountered significant resistance due to coding decisions and other aspects (see, e.g., Songer and Lindquist 1996; Brenner and Stier 1996).

to pursue policy alone, but they are constrained from doing so by external expectations.

In recent years, scholars have employed more sophisticated empirical models to make the point and to challenge the theory that legal change is purely a function of judicial preference. Like Knight and Epstein (1996), these scholars suggest that law changes as a function of justices' policy preferences and a host of broader contextual components that limit justices' choices. Consider the approach taken by Bailey and Maltzman (2008). They analyze whether law influences justices to cast votes contrary to their policy goals. In a clever research design, the authors argue that to examine how law influences justices, one must disentangle legal motivations and policy-based motivations. Doing so, however, is not easy (see, e.g., Segal and Spaeth 1999). One must be able to predict how a judge would vote in the absence of legal norms. To determine this baseline policy motivation, the authors looked to statements made by members of Congress and presidents regarding Supreme Court decisions. Politicians, they argued, care primarily about the policy implications of cases rather than the legal niceties of them. Thus, to estimate where the policy outcome of a case was, one could look to comments made by the elected branches. Using those comments to establish baseline ideologies for each case, the authors found that justices often cast counterideological votes. Many conservative (liberal) justices voted against the conservative (liberal) position in cases, leading the authors to believe that law did in fact constrain justices at least part of the time.

Looking at the Court's decisions at the agenda-setting stage, Black and Owens (2009a) also discovered strong evidence that the law influences justices. Justices expected to cast policy-based votes failed to do so in the presence of important legal considerations. When legal and policy goals diverged, their results showed, legal considerations limited justices' abilities to maximize their policy goals. In fact, in some instances, justices were 33 percent less likely to engage in policy-based behavior simply because of the presence of critical legal considerations. Conversely, when legal and policy goals converged, the law made it easier for justices to seek policy. The results of the study suggested, then, that law was a constraint on justices but could also, when pointed in the same direction as their policy goals, be a strong legitimizer.

Richards and Kritzer (2002) argue that when justices adopt new "jurisprudential regimes," they can redefine how justices interpret law in future cases (see also Luse et al. 2011; Richards et al. 2006; Kritzer and Richards 2005; Kritzer and Richards 2003). The authors argued that justices create legal tests that look to certain facts in cases to determine how much scrutiny to apply to a governmental act. When facts *a* and *b* are present, the Court will apply one type of test; when facts *c* and *d* are present, the Court will apply a different level of scrutiny. Richards and Kritzer examined whether a change in these legal tests was correlated with case outcomes. It was. By making some facts more or less relevant to the legal outcome, the new regime made victory for some litigants harder than for others. Legal change, then, occurred because justices created tests that limited the discretion of future justices in future cases. And while policy preferences mattered in the creation of the test, once the test took hold and became precedential, it could influence future judicial outcomes.[6]

Bartels (2009) also finds that judicial tests can limit justices' discretion. Like Richards and Kritzer (2002), Bartels argues that law may act as an independent force on justices, either with their policy goals or against them.[7] He finds that both ideology and law matter, but with a twist. When the Court adopts a test that involves strict scrutiny analysis, justices enjoy little discretion to impose their policy preferences in a case. Conversely, when justices agree that the test to apply in the case is lower-level scrutiny, such as the rational basis test, or intermediate-level scrutiny, they enjoy more discretion to impose their preferences. The law, then, can constrain justices' policy-driven behavior, but only when they are faced with fact scenarios that generate strict scrutiny. Thus, like Richards and Kritzer (2002), the study suggests that legal change is a function of justices' preferences but also the constraints imposed on them by existing law and legal tests.

In a similar manner, Hansford and Spriggs (2006) examine how law changes by focusing on the interactive relationship between justices' policy preferences and "precedent vitality." The authors analyze the conditions under which the Court treats precedent positively (by applying it) or negatively (by distinguishing or overruling it). They find that precedent vitality – the Court's past treatment of the precedent – influences justices' policy-seeking behavior. As a case receives more positive treatment over time, it becomes more vital. As it garners more negative treatment it becomes less vital. Hansford and Spriggs's findings showed that justices are more likely to overrule ideologically distant–high-vitality cases than all others. They do so to drive down the value of strong but ideologically distant law. Relatedly, justices who are ideologically close to a precedent are more likely to treat it positively if it has low vitality than if it is highly vital. Seeking to resuscitate close but weak law, they will positively interpret it when they can. Justices, in short, use law instrumentally to

---

[6]   For a study challenging these results, see Lax and Rader (2010).

[7]   Bartels (2009, 475) refers to models that claim that "law exerts an independent and concurrent influence" as "hybrid models."

achieve their policy goals, and the existing health or strength of the precedent influences their treatment of it.

Recent innovations in network analysis provide perhaps the most promising insight for research into legal development on the Court. Fowler et al. (2007) apply network analysis to examine how precedents cite each other and to "identify the most legally relevant precedents in the network of Supreme Court law at any given point in time" (324). The authors examined every published Supreme Court opinion between the 1791 and 2005 terms. They created two measures that reflected a precedent's importance and its connection to other precedents: outward centrality and inward centrality. Outward centrality captures the number of precedents each opinion cites, whereas inward centrality measures the number of times the case under study was later cited by other Court precedents. Thus cases with large values of inward centrality are more important in the legal network. The results show the most important cases in the legal network. They also show how the Court has employed stare decisis broadly over time. One interesting finding, for example, is that the Court's application of stare decisis has changed dramatically. During its early years, the Court cited very few cases to support its decisions, yet, as time went on, the Court began to cite more of its own precedents to support its decisions.[8]

All these studies are clearly important. They suggest that law evolves as a function of justices' policy preferences – and sometimes as a function of the pursuit of those policies within broader constraints. Yet they do not directly examine whether the OSG plays a role in influencing doctrinal development. The study that comes closest to examining OSG influence is Wahlbeck's study on legal change. In an interesting approach, Wahlbeck (1997) analyzes the factors that lead the Court to restrict or expand rights, finding that change in search and seizure law is a function of attorney experience, amicus curiae support, presidential preference, and, most important for our purposes, government party status; that is, when the federal government is a party to the case, the Court is much less likely to engage in expansive legal change.[9] But even these results are limited. Although Wahlbeck finds a connection between the presence of the government and the probability of engaging in expansive change,

---

[8] Other studies examine more specific matters such as the role of interest groups in doctrinal development (Epstein and Kobylka 1992; Collins 2004, 2008b), the prestige of circuit judges (Klein and Morrisroe 1999), and how the use of constitutional (Gates and Phelps 1996; Phelps and Gates 1991) or statutory interpretive methods (Brudney and Ditslear 2005) leads to (or fails to lead to) jurisprudential outcomes.

[9] As we stated in Chapter 6, Corley (2008) and Spriggs and Wahlbeck (1997) find that the language in Supreme Court opinions is partly a function of the arguments made in OSG briefs.

it is unclear why this might be the case or what the underlying dynamics are that generate this outcome.

Put simply, we have learned much in recent years about the effects of law and its evolution, but we still know little about whether the OSG influences that development. Our goal in this chapter is to build on these valuable studies, expand the focus to the OSG, and answer whether justices become more likely to treat precedent positively or negatively when the OSG so recommends.

DATA, MEASUREMENT, AND MATCHING

To determine whether the OSG influences how the Court interprets precedent, we once again followed the matching strategy described in our previous chapters. We started by using data from Hansford and Spriggs (2006) that identify all Supreme Court precedents that were either cited or substantively interpreted by subsequent decisions of the Court. These data identify how a citing case (i.e., the subsequent case) treated a cited case (i.e., the initial precedent). In the introduction to this chapter, for example, the citing case of *Tahoe-Sierra* interpreted the cited case of *Lucas*. We restrict our universe of citing cases to those between the Court's 1984 and 2004 terms. Similarly, we focus on cited cases decided starting with the Court's 1946 term.[10] Our dependent variables are two dichotomous measures that assess whether the Court negatively interpreted a cited case in a citing case and whether it positively interpreted a cited case in a citing case.

Our key independent variable is whether the OSG recommended that the Court substantively interpret a cited precedent in a citing case. To generate this measure, we started by determining whether the OSG submitted a merits brief in each of the citing cases (i.e., those from 1984 to 2004). If it did, we coded all the Supreme Court precedents cited in any OSG brief filed during the merits stage. For each of the cited precedents, we applied the coding rules used by Hansford and Spriggs (2006) to determine if the OSG recommended that the Court positively or negatively interpret the cited case.[11] Through this process,

---

[10] The citing window bounds were determined by data availability. Electronic briefs are not systematically available on Westlaw prior to the Court's 1984 term. The treatment data, which were generously provided to us by Hansford and Spriggs, end with the Court's 2004 term. The cited window bound was chosen because data for a host of variables are unavailable prior to the beginning of the Vinson Court. We have no reason to believe that our results would systematically differ by extending any of these time limits.

[11] These coding rules follow the same process applied by *Shepard's*, which is the service LexisNexis uses to determine had the Court treats precedent – whether the Court follows precedent, distinguishes it, overrules it, etc. We code as positive treatment when the OSG brief asks that the Court follow a cited case. We code as negative treatment when the OSG brief distinguishes, criticizes, or recommends overruling the cited case. Spriggs and Hansford

we coded 751 cases in which the OSG submitted a merits brief.[12] Across these 751 cases, OSG briefs cited a cumulative total of 14,619 precedents (about 19.5 per case) and argued for positive or negative treatment in 1,319 (about 1.8 per case) and 976 (about 1.3 per case) of them, respectively.

As in our previous chapters, we control for potential confounding variables by matching our treated observations with similar untreated observations. More specifically, we match treated and untreated observations on the cited precedent's vitality, the ideological distance from the cited precedent, the cited precedent's inward centrality, and the number of opinions filed in the cited precedent.

Precedent Vitality

As Hansford and Spriggs (2006) document, the extent to which a precedent has been positively (or negatively) interpreted in the past influences how it will be treated in the future. Accordingly, it is necessary to isolate and balance the confounding influence of vitality. Following Hansford and Spriggs (2006), we measure *Precedent Vitality* as the number of previous positive interpretations minus the number of previous negative interpretations (up to, but not including, the year in which a case was decided).[13] Positive values thus correspond to precedents that are still considered to be "good law," and negative values represent precedents viewed as being not so good.

Ideological Distance

Hansford and Spriggs (2006) and others (e.g., Segal and Spaeth 1999) show that the Court's ideological distance from a precedent can influence how it interprets that precedent. All else being equal, the more distant the Court is ideologically from a precedent, the less likely it will be to interpret it positively

---

(2000) show that, as applied by the staff attorneys at *Shepard's*, these coding rules are both a reliable and valid way of capturing legal change. Our own analysis of a subset of our coding verifies their reliability when applied to the coding of OSG briefs. Treating the coding as a trichotomous variable, where the OSG brief recommends positive treatment, negative treatment, or no treatment (i.e., only cites it), we obtain 86.5% agreement across a sample of 282 cited cases that appear in twelve randomly chosen briefs. This corresponds to a Kappa value of 0.59 ($p < 0.001$), which represents "moderate" (Landis and Koch 1977, 165) and "fair to good" (Fleiss 1973) agreement according to two commonly used metrics.

[12] This 751 number includes the universe of OSG amicus briefs – both invited and voluntary – and 375 randomly selected cases in which the OSG was a direct party (roughly a 60% sample of the population).

[13] As in previous chapters, we use the default automatic method of cut point selection for the models we estimate (i.e., Sturges's rule). This process tends, in our experience, to result in a greater reduction in data imbalance than coarsening by hand.

(and the more likely it will be to interpret it negatively). As such, to avoid making spurious claims about OSG influence, we match treated and untreated observations on ideological distance. To do so, we follow Hansford and Spriggs (2006) and measure the absolute value of the distance between the ideal point of the median of the majority coalition in the cited case and the citing case (see also Spriggs and Hansford, 2001, 2002). To estimate a justice's ideal point, we rely on estimates provided by Martin and Quinn (2002).

Inward Centrality

As we discussed earlier, Fowler et al. (2007) use network analysis to generate scores of inward centrality. In essence, inward centrality captures the importance of a case to the legal network. As Fowler and his colleagues (2007, 330) note, "an inwardly relevant case is one that is widely cited by other prestigious decisions, meaning that judges see it as an integral part of the law." We match treated and untreated cases on inward centrality to ensure, again, that our inferences of OSG influence are not due, instead, to the importance of the case.[14] For example, if we compared the Court's treatment of an inwardly central precedent that received a positive OSG recommendation with the Court's treatment of precedent with little inward centrality that received no positive OSG recommendation, the Court might be more likely to render a positive treatment simply because of the importance of the case rather than because the OSG so recommended. Matching on inward centrality allows us to account for this potential problem.

Number of Opinions

Finally, we matched on the the total number of opinions in the cases; that is, we looked to determine the number of majority and separate opinions filed in the treated cases and the number in the untreated cases. We do so to account for the potential that separate opinions might water down the strength of existing precedent. Brenner and Spaeth (1995), for example, argue that a lack of agreement in Court opinions can weaken them and decrease the likelihood that justices will follow them. Murphy (1964) makes a similar argument. We looked to the Supreme Court Database to determine the number of opinions in each case.

[14] Fowler et al. (2007) also generate a measure of outward centrality, based on the extent to which a cited case itself cites a large number of other cases. We confine our matching to inward centrality as it speaks most directly to the continuing importance of a cited case. Outward centrality, by contrast, is less dynamic because the inputs (i.e., the cases cited within an opinion) are necessarily static.

METHODS AND RESULTS

Because our dependent variable is binary, we estimate a series of logistic regression models that examine whether the Court positively or negatively interpreted a cited precedent in a citing case. Each regression model contains a specific treatment variable of interest and the full set of pretreatment covariates described earlier. As in our earlier chapters, we include the matched variables in our statistical estimations to reduce any remaining imbalance that exists after our matching preprocessing (Ho et al. 2006). Following our practice thus far, we present our parameter estimates in the chapter's appendix. Using parameter estimates from each model, we generate simulations to quantify the impact our treatment variables had on the probability the Court would positively or negatively interpret a precedent. We present these results visually in Figures 7.1, 7.2, 7.3, and 7.4.

Consider, first, Figure 7.1, which focuses on the Court's propensity to interpret a cited precedent positively. The top line in the main panel presents the most basic comparison of when the OSG – in any capacity – recommends positive treatment. The control group consists of all other instances in which no OSG recommendation is present. This numerical result answers the following question: is the Court more likely to interpret a precedent because of the existence of the OSG's positive recommendation? As the plot makes clear, the answer to this question is a resounding yes. Even after neutralizing the confounding effects of ideology, vitality, and a host of other variables, we still observe a 0.31 increase in the probability that the Court will positively interpret a precedent because the OSG asked it to do so. Simply put, a positive OSG recommendation goes far.

This figure further breaks down the Court's positive interpretation of precedent by the OSG's mode of participation. When the OSG participates as a party in a case, we continue to observe a robust effect that is both statistically and substantively significant. Indeed, we estimate a 0.29 bump in the probability of positive interpretation when the OSG is a direct party to a case and recommends positive treatment. Similarly, when the OSG's brief comes as either an invited or voluntary amicus and asks the Court to positively interpret a cited case, we estimate a 0.34 increase in the likelihood that the Court will do so. Note that although the point estimates suggest that the Court might be more likely to interpret positively when the OSG brief comes as an amicus versus a party, these results are not directly comparable as they come from distinct data sets. If we set OSG party as the treatment and OSG amicus as the control and estimate a treatment effect, we fail to recover a statistically significant difference (80% two-tailed confidence interval $[-0.06, 0.06]$; matched $N = 935$).

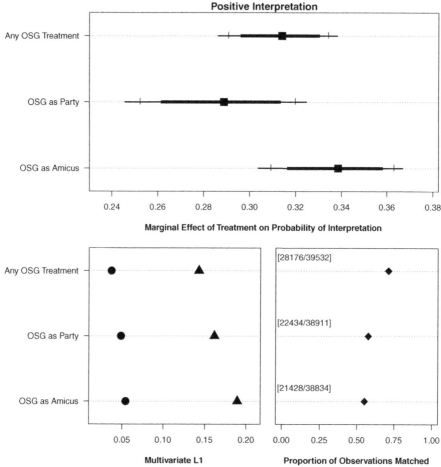

FIGURE 7.1. Dot plots of treatment effects and model diagnostic information. Each line in the top panel corresponds to a separate regression and effect estimate, which are denoted by the labels on the *y* axis. The value listed in the *y* label indicates the treatment group. The control group is defined as all nontreatment observations. Plotted values indicate how much more likely the Court is to positively interpret a treatment case than a control case. Squares represent point estimates. Thin horizontal lines, vertical tick marks, and thicker horizontal lines denote 95, 90, and 80 percent confidence intervals (two-tailed), respectively. These values were obtained through stochastic simulations using model parameter estimates reported in the chapter's appendix. The lower left panel presents the multivariate value of $\mathcal{L}_1$ for the unmatched (triangle point) and matched (circle point). Note 12 in Chapter 5 provides additional details on the calculation of these values. The lower right panel presents the proportion of observations retained by our matching solution for each treatment–control pairing. The numbers in square brackets provide the raw values for the matched and unmatched data, respectively.

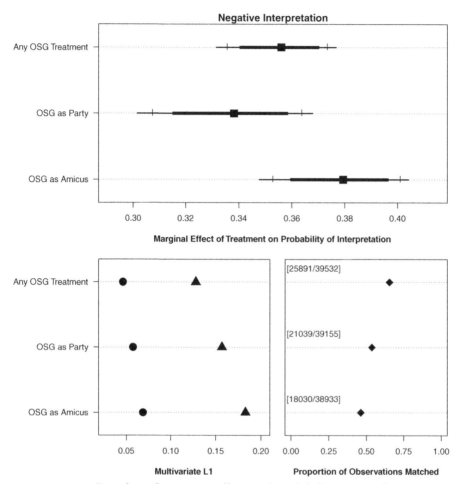

FIGURE 7.2. Dot plots of treatment effects and model diagnostic information. Marginal effects in the top panel denote increase in probability of negative treatment. See the caption to Figure 7.1 for additional information.

What, then, can we say about these first-round results? The OSG makes the Court nearly one-third more likely to treat precedent positively simply because of its recommendation. That, we believe, is sizable evidence of influence.

What is more, the OSG's influence appears to be even more significant when it asks the Court to interpret one of its previous decisions negatively. Figure 7.2 illuminates. When the OSG recommends that the Court negatively interpret precedent, the probability that the Court will do so increases by 0.36 versus when the OSG does not make such a recommendation. When we break down the OSG's mode of participation, we again see consistently impressive levels of influence. When the OSG is involved as a direct party to the case, we estimate a 0.34 increase in the probability that the Court will negatively interpret a specific precedent versus when the OSG's recommendation is absent. In a similar vein, when the OSG is participating as a friend of the court, we recover a 0.38 probability increase.

What is more, unlike the null result for the difference between party and amicus participation we reported earlier, we *do* find a statistically significant difference between the OSG's participation as a party and its participation as amicus. In particular, we estimate a 0.15 probability advantage when the OSG recommends negative treatment as amicus versus when it does so as a direct party.[15] This finding highlights that while the OSG is clearly influential across the board, that influence can be conditioned by factors relating to how it appears before the Court.

Can we falsify any of the existing theories of OSG success? Yes. When we compare the OSG against itself, we discover that both the strategic selection theory and the separation-of-powers theory fail. Consider, first, the strategic selection argument, which argues that discretion on the part of the OSG helps inflate its success rate. To gain empirical leverage on this theory, we need to construct counterfactuals in which the office has discretion to pursue a case versus in which it does not have such discretion. In so doing, we can test the claim that this discretion is ultimately what drives the success we observe.

Figure 7.3 does exactly this for the Court's decision to interpret its previous decisions positively. Despite deploying multiple counterfactuals that pit discretion against no discretion, we find no evidence of a selection effect. The first line of the top panel compares the OSG as the petitioner (i.e., has discretion) and when it is the respondent in a case (i.e., has no discretion). The point estimate is actually in the wrong direction, and we fail to find a significant effect. Similarly, when we compare the Court's positive treatment of precedent when the OSG is petitioner (has discretion) with when it is an invited amicus (has no discretion), we actually observe the OSG to be more successful when invited. Furthermore, when we compare the OSG as respondent (has no discretion) versus voluntary amicus (has discretion), there are no differences

---

[15] The two-tailed 95% confidence interval for this estimate is [0.06, 0.23], and the matched data set contains 653 observations. If we further disaggregate amicus participation by invited (i.e., CVSG) versus voluntary participation, we see that the Court is more likely to negatively interpret in either type of amicus participation versus when the OSG is a party (the amicus advantage is 0.15 and 0.18 for voluntary and CVSG cases, respectively). In terms of pitting voluntary versus invited amicus participation against each other, as we display in the bottom line of Figure 7.4, we find that the Court privileges invited participation over voluntary appearances by the OSG.

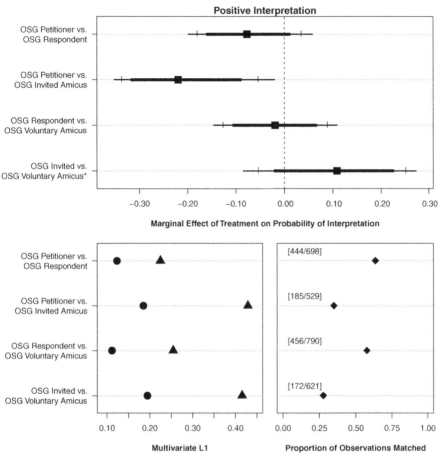

FIGURE 7.3. Dot plots of treatment effects and model diagnostic information. The first value in the *y* axis label denotes the treatment group. The second value (i.e., after the "vs.") denotes the control group. Asterisks indicate that the underlying model used was a bivariate regression between the dependent variable and the treatment variable. Marginal effects in the top panel denote an increase in probability of positive treatment. See the caption to Figure 7.1 for additional information.

in the Court's propensity to treat precedent positively. Finally, when we pit the OSG against itself as invited amicus (has no discretion) versus voluntary amicus (has discretion), we also fail to document a difference. Simply put, there is not a shred of evidence that a selection-type effect drives the OSG's overall influence in persuading the Court to treat precedent positively.

Nor does strategic selection generate OSG success in influencing the Court to treat precedent negatively. Consider again the comparisons of discretionary

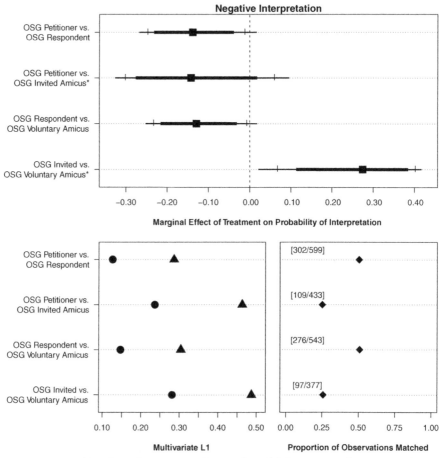

FIGURE 7.4. Dot plots of treatment effects and model diagnostic information. The first value in the *y* axis label denotes the treatment group. The second value (i.e., after the "vs.") denotes the control group. Asterisks indicate that the underlying model used was a bivariate regression between the dependent variable and the treatment variable. Marginal effects in the top panel denote an increase in probability of negative treatment. See the caption to Figure 7.1 for additional information.

OSG behavior versus nondiscretionary behavior. As line 1 of Figure 7.4 shows, the Court is somewhat less likely ($p = 0.08$) to treat precedent negatively when so recommended by the OSG petitioner (has discretion) than the OSG respondent (has no discretion). We also fail to find evidence of selection in pairing the OSG as petitioner (has discretion) versus when it is invited amicus (has no discretion) or when it is invited to participate (has no discretion) versus when it comes in as voluntary amicus (has discretion). The only evidence we

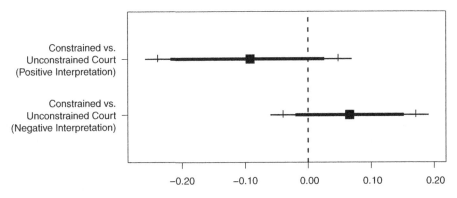

Marginal Effect of Treatment on Probability of Interpretation

FIGURE 7.5. Dot plot of treatment effect of precedent interpretation recommendation made by the OSG under a constrained versus unconstrained court. The first value in the *y* axis label denotes the treatment group. The second value (i.e., after the "vs.") denotes the control group. These values were derived from pooling seven potential ways of operationalizing a spatial model of the separation of powers (see the appendix to Chapter 6 for additional details concerning these models). Squares denote point estimates. Thin horizontal lines, vertical tick marks, and thick horizontal lines denote 95, 90, and 80 percent confidence intervals, respectively (all two-tailed values).

recover in support of a selection effect comes from comparing the OSG as respondent, when it lacks discretion, and when it is voluntary amicus. Under this, and only this, configuration, we find some evidence that the Court will be more likely to adopt the OSG's recommendation when the OSG has discretion ($p = 0.08$). Viewed as a whole, however, these findings overwhelmingly weigh against the strategic selection theory.

Consider next the separation-of-powers argument. Recall that the separation-of-powers theory held that the OSG was successful because the Court may need to defer to the elected branches or otherwise mollify them to protect their decisions – and their legitimacy – from attack by hostile politicians. We examined this theory by including a treatment variable for whether the Court was in a constrained or unconstrained regime. If the OSG wins more often for separation-of-powers considerations, then we would observe a positive relationship between our constrained regime treatment and the Court's probability of positively (negatively) interpreting precedent when the OSG so recommends. As we illustrate in Figure 7.5, for instances of both positive and negative interpretation, we find that a constrained court is no more likely to favor the OSG than an unconstrained court. The data clearly debunk the separation-of-powers theory. In neither model does the separation-of-powers coefficient approach conventional levels of statistical significance. The Court's decision to follow OSG recommendations is not tied to a separation-of-powers concern, and so that theory, like the strategic selection theory, fails.

DISCUSSION

So what does explain the OSG influence that we observe in this chapter? The data seem to suggest, once again, that the OSG's overall professionalism wins the day. Consider where the OSG appears to be most influential – the invited cases. The OSG appears most influential as an invited amicus, next most influential as a voluntary amicus, and least influential as a party (and, perhaps, when a petitioner). To us, this suggests that the Court trusts the OSG's information most when it has strong reason to believe in the objectivity of it. To be sure, the OSG is influential across the board – and we believe this overall influence is because of the office's professionalism. Yet, when we pit the OSG against itself, we observe that it is most influential in those cases where it had the least incentive to pursue a partisan or ideological argument. That is not to say that the invited cases are not partisan or that the OSG does not fulfill important duties in invited cases. It is rather to say that on average, those cases are least likely to be partisan. And in those cases, the OSG does best. Though this is, to be sure, a post hoc analysis, it does follow the important results of Wohlfarth (2009), who discovered that the OSG suffers more losses as it becomes more partisan. Thus our findings cast doubt once again on two existing theories and support the professionalism theory.

We began this chapter with a discussion of the Court's shifting regulatory takings doctrine. In *Lucas*, the Court took a strong stand against regulation and in favor of landowners' rights. Yet, just ten years later, in *Tahoe-Sierra*, the Court appeared to drop *Lucas* as an unworkable standard. We asked what might have caused such a shift. One reasonable response, of course, was that the composition of the Court changed, and the conservative majority justices in *Lucas* were replaced by the liberals who took charge in *Tahoe-Sierra*. Yet this was not the case – only one of the majority justices in *Lucas* was replaced. Rather, the cause of the shift was the changing votes of Justices O'Connor and Kennedy. And just why did those justices switch positions? If our results have anything to say about the matter, they switched because of the arguments proffered by the OSG.

Across the board, the OSG is able to influence the Court's interpretation of precedent. When positively interpreting precedent – applying it, and even expanding it, in cases – a positive OSG recommendation makes it considerably more likely that the Court will treat the precedent favorably. On the other side of the ledger, a negative OSG recommendation makes it considerably more likely that the Court will negatively treat precedent by distinguishing it or overruling it. OSG recommendations, in short, drive doctrinal change, and this, we believe, is yet further evidence of OSG influence over judicial outcomes.

8

Conclusion

In 1915, Albert Einstein proposed the theory that gravity could influence light to bend, something that has come to be known as gravitational lensing. His theory was that the gravity from mass (e.g., a star or black hole) would pull on light photons as they traveled by, moving them out of their original trajectories. Of course, at the time, the sun was the only thing with enough mass to bend light that was close enough for scientists to observe. Thus, to test the theory, scientists needed to compare the observed position of the stars in the presence versus the absence of the sun. During the night, there would be no gravitational lensing, as the sun was not present. Conversely, during the day, the sun would theoretically bend the same light. Einstein's theory would be correct only if the position of the stars near the sun during the day appeared different than at night.

Though many people believed Einstein's theory was correct, there was one problem: no one could test it. During the day, the sun was so bright that no one could see the stars, let alone gauge whether their position appeared to shift as a result of gravitational lensing. No one could test the theory, that is, until Sir Arthur Eddington took advantage of a total solar eclipse. As fate would have it, when the moon passed between the sun and the earth in 1919, it blocked out the sun's rays such that Eddington could actually see the stars immediately around the sun. His observations confirmed Einstein's theory. Eddington noticed that stars that had light rays traveling near the sun appeared slightly out of place – their light had curved owing to the sun's gravitational pull. In short, just as Einstein had theorized, gravity influenced light to bend.

This discussion, strange as it may seem at first glance, highlights two things that are relevant to the Office of the Solicitor General's (OSG's) relationship with the Supreme Court. First, influence makes a person or object do something it otherwise would not do. In the absence of gravity, a ray of light will move in a constant direction, but when gravity is present, that light bends. And, when the United States Solicitor General's office is absent from a case, the Court will behave differently. It will set its agenda differently. It will rule on cases differently. It will write different opinions and even treat precedent differently. Every aspect of the Court's decision-making process will be different when the OSG does not participate. The OSG, in short, is like gravity bending a ray of light.

Second, the example shows that influence can be tested with an appropriate research design under the right conditions. Although many scholars believed Einstein's theory, they could not test it until the solar eclipse presented itself, and when it did, Eddington was able to observe and compare. In the case of solicitor general (SG) influence, most scholars have believed for years that the OSG influences the Court, yet no one has been able to offer a rigorous test of such influence. We took advantage of recent innovations in matching to test for that influence. Our ability to compare nearly identical cases – save for the presence or absence of the OSG – allowed us to make inferences about OSG influence. In short, like Eddington (but not nearly as cleverly!), we tested an existing belief about the influence of one entity (the OSG) on another (the Court), and our results provide strong evidence of influence.

SOLICITOR GENERAL INFLUENCE

The OSG influences every major aspect of the Court's decision-making process. At the agenda stage, justices who agree and disagree with the SG accept his recommendation. Regardless of a justice's level of general ideological agreement with the OSG, there is a substantial probability that the justice will ultimately follow the OSG's recommendation – and this is in cases where the justice desires an outcome other than what the OSG recommends. Simply put, if we assume that justices consider the SG's ideology in addition to other features of a case, we find that even those most opposed to the SG still follow his recommendations in a sizeable number of cases. This is strong evidence of influence.

We also examined whether the OSG influences the Court's ultimate rulings in cases. We analyzed how the Court would rule in the presence and absence of the OSG. In essence, we compared cases that were identical in all relevant respects, with the exception that one case saw the OSG arguing and the other did not, and found that the Court is more likely to side with the OSG. The Court is more likely to side with the OSG versus an attorney who never worked in the office and is more likely to side with the OSG versus an otherwise identical attorney who once worked in the OSG. When one considers that the only difference between the two cases is the presence of the OSG, the results, once again, show compelling evidence of OSG influence.

We next examined whether the OSG influences the language of Court opinions. We compared Court opinions when the OSG filed a brief in the case versus the Court's opinions when the OSG did not file a brief, and once again, we observed strong evidence of influence. Even after controlling for such features as the quality of the brief, attorney experience, and other relevant factors, we still found that the OSG affected the Court's opinions. The Court borrows significantly more content in its majority opinions from OSG briefs than from similar non-OSG briefs. And perhaps more important, we found that although the Court, on average, borrows more language from winning briefs than from losing briefs, this dynamic does not apply when the OSG loses and a non-OSG attorney wins – The Court is just as likely to borrow from a losing OSG brief as it is from a winning non-OSG brief. Simply put, the Court turns to the OSG's briefs much more than to briefs filed by otherwise identical non-OSG actors in otherwise identical cases: influence, yet again.

Finally, we analyzed whether the OSG can influence the Court's treatment of precedent. We compared the Court's treatment of precedent in the presence of a recommendation by the OSG to its treatment with no such OSG recommendation. The results were impressive as far as influence goes. We observed a significant increase in the probability that the Court would positively and negatively interpret precedent, simply because the OSG asked it to do so. To be sure, these figures rise and fall depending on other characteristics such as mode of participation – but not much. Put plainly, the OSG is considerably influential in persuading the Court to treat precedent positively or negatively.

All in all, then, the OSG influences the Court at all stages of its decision-making process, and if the mark of influence is how often the SG persuades the Court to take a position it would not have taken without his or her advocacy (McConnell 1988, 1115), the OSG is remarkably influential.

THE EXPLANATION FOR SOLICITOR GENERAL INFLUENCE

Though our central goal was to provide a rigorous analysis of OSG influence, we also sought to bring clarity to the overall picture of what drives OSG influence. We believe we have satisfied our first goal. As to the second, the data are less clear, but they do appear to line up behind one theory: that OSG success comes from its objectivity and professionalism. Throughout the book, theories like attorney experience, the separation of powers, attorney quality, ideology, and strategic selection fell by the wayside. To be sure, this is not to say that these factors do not matter; it is, rather, to make the argument that these factors do not *systematically* generate OSG influence. Instead, our belief is that OSG objectivity, professionalism, and independence likely lead to its influence. To bolster this argument, we look, of all places, to the history of the Federal Reserve, the National Labor Relations Board (NLRB), and turn-of-the-century spoilage reform. These histories provide evidence that long-term success and credibility, as enjoyed by the OSG, come from professionals who exercise objectivity and independence from short-term political appetites.

Consider the history of the Federal Reserve. The Fed is charged with the important task of setting the country's monetary policies, and despite the wishes of more than a handful of politicians, it largely – at least historically – has done so without political interference. For example, its decisions do not need the approval of Congress; the members of the Board of Governors serve for fourteen-year fixed terms, and they cannot be removed from office for their policy views. In short, the Fed is well insulated from political control. And according to Jeong, Miller, and Sobel (2009) and others (Franzese 1999; Grilli, Masciandaro, and Tabellini 1991; Keefer and Stasavage 2003), the objectivity with which its members act has led to long-term fiscal stability. The Fed's independence has "reduced bureaucratic inefficiency and mismanagement, helped stabilize monetary policy, and constrained the increasing bouts of financial distress" that afflicted the U.S. economy prior to its creation (Jeong, Miller, and Sobel 2009, 474). Delegating monetary policy to the professionalized Fed led to long-term stability to the extent that it avoided "policy losses from flip-flopping presidential economic policy" (Lewis 2003, 161; see also North and Weingast 1989). In short, by placing control of monetary policy in the hands of professionals who could be trusted to act objectively in the long-run interests of the country, the banking system and monetary policy became more stable and less subject to artificial market ebbs and flows. Investors, risk takers, and the general public could trust what the Fed did without fear of aggrandizement or other symptoms of short-term policy gains typically sought by reelection-seeking politicians.

The NLRB's history also shows how professionals can generate stability and trustworthiness. During the board's early years, liberals and conservatives fought aggressively over who would control board (i.e., labor) policy. When Democrats controlled the levers of government, labor tended to win out. When Republicans controlled it, business won out (Moe 1987). Over time, a class of labor lawyers at the NLRB developed. These lawyers kept a close eye on both sides, which largely led them to lay down their arms. Eventually, both sides figured out that peace was the better policy. At any rate, the emergence of professionals at the board led to more stability, clarity, and expertise. In the end, objectivity and professionalism prevailed. Both labor and business recognized the NLRB as a mediator of sorts that could be trusted (Moe 1987).

Why did they come to trust the board? Because the professionals within it displayed behavior that was objective, consistent, and trustworthy.

Our belief that objectivity and independence lead to OSG influence is further buttressed by the consequences of turn-of-the-century spoilage reforms. Boss politics in many cities in the late 1800s and early 1900s encouraged personal ties between economic groups and party bosses. Unqualified partisan hacks and other shysters were appointed to important positions simply because they could deliver votes for politicians. With such extreme back scratching occurring, business could not advance under true capitalist form. Without certainty as to the future rules of the game, business found it difficult to engage in long-term planning and hiring. Once the spoils system was eliminated, however, and (qualified) professionals filled important policy-making positions, businesses found themselves able and willing to operate and invest. As Miller (1989, 691) states, business could now invest "without having to worry that the next change in party control in their city government would result in a new round of extortion or elimination of their property rights."

These examples all have the same thing in common: objective, professional actors with independence to do their jobs led to overall credibility. Other actors find their information to be more trustworthy and credible, and they will change their behavior because of it. This is, in short, what we witness between the Court and the OSG.

The OSG largely enjoys independence from the president. To be sure, the SG is nominated by the president and serves at his pleasure, and there have been noteworthy instances of presidents ordering SGs to take certain positions in cases (Fraley 1996). Yet norms have evolved over time that afford the SG a degree of independence. And even when the SG himself or herself takes on a heightened political role, the deputy SGs and assistant SGs – actors not affiliated directly with the administration – provide a further internal check on partisan behavior. Indeed, the following quote by Moe is particularly apt when thinking about the OSG:

> Professionals are difficult to control, but their behavior is fairly easy to predict. And that, of course, is at the heart of all this. A professional, if given total autonomy and insulated from external pressures, can be counted upon to behave in a manner characteristic of his type. That is what true professionalism is all about. This very predictability ensures . . . [that] stability, clarity, and expertise will be protected. (Moe 1987, 259)

Perhaps the strongest reason to believe that OSG influence is tied to its professionalism and objectivity is to examine what happens when that objectivity is questioned.[1] As we stated in previous chapters, Wohlfarth (2009) examines whether the Court becomes less likely to side with the OSG when that office takes more polarizing, political positions in its amicus briefs. His findings are quite clear: the Court defers less to the OSG when the office becomes politicized. In short, the less the OSG toes the president's line in Court, the more effective it is.

These studies, combined with our findings throughout this book, suggest, then, that the considerable influence wielded by the OSG is a function of a professional, objective, and largely independent office. And regardless of the political field that seems to generate more polarization – and place more ideologically extreme justices on the Court – OSG influence will survive so long as independent professionals remain at the helm.

---

[1] We, of course, take no normative position on whether the OSG should follow the president's wishes or take its own path.

Appendices

Operationalizing the Separation of Powers

In note 16 in Chapter 4, we describe the ongoing debate over the legislative decision-making process, which directly affects our ability to operationalize any separation-of-powers variable. The key disagreement in the literature stems from whose preferences within the legislature are pivotal. At present, four viable candidates exist: the Senate filibuster pivot and the veto override pivots (Krehbiel 1998), the chamber median (Riker 1962; Krehbiel 1995), party gatekeepers (Cox and McCubbins 2005), and the judiciary committee (see, generally, Smith 1989). An additional complication stems from debate over whether to include the president in the latter three of these spatial models. Some studies include the president (Owens 2010), while others do not (Harvey and Friedman 2006).

Lacking private information about which of these constitutes the "right" model, we take an approach of complete agnosticism while conducting our data analysis. In particular, we reestimated our underlying model using each of the unique combinations of legislative preferences and inclusion of the president (the filibuster–veto pivots perspective assumes the presence of the president). We then used these parameter estimates to simulate marginal effects. Effect estimates in hand, we then simply pooled all sets of simulation results together before computing the percentile values. The *Constrained Court* variable never achieves statistical significance in the expected direction. Accordingly, our 95 percent confidence interval for the marginal effect of the Court being constrained on the Office of the Solicitor General's (OSG's) influence is very wide (i.e., $[-0.43, 0.07]$).

Model Parameter Estimates

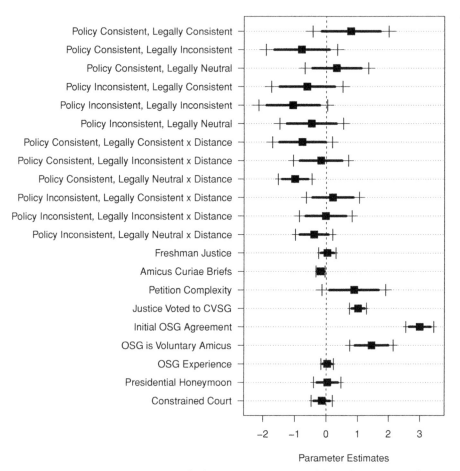

Parameter Estimates

FIGURE A1. Parameter estimates for logistic regression model used to generate the predicted probabilities in Figures 4.3, 4.4, and 4.5.

In Chapter 4 we jumped directly to the visual presentation of our results. Here, in Figure A1, we include a visual depiction of the parameter estimates of that model.

Evidence of CVSG Case Importance

To gain empirical leverage on the question of solicitor general (SG) influence – and eliminate the damage posed by selection effects where the SG makes the discretionary decision to participate in a case (see Nicholson and Collins 2008) – we focus primarily on instances in which SG participation is forced by the Court via the justices voting to call for the views of the solicitor general (CVSG). As we discuss, our results suggest that the SG can motivate justices to depart from their policy preferences, a finding we deem as evidence of the SG's influential power. An alternative explanation for these results is that invited cases are simply unimportant, and neither justices nor SGs care significantly about them. Thus our finding of SG influence might simply be the result of justices acting on some other nonideological consideration.

Given the potential for this claim to undermine the inferences we make, we have assembled an exhaustive and multifaceted body of empirical evidence that strongly suggests that invited cases are just as important as noninvited cases. In what follows, we describe these data and discuss how they support our belief that invited cases are important to both the justices and the SG.

Justices' CVSG Voting Behavior

To show that invited cases are important to justices, we begin by analyzing the conditions under which justices vote to CVSG. Because the following analysis examines justices' votes, we believe it represents a careful and critical test of whether justices themselves believe that invited cases are important. If invited cases are important, factors related to case importance will increase the probability that a justice will CVSG. Conversely, if justices vote to CVSG in unimportant cases, factors related to a case's importance will depress the probability that a justice votes to CVSG. Again, since this test examines CVSG behavior from the justice's point of view, it provides the most direct test of case importance.

To examine the conditions under which justices CVSG, we began by visually examining the docket sheet in every paid, non–death penalty petition originating from a federal court of appeals that made the discuss list during the Court's 1986–93 term ($N = 1227$).[1] We obtained our docket sheets from Epstein, Segal, and Spaeth (2007). Because of the overall infrequency of

---

[1] We exclude capital petitions because during the time period of our study, they were treated differently than their noncapital counterparts (Woodward and Armstrong 1979). We examine only petitions from federal courts of appeals because there are no measures that map state supreme court justices on the same ideological scale as U.S. Supreme Court justices (part of a related project not reported here). We sample petitions from the Court's discuss list because these are petitions that have a nonzero probability of being granted because at least one justice deemed it worthy of some discussion. We excluded those cases in which the United States was a party or where it already filed an amicus brief because justices have no option to CVSG in them.

CVSG votes, we followed the advice of King and Zeng (2001a, 2001b) and utilized a rare events sampling approach to our data. In so doing, we automatically included a case in our analysis if it contained at least one justice vote to CVSG. This process revealed a total of 839 CVSG votes cast across 197 petitions. We then supplemented these petitions with a random sample of 208 petitions in which no justice voted to CVSG. This is roughly 20 percent of the remaining population of interest (i.e., 1,227 minus 197). The results we report subsequently use the appropriate weights to adjust the estimates given our sampling procedures. Our unit of analysis is the justice vote, and our dependent variable is coded as 1 if a justice voted to CVSG, and 0 otherwise. In sum, our data include 405 petitions and 3,582 justice votes.[2]

Our motivation is to determine whether justices vote to CVSG in important cases. Accordingly, we regress each justice's agenda vote (i.e., to CVSG or not) on a host of independent variables that tap into case importance:

1. *Amicus participation.* The submission of amicus curiae briefs at the agenda-setting stage provides a valuable cue for justices as to a petition's salience (Caldeira and Wright 1988, 1998, Black and Owens 2009a).[3] Accordingly, we counted the total number of amicus briefs filed in support of or in opposition to the grant of certiorari prior to the CVSG vote.

2. *Media coverage.* Following the general approach suggested by Epstein and Segal (2000), we turn to the legal periodical *U.S. Law Week*, which "provides current and comprehensive reporting and analysis on the most significant federal and state cases" and "[alerts] the legal profession to the most important cases and why they are important" (Source Information, LexisNexis). We counted the total number of words *U.S. Law Week* dedicated to each case after it was decided in the lower court but before a cert petition was filed in the Supreme Court. To account for the fact that coverage is unlikely to be linear (i.e., going from zero words to one hundred is more important than going from five hundred words to

---

[2] We have 63 fewer observations than the theoretically full complement of 3,645 votes (i.e., 383 × 9) owing to missing data (i.e., discretionary recusals by the justices) and votes that were unclear.

[3] Note that we refer specifically to the importance-based role of amicus briefs at the agenda-setting stage and not at the merits stage. Although previous research has argued for using amicus briefs as an indicator of salience at the merits stage (e.g., Maltzman, Spriggs, and Wahlbeck 2000), a recent book by Collins suggests that at the merits stage, amicus participation is a better indicator of a case's complexity and not its salience. Importantly, however, Collins suggests that its continued use as a measure of salience at the agenda-setting stage remains appropriate (Collins 2008b, 133n120).

six hundred words), we transformed the variable by taking (1+) the natural logarithm of the number of words.

3. *Lower court opinion characteristics.* A long line of research on agenda setting suggests that various aspects of lower court opinions provide justices with evidence as to the overall importance of a petition (e.g., Tanenhaus et al. 1963; Ulmer, Hintz, and Kirklosky 1972; Brenner 1979; Songer 1979; Caldeira, Wright, and Zorn 1999; Black and Owens 2009a). Among the cues that suggest a petition is important are whether it was decided en banc (i.e., with all judges presiding in the circuit court below), whether the circuit court reversed the trial court, and whether the opinion observed a dissent. Conversely, if the lower court elected not to publish the opinion, it is generally deemed nonprecedential and less important. Using the discussion contained in the cert pool memos written in each case, we coded dummy variables for each of these characteristics (1 means the attribute was present; 0 means it was not).

4. *Legal conflict.* Finally, justices might simply CVSG to determine how much conflict exists among the lower courts in a given petition, and such a determination of legal conflict might swamp policy importance. Alternatively, legal conflict might be correlated with our case importance variables. For example, lower court decisions might generate heightened media coverage when they produce circuit splits. Accordingly, we include *Weak Conflict* and *Strong Conflict* in our model. We code *Weak Conflict* as 1 if the petitioner alleges the existence of conflict and the pool clerk notes that while some tension exists, the conflict is otherwise tolerable (is shallow, has not sufficiently percolated, will resolve itself, etc.). We code *Strong Conflict* as 1 if the petitioner alleges the existence of conflict and the pool clerk notes such conflict and does not discount it.

In sum, we are going to fit a statistical model to determine whether justices invite the SG to participate in important cases or whether they invite the SG to participate only in unimportant cases. If they invite SGs to participate in important cases, the coefficients on all our covariates but *Lower Court Unpublished* will be positive and statistically significant, while the coefficient on *Lower Court Unpublished* will be negative and statistically significant. What is more, these coefficients should take on significance even while controlling for legal conflict.

As the parameter estimates for our logistic regression model in Table A1 show, justices invite the SG in important cases. The coefficients on nearly

Appendices

TABLE A1. *Logistic regression model of a justice's decision to call for the views of the solicitor general (CVSG). Parameter estimates in the second column are maximum likelihood. The third column contains the substantive effect of each variable on the baseline probability (i.e., 0.04) that a justice votes to CVSG, holding all else constant (calculated using the prvalue command in Stata 11).*

	Coefficient (robust S.E.)	Baseline pred. prob. 0.04 [0.03, 0.05]
Amicus Briefs	0.387*	+0.02
	(0.054)	[0.01, 0.03]
USLW Coverage	0.053*	+0.02
	(0.013)	[0.01, 0.03]
Lower Opinion Unpublished	−0.657*	−0.02
	(0.203)	[−0.03, −0.01]
Lower Opinion En Banc	−0.851*	−0.02
	(0.211)	[−0.03, −0.02]
Lower Opinion Reverses Trial Court	0.224*	+0.01
	(0.088)	[0.00, 0.02]
Lower Opinion Contains Dissent	0.246*	+0.01
	(0.108)	[0.00, 0.02]
Weak Conflict	0.706*	+0.04
	(0.100)	[0.03, 0.05]
Strong Conflict	0.445*	+0.02
	(0.109)	[0.01, 0.03]
Constant	−3.150*	
	(0.091)	
Observations	3582	
Log likelihood	−2801.188	

* $p < 0.05$ (two-tailed test).

every variable are signed in the expected direction and are statistically significant. Note, furthermore, the third column in the table, which provides the substantive magnitude for each variable's effect. These magnitudes are the difference between the baseline hypothetical (i.e., all dummy variables are set at their modal value of 0) and a hypothetical where the dummy variable is set at a value of 1. For Amicus Briefs, the substantive effect is the difference between a case with zero amicus briefs and one brief. For *Media Coverage*, the difference is between a case with no media coverage (the mode) and a case with the maximum value of media coverage.

The results show, first, that justices are more likely to CVSG in cases with an amicus brief than in those without such a brief. A justice's CVSG probability increases by 0.02 when an organized interest has filed a brief at the agenda stage. We also find, as expected, that pre-cert coverage in the media is positively related with a justice's CVSG probability. Additionally, a justice is less likely to CVSG in cases disposed of in the circuit below with an unpublished opinion than in cases that were published. Similarly, a justice is more likely to CVSG when the lower court reverses the trial court and when the lower court opinion contained a dissenting opinion. While the raw size of these substantive effects is not especially large, neither is the baseline probability that a justice votes to CVSG (i.e., 0.04). Viewed as relative differences, then, the effect sizes are quite sizeable (e.g., justices are 50% more likely to CVSG when there is an amicus brief than when there is none).

Somewhat surprisingly, our findings suggest that justices are actually less likely to CVSG when the lower court decision was rendered en banc. While we are at somewhat of a loss to explain why this relationship appears to exist, we are ultimately unfazed by it, as existing studies on agenda setting more broadly find little evidence to suggest that justices are any more likely to grant review to cases that were decided en banc by the lower court (Black and Owens 2009a). More broadly, we have no reason to believe that this single discrepant result impeaches the otherwise clear results from the other five indicators of case importance that perform as expected, even after controlling for legal conflict; that is, viewing the results as a whole, we believe there is more than sufficient systematic evidence to show that justices vote to CVSG in important cases and, therefore, that invited cases are important.

Front-Page Coverage by the New York Times

Epstein and Segal (2000) argue that front-page coverage of a decision by the *New York Times* serves as a reliable proxy for case salience. The measure is frequently used in judicial research (e.g., McAtee and McGuire 2007) and has been called the "standard measure of case salience for judicial scholars" (Maltzman and Wahlbeck 2003, 3). We employ this measure to examine, from another perspective, whether invited cases are important. If invited cases are substantially less important than noninvited cases, then we should observe significantly fewer invited cases making the cover of the *Times*. We do not.

To examine the extent to which the *Times* covered invited and noninvited cases, we began by obtaining the data Rich Pacelle used in his 2006 *Judicature* article on the SG. We updated these data and merged them with data available in Epstein et al. (2007) concerning whether a case received coverage by the *Times*. Of the 223 cases in which the SG was invited to

TABLE A2. *Relationship between type of U.S. involvement in a case and the frequency of dissenting votes*

Case type	Average dissent votes	0 Votes	1 Vote	2 Votes	3 Votes	4 Votes
SG invited	1.48	40.74	12.17	17.99	16.93	12.17
SG voluntary	1.69	39.09	8.8	14.55	18.95	18.61
US party	1.65	36.75	12.19	15.9	19.53	15.63
US uninvolved	1.61	38.5	11.77	15.06	19.28	15.38

Pearson Chi-Square Statistic (12 d.f.) = 13.59; $p = 0.33$.

participate between 1953 and 2007, 18.4 percent ultimately received front-page treatment by the *Times*. Of the 736 cases in which the SG was not invited, 21.2 percent were covered by the *Times*. This difference in proportions is neither statistically ($p = 0.36$) nor substantively significant.[4] In short, the *Times* reported on invited cases to the same degree as it reported on noninvited cases.

Final Merits Coalition Sizes

If invited cases are easier cases, or cases in which justices do not operate pursuant to their ideological preferences, we would expect to see a significantly higher percentage of invited cases decided unanimously than other cases. Accordingly, we examined all cases decided between 1953 and 2000 to see if invited cases were significantly more consensual than other cases decided by the Court. As Table A2 shows, there are few differences among coalition sizes, and what differences do exist are generally quite small. Indeed, the high p value for the chi-square statistic shows that we cannot reject the

[4] If we look at the entire population of cases, there are four case types: (1) SG invited participation, (2) SG voluntary participation, (3) United States as direct party, and (4) United States not involved. From 1953 to 2000, the percentages of cases receiving coverage by the *Times* are as follows: SG invited (20.6%), SG voluntary (23.5%), United States direct party (13.8%), and United States uninvolved (15.0%). Viewed as an entire population, invited cases actually receive significantly more coverage than both cases where the United States is a direct party ($p = 0.01$) and where the United States isn't involved at all ($p = 0.04$). If we substitute the *Times* measure for the list of cases created by *Congressional Quarterly* (CQ), we obtain similar results. The percentages are as follows: SG invited (9.0%), SG voluntary (10.8%), United States direct party (4.2%), and United States uninvolved (5.2%). We focus on the *Times* measure as Epstein and Segal (2000, 69) note several important limitations with the CQ measure.

null hypothesis of no relationship between the *Case Type* and *Number of Dissenting Votes* variables; that is, we cannot claim from these data that there are systematic coalitional differences between invited cases and noninvited cases.

If we simply count the average number of dissenting votes for each of the values of *Case Type* (second column of Table A2), we find that while invited cases appear to have a slightly lower number of dissenting votes than, for example, voluntary cases, neither the statistical ($p = 0.11$) nor the substantive strength of the difference is overpowering. In short, here, too, we fail to find significant evidence that would corroborate the claim that invited cases are less important than noninvited cases.

Case Centrality in the Legal Citation Network

While contemporaneous variables such as coverage by the *New York Times* or size of the overall voting coalition can provide a useful indicator of a case's importance, such indicators are just a brief snapshot of a case's overall history. An alternative way to examine legal impact is to employ network analysis to scrutinize how a decision stands up over time. Accordingly, we follow Fowler et al. (2007) and compare the inward and outward centrality of invited (and other) cases. Critically, the inward and outward centrality of cases can go a long way toward explaining their importance to the legal community.

We merged the aforementioned data obtained from Pacelle with Fowler et al.'s centrality data, which estimate year-by-year inward and outward centrality scores for every Supreme Court opinion. For ease of exposition, we present these results visually using the box plots in Figure A2.

The *x* axis of the figure presents the four case types in our data (SG invited, SG voluntary, United States a direct party, and United States not involved), spanning from 1953 to 2000. Within each case type, we display both the outward and inward centrality measures. The darker box plot represents the distribution of that type of case's outward centrality (i.e., opinion breadth), and the lighter box plot represents the distribution of that type of case's inward centrality (i.e., opinion importance). Both inward and outward centrality can range between 0 and 1, with higher values indicating that an opinion is more central in the legal network.

After comparing median values (i.e., the white horizontal bars within each box plot) across all four case types, we find, once again, that invited cases decided on the merits are just as important as noninvited cases decided on the merits. The median outward centrality score for invited cases is 0.84.

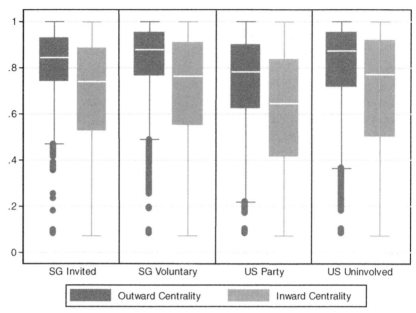

FIGURE A2. Comparative box plots of case centrality, conditional on the type of U.S. participation in a case.

For voluntary cases, the same quantity is 0.88. In terms of inward centrality, the median scores for invited and voluntary cases are 0.74 and 0.76, respectively. Once again, this is hardly a difference at all; that is, though there are some distributional differences across cases, we fail to see evidence that, by our viewing, could lead anyone to conclude that invited cases are unimportant.

Nevertheless, to check the robustness of these results, we estimated two linear regression models in which the dependent variables were a case's outward centrality score and the case's inward centrality score and the independent variables were dummies for each of the four case types (SG invited, SG voluntary, United States direct party, and United States not involved).

Because we want to compare invited cases to all others, we used invited cases as the omitted baseline category in the models. Parameter estimates are ordinary least squares. To account for the presence of multiple observations for each case,[5] we cluster our standard errors on each of the 5,677 unique opinions included in the data. Because the baseline value is an invited case,

---

[5] The unit of analysis for these data is the opinion-year, which is to say that an opinion released in 1990 would have a separate observation for each of the subsequent years in which it exists in the network.

TABLE A3. *Linear regression of case outward (middle column) and inward (right column) case centrality on the type of U.S. involvement in a case*

Variable	Outward centrality	Inward centrality
SG Voluntary	0.0245	0.0161
	(0.0145)	(0.0197)
US Party	−0.0743[*]	−0.0722[*]
	(0.0133)	(0.0178)
US Uninvolved	−0.0181	−0.0023
	(0.0133)	(0.0178)
Constant	0.8115[*]	0.6728[*]
	(0.0124)	(0.0169)
R2	0.024	0.015
Root MSE	0.211	0.288
Observations		158,713

[*] $p < 0.05$ (two-tailed test).

the parameter estimates for each of the three remaining dummy variables represent whether those cases enjoy systematically different levels of centrality than invited cases. Looking first in Table A3, at outward centrality, we find that invited cases are significantly more outwardly central than those in which the United States is a party. We also find some limited evidence to suggest that voluntary cases are more outwardly central than invited cases ($p = 0.09$). However, the effect size – a 0.02 increase – is less than one-tenth of a single standard deviation in terms of the dependent variable.

As it taps into subsequent citation by judges in other cases, the more meaningful test of case importance is whether the case is inwardly central, and on this score, invited cases clearly show themselves to be just as important as other cases. Here, too, invited cases are significantly more inwardly central than those in which the United States is a party. What is more, we find no evidence to suggest that invited cases are less inwardly central than either voluntary cases ($p = 0.41$) or cases in which the United States is not involved at all ($p = 0.90$). Simply put, one of the most cutting-edge measures of case importance provides no evidence that invited cases are less important than noninvited cases. Indeed, some measures of centrality even suggest that invited cases may hold more importance than noninvited cases.

Archival Evidence

Analysis of the archival materials shows that SGs tell the Court that invited cases are important. Indeed, in one case, *Matsushita Electrical Co. v. Zenith*

Radio Corp., 475 U.S. 574 (1986), the SG urged review because of (in his words) the "significant practical implications for both antitrust policy and the conduct of the nation's foreign trade policy."

Consider further the SG's recommendation in *Airline Pilot's Association v. O'Neill*, 499 U.S. 65 (1991). After the Court invited the SG's views on whether to grant review to the case, the SG stated that the case presented "an excellent opportunity to clarify the standards for determining whether a union has acted arbitrarily.... The standards circumscribing a union's [actions] are an important element of federal labor law. The problems of labor disputes in interstate transportation industries is a recurring one."

Justices' law clerks also discuss the importance of invited cases. Take, for example, *Puerto Rico Dept. of Consumer Affairs v. Isla Petroleum Corp.*, 485 U.S. 495 (1988), in which the cert pool memo writer stated:

> [This case] presents important pre-emption issues as well as questions on the statutory interpretation [of] EPAA and the ongoing authority of TECA [Temporary Emergency Court of Appeals] to consider pre-emption claims.... Because the case concerns the interpretation of a federal statute, the Court might wish to seek the views of the Solicitor General, but I am inclined to recommend an outright grant.

It is worth pointing out that the case involved preemption issues, a federalism dispute that often split conservatives and liberals.

Consider, furthermore, *Lorance v. AT&T*, 490 U.S. 900 (1989), in which the cert pool writer noted, "This case involves a seemingly significant question of federal anti-discrimination law." Indeed, Justice Blackmun's clerk stated, "The recommendation to obtain the SG's views seems wise, although this looks like a grant to me. Perhaps the SG may have some perspective not flushed out by the parties." These and other comments by clerks suggest that invited cases are not systematically unimportant.

Additional Considerations

If these cases are important, then why does the SG not file amicus briefs voluntarily at the agenda-setting stage in them? While there are probably a host of reasons, appearances and workload considerations are likely among them. There is a norm in the OSG not to file briefs in too many cases. As Johnson (2003) states, the government voluntarily files amicus briefs in only 8 percent of all cases that can be considered presidential priorities. Indeed, Johnson cites former SG Rex Lee, who explained that "it is a mistake to file in too many [cases]" because "the ability of the Solicitor General to serve any of the president's objectives would suffer" as a result (Lee 1986, 599–600). Salokar (1992, 141) also suggests that SGs cannot "become involved in so many cases that the Court should begin to expect the government's views, and as a result, give them less weight."

We think it is further likely that the workload of preparing their own cert petitions, responding to CVSGs, and authoring merits briefs makes authoring all but the smallest number of voluntary agenda-setting amicus briefs difficult for the OSG. In short, that the SG does not file an amicus brief voluntarily in a case does not mean that the petition is unimportant. If it did, one would have to accept the conclusion that out of the tens of thousands of petitions filed between the Court's 1984 and 1993 terms, the OSG found only nineteen important – a remarkable assumption indeed. (Recall that the OSG voluntarily filed only nineteen amicus briefs at the agenda stage between the Court's 1984 and 1993 terms.)

APPENDIX TO CHAPTER 5: SOLICITOR GENERAL INFLUENCE
AND MERITS OUTCOMES

Operationalizing the Separation of Powers

As we have mentioned at a few previous points (see, e.g., note 17), there is no clear answer in terms of how to model the separation-of-powers game. For the results reported in this and subsequent chapters, we generated seven treatment–control pairings using each of the unique combinations of legislative preferences and inclusion of the president (the filibuster–veto pivots perspective assumes the presence of the president). We then preprocessed and estimated models for each of these seven treatment variables. Using these parameter estimates, we simulated marginal effects and then simply pooled all seven sets of simulation results together before computing the percentile values that are reported in the top panel of Figure 5.2. To populate the values for the lower panels in our figure, we took the median value of the seven multivariate $\mathcal{L}_1$ values that we obtained, and we did the same for the proportion of observations to matched values that is reported in the lower right panel of this figure.

Model Parameter Estimates

Figures A3–A5 provide the parameter estimates for the underlying logistic regression models used to generate treatment effect estimates presented in

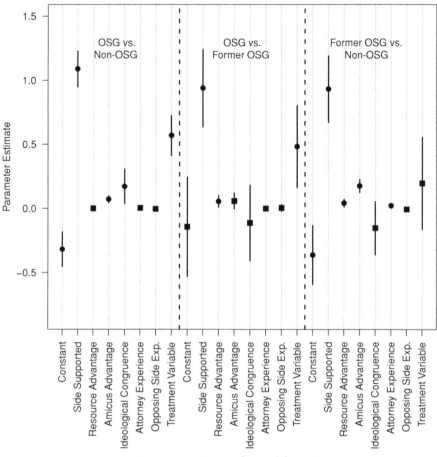

FIGURE A3. Parameter estimates for models in Figure 5.1.

Chapter 5. Circles mean statistically significant ($p < 0.05$, two-tailed test), and squares indicate not statistically significant. The vertical whiskers denote the 95 percent confidence interval around the estimates (two-tailed).

APPENDIX TO CHAPTER 6: SOLICITOR GENERAL INFLUENCE
AND BRIEFS

In this chapter we include, as pretreatment covariates, brief clarity and the separation-of-powers regime in place when the case was decided. For both these concepts, there are a considerable range of measurement options

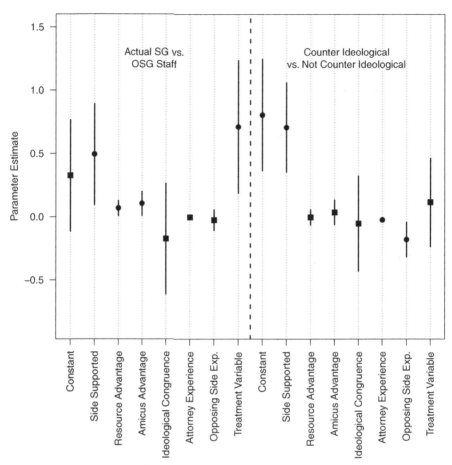

FIGURE A4. Parameter estimates for models in Figure 5.2.

and, unfortunately, no clear consensus about which approach is "right." In surveying the research on measuring readability, we discovered a total of five other measures: Automated Readability Index (Smith and Senter 1967), Flesh–Kincaid readability (Kincaid et al. 1975), Flesh–Kincaid grade (id.), Gunning-Fox Index (Gunning 1952), and the SMOG Grade (McLaughlin 1969).

For the separation-of-powers literature, the key disagreement in the literature stems from whose preferences within the legislature are pivotal. In addition to the filibuster veto pivot, which we use in Chapter 6, three others exist. They are the chamber median (Riker 1962; Krehbiel 1995), the party

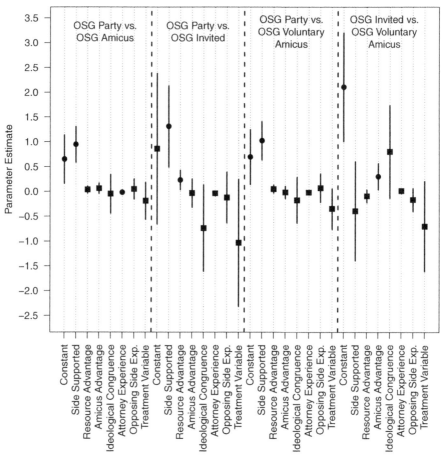

FIGURE A5. Parameter estimates for models in Figure 5.3.

gatekeeping (Cox and McCubbins 2005), and the judiciary committee (see, generally, Smith 1989). An additional complication stems from debate over whether to include the president in these spatial models. Some studies include the president (Owens 2010), while others do not (Harvey and Friedman 2006).

In Figure A6, we plot estimated treatment effects for all treatment–control pairings described in Chapter 6. For each counterfactual, we show the result that we report in Chapter 6 (i.e., using the Coleman–Liau Index and the filibuster veto pivot). We then provide, immediately below it, the "pooled effect," which represents the treatment effect if we were to combine simulation results from each of the six measures of brief clarity described earlier. To generate this value, we preprocessed the data for each clarity variable and

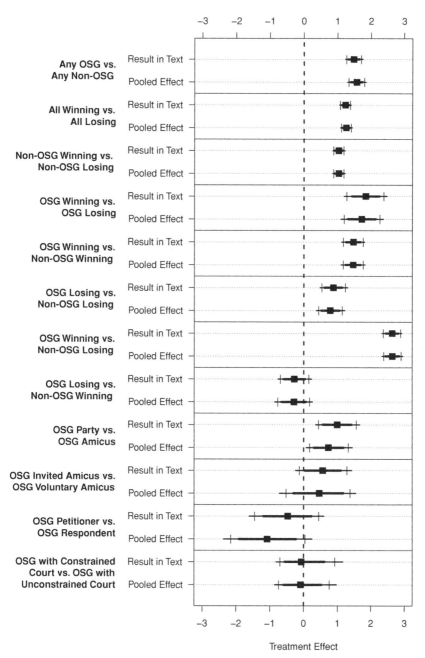

FIGURE A6. Treatment effect estimates for alternative operationalizations of our readability variables. Plotted values indicate how much more the Court will borrow from a treatment brief than a control brief. Squares represent point estimates. Thin horizontal lines, vertical tick marks, and thicker horizontal lines denote 95, 90, and 80 percent confidence intervals (two-tailed), respectively.

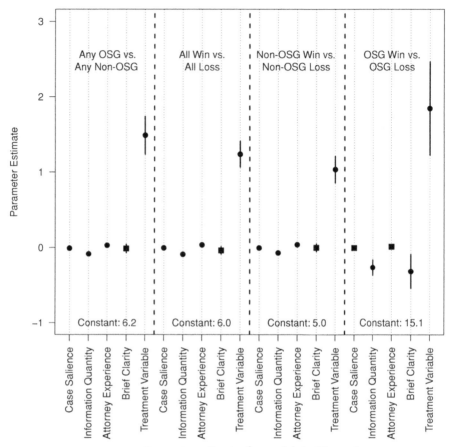

FIGURE A7. Parameter estimates for models in Figure 6.1.

then estimated our linear regression model on the matched data. We then used these regression results to perform stochastic simulations that yielded six sets of predicted values. Finally, we merged these six sets of values and took the appropriate quantiles to generate the plotted values.

Model Parameter Estimates

Figures A7–A9 provide the parameter estimates for the underlying linear regression models used to generate treatment effect estimates presented in Chapter 6. Circles mean statistically significant ($p < 0.05$, two-tailed test), and squares indicate not statistically significant. The vertical whiskers denote the 95 percent confidence interval around the estimates (two-tailed).

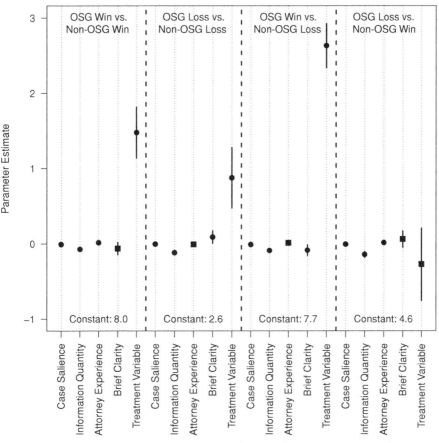

FIGURE A8. Parameter estimates for models in Figure 6.2.

APPENDIX TO CHAPTER 7: SOLICITOR GENERAL INFLUENCE
AND LEGAL DOCTRINE

Model Parameter Estimates

Figures A10–A13 provide the parameter estimates for the underlying logistic regression models used to generate treatment effect estimates presented in Chapter 7. Circles mean statistically significant ($p < 0.05$, two-tailed test), and squares indicate not statistically significant. The vertical whiskers denote the 95 percent confidence interval around the estimates (two-tailed).

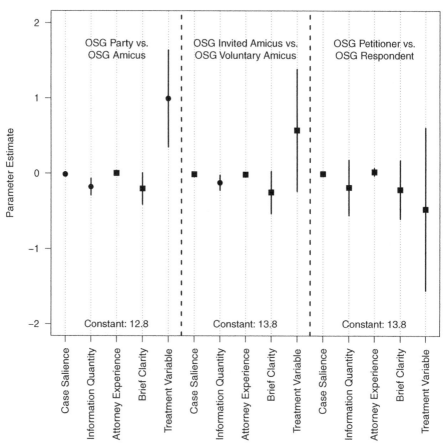

FIGURE A9. Parameter estimates for models in Figure 6.3.

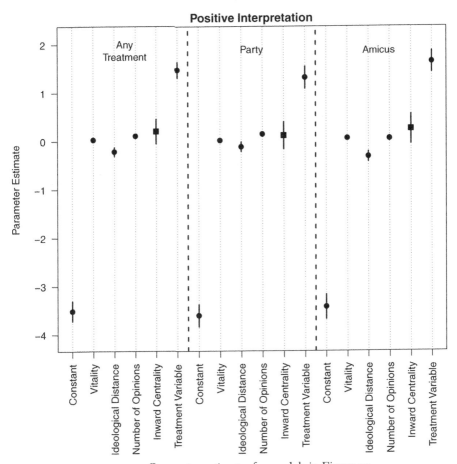

FIGURE A10. Parameter estimates for models in Figure 7.1.

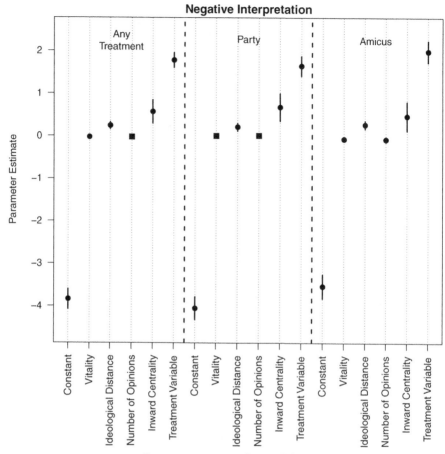

FIGURE A11. Parameter estimates for models in Figure 7.2.

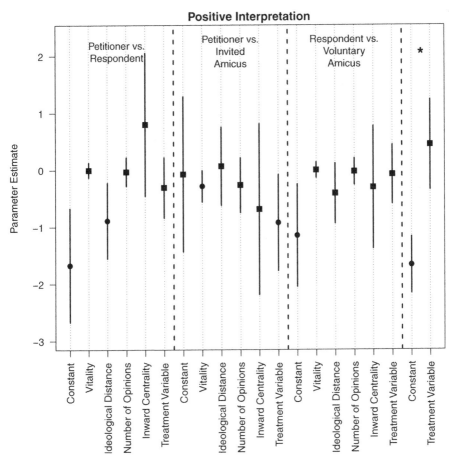

FIGURE A12. Parameter estimates for models in Figure 7.3. The asterisk denotes the estimates for the OSG Invited Amicus vs. OSG Voluntary Amicus counterfactual.

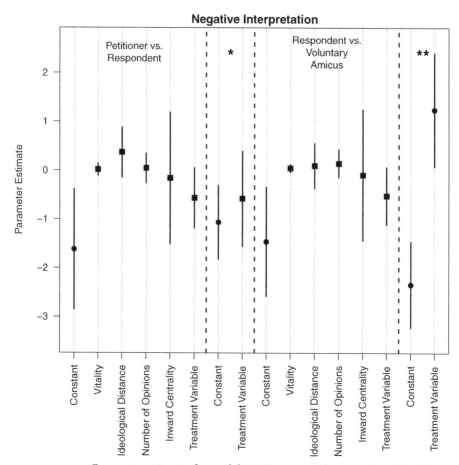

FIGURE A13. Parameter estimates for models in Figure 7.4. The asterisk and double asterisks denote the estimates for the OSG Petitioner vs. OSG Invited Amicus and OSG Invited Amicus vs. OSG Voluntary Amicus counterfactuals, respectively.

References

Ai, Chunrong, and Edward C. Norton. 2003. "Interaction Terms in Logit and Probit Models." *Economic Letters* 80: 123–29.

Bailey, Michael A., Brian Kamoie, and Forrest Maltzman. 2005. "Signals from the Tenth Justice: The Political Role of the Solicitor General in Supreme Court Decision Making." *American Journal of Political Science* 49 (1): 72–85.

Bailey, Michael A., and Forrest Maltzman. 2008. "Does Legal Doctrine Matter? Unpacking Law and Policy Preferences on the U.S. Supreme Court." *American Political Science Review* 102 (3): 369–84.

Bartels, Brandon L. 2009. "The Constraining Capacity of Legal Doctrine on the U.S. Supreme Court." *American Political Science Review* 103 (3): 474–95.

Baum, Lawrence. 2009. *The Supreme Court*. 10th Ed. Washington, D.C., Congressional Quarterly Press.

Benesh, Sara C., Saul Brenner, and Harold J. Spaeth. 2002. "Aggressive Grants by Affirm-Minded Justices." *American Politics Research* 30 (3): 219–34.

Benson, Robert W., and Joan B. Kessler. 1987. "Legalese v. Plain Language: An Empirical Study of Persuasion and Credibility in Appellate Brief Writing." *Loyola of Los Angeles Law Review* 20: 301–22.

Bergara, Mario, Barak Richman, and Pablo T. Spiller. 2003. "Modeling Supreme Court Decision Making: The Congressional Constraint." *Legislative Studies Quarterly* 28 (2): 247–80.

Berry, William D., Jacqueline H. R. DeMeritt, and Justin Esarey. 2010. "Testing for Interaction in Binary Logit and Probit Models: Is a Product Term Essential?" *American Journal of Political Science* 54 (1): 248–66.

Black, Ryan C., and Timothy R. Johnson. 2008. "Judicial Politics and the Search for the 'Holy Grail' of Salience." Paper presented at the 2008 meeting of the Southern Political Science Association, New Orleans, LA.

Black, Ryan C., Anthony J. Madonna, Ryan J. Owens, and Michael S. Lynch. 2007. "Adding Recess Appointments to the President's 'Tool Chest' of Unilateral Powers." *Political Research Quarterly* 60 (4): 645–54.

Black, Ryan C., and Ryan J. Owens. 2009a. "Agenda-Setting in the Supreme Court: The Collision of Policy and Jurisprudence." *Journal of Politics* 71 (3): 1062–75.

Black, Ryan C., and Ryan J. Owens. 2009b. "Analyzing the Reliability of Supreme Court Justices' Agenda Setting Records." *Justice System Journal* 30 (3): 254–65.

Black, Ryan C., and Ryan J. Owens. Forthcoming. "Solicitor General Influence and the United States Supreme Court." *Political Research Quarterly.* Available at: http://prg.sagepub.com/content/early/2011/01/26/1065912910388185.abstract.

Black, Ryan C., Sarah A. Treul, Timothy R. Johnson, and Jerry Goldman. 2011. "Emotions, Oral Arguments, and Supreme Court Decision Making." *Journal of Politics* 73 (2): 572–81.

Black, Ryan C., and Christina L. Boyd. Forthcoming 2012. "US Supreme Court Agenda Setting and the Role of Litigant Status." *Journal of Law, Economics, and Organization* 28 (1). Advanced online access available at http://jleo.oxfordjournals.org/cgi/content/full/ewq002?ijkey=54K01n3PGcmHTjL&keytype=ref.

Blackwell, Matthew, Stefano Iacus, Gary King, and Giuseppe Porro. 2009. "CEM: Coarsened Exact Matching in Stata." *Stata Journal* 9 (4): 524–46.

Blackwell, Matthew, Stefano Iacus, Gary King, and Giuseppe Porro. 2010. "CEM: Coarsened Exact Matching in Stata." Extended user's guide, February 22. http://gking.harvard.edu/files/cem-stata.pdf.

Bloch, Susan Low. 1989. "The Early Role of the Attorney General in Our Constitutional Scheme: In the Beginning There Was Pragmatism." *Duke Law Journal* 1989: 561–653.

Bloomfield, Louis A. 2009. "WCopyfind (Version 2.7)." Windows computer program. http://www.plagiarism.phys.virginia.edu/Wsoftware.html.

Boucher, Robert L. Jr., and Jeffrey A. Segal. 1995. "Supreme Court Justices as Strategic Decision Makers: Aggressive Grants and Defensive Denials on the Vinson Court." *Journal of Politics* 57 (3): 824–37.

Boyd, Christina L., Lee Epstein, and Andrew D. Martin. 2010. "Untangling the Causal Effects of Sex on Judging." *American Journal of Political Science* 54 (2): 389–411.

Brambor, Thomas, William Roberts Clark, and Matt Golder. 2006. "Understanding Interaction Models: Improving Empirical Analysis." *Political Analysis* 14 (1): 63–82.

Brand, Norman. 1979. "Legal Writing, Reasoning and Research: An Introduction." *Albany Law Review* 44: 292–97.

Brenner, Saul. 1979. "The New Certiorari Game." *Journal of Politics* 41 (2): 649–55.

Brenner, Saul, and Harold J. Spaeth. 1995. *Stare Indecisis: The Alteration of Precedent on the U.S. Supreme Court, 1946–1992.* New York: Cambridge University Press.

Brenner, Saul, and Marc Stier. 1996. "Retesting Segal and Spaeth's Stare Decisis Model." *American Journal of Political Science* 40 (4): 1036–48.

Brudney, James J., and Corey Ditslear. 2005. "Canons of Construction and the Elusive Quest for Neutral Reasoning." *Vanderbilt Law Review* 58 (1): 1–116.

Caldeira, Gregory A., and John R. Wright. 1988. "Organized Interests and Agenda Setting in the U.S. Supreme Court." *American Political Science Review* 82 (4): 1109–27.

Caldeira, Gregory A., and John R. Wright. 1998. "Organized Interests before the Supreme Court: Setting the Agenda." Paper presented at the annual meeting of the American Political Science Association. Boston, MA.

Caldeira, Gregory A., John R. Wright, and Christopher J. W. Zorn. 1999. "Sophisticated Voting and Gate-Keeping in the Supreme Court." *Journal of Law, Economics, and Organization* 15 (3): 549–72.

Calvert, Randall L. 1985. "The Value of Biased Information: A Rational Choice Model of Political Advice." *Journal of Politics* 47 (2): 530–55.

Caplan, Lincoln. 1987. *The Tenth Justice: The Solicitor General and the Rule of Law.* New York: Knopf.

Carrubba, Clifford, Barry Friedman, Andrew D. Martin, and Georg Vanberg. 2007. "Does the Median Justice Control the Content of Supreme Court Opinions?" Paper presented at the second annual conference on Empirical Legal Studies. New York, NY.

Chamberlain, Ronald S. 1987. "Mixing Politics and Justice: The Office of the Solicitor General." *Journal of Law and Politics* 4: 379–428.

Charrow, Robert P., and Veda R. Charrow. 1979. "Making Legal Language Understandable: A Psycholinguistic Study of Jury Instructions." *Columbia Law Review* 79 (7): 1306–74.

Clement, Paul D. 2005. "Confirmation Hearing on the Nomination of Paul D. Clement to be Solicitor General of the United States." Hearing Before the Committee on the Judiciary, United States Senate (109th Congress, First Session). April 27. Available online at: http://www.access.gpo.gov/congress/senate/pdf/109hrg/21706.pdf.

Coffin, Frank M. 1994. *On Appeal: Courts, Lawyering, and Judging.* New York: W.W. Norton.

Coleman, Meri, and T. L. Liau. 1975. "A Computer Readability Formula Designed for Machine Scoring." *Journal of Applied Psychology* 60 (2): 283–84.

Collins, Paul M., Jr. 2004. "Friends of the Court: Examining the Influence of Amicus Curiae Participation in U.S. Supreme Court Litigation." *Law and Society Review* 38 (4): 807–32.

Collins, Paul M., Jr. 2007. "Lobbyists before the U.S. Supreme Court: Investigating the Influence of Amicus Curiae Briefs." *Political Research Quarterly* 60 (1): 55–70.

Collins, Paul M., Jr. 2008a. "Amici Curiae and Dissensus on the U.S. Supreme Court." *Journal of Empirical Legal Studies* 5 (1): 143–70.

Collins, Paul M., Jr. 2008b. *Friends of the Court: Interest Groups and Judical Decision Making.* New York: Oxford University Press.

Cooper, James L. 1990. "The Solicitor General and the Evolution of Activism." *Indiana Law Journal* 65: 675–96.

Corley, Pamela C. 2008. "The Supreme Court and Opinion Content: The Influence of Parties' Briefs." *Political Research Quarterly* 61 (3): 468–78.

Corley, Pamela C., Paul M. Collins, Jr., and Bryan Calvin. 2011. "Lower Court Influence on U.S. Supreme Court Opinion Content." *Journal of Politics* 73 (1): 31–44.

Cox, Gary W., and Mathew D. McCubbins. 2005. *Setting the Agenda: Responsible Party Government in the U.S. House of Representatives.* New York: Cambridge University Press.

Cozine, R. Kirkland. 1994. "The Emergence of Written Appellate Briefs in the Nineteenth-century United States." *American Journal of Legal History* 38 (4): 482–530.

Days, Drew S. 1995. "The Solicitor General and the American Legal Ideal." *Southern Methodist Law Review* 49: 73–82.

Deen, Rebecca, Joseph Ignagni, and James Meernik. 2003. "The Solicitor General as Amicus 1953–2000: How Influential?" *Judicature* 87 (2): 60–71.

Deen, Rebecca. E., Joseph Ignagni, and James Meernik. 2005. "Individual Justices and the Solicitor General: The Amicus Curiae Cases 1953–2000." *Judicature* 89 (2): 68–77.

Dreeben, Michael. 2010. "Lecture with Michael Dreeben, Criminal Deputy Solicitor General at the U.S. Department of Justice." Available at: http://www.youtube.com/watch?v=EmeHI4Trylw.

Ehrenberg, Suzanne. 2004. "Embracing the Writing-Centered Legal Process." *Iowa Law Review* 89: 1160–99.

Epstein, Lee, Daniel E. Ho, Gary King, and Jeffrey A. Segal. 2005. "The Supreme Court During Crisis: How War Affects Only Non-war Cases." *New York University Law Review* 80 (1): 1–116.

Epstein, Lee, and Joseph F. Kobylka. 1992. *The Supreme Court and Legal Change: Abortion and the Death Penalty*. Chapel Hill, NC. University of North Carolina Press.

Epstein, Lee, and Jack Knight. 1998. *The Choices Justices Make*. Washington, DC: Congressional Quarterly Press.

Epstein, Lee, and Jack Knight. 1999. "Mapping Out the Strategic Terrain: The Informational Role of *Amici Curiae*." In *Supreme Court Decision-Making: New Institutional Approaches*, ed. Cornell W. Clayton and Howard Gillman 215–35. Chicago: University of Chicago Press.

Epstein, Lee, Jack Knight, and Andrew D. Martin. 2001. "The Supreme Court as a Strategic National Policymaker." *Emory Law Journal* 50 (2): 583–612.

Epstein, Lee, Andrew D. Martin, Kevin M. Quinn, and Jeffrey A. Segal. 2007. "Ideological Drift among Supreme Court Justices: Who, When, and How Important?" *Northwestern University Law Review* 101 (4): 1483–1542.

Epstein, Lee, Andrew D. Martin, Jeffrey A. Segal, and Chad Westerland. 2007. "The Judicial Common Space." *Journal of Law, Economics, and Organization* 23 (2): 303–25.

Epstein, Lee, and Jeffrey A. Segal. 2000. "Measuring Issue Salience." *American Journal of Political Science* 44 (1): 66–83.

Epstein, Lee, Jeffrey A. Segal, and Harold J. Spaeth. 2007. "Digital Archive of the Papers of Harry A. Blackmun." http://epstein.law.northwestern.edu/research/BlackmunArchive/.

Epstein, Lee, Jeffrey A. Segal, Harold J. Spaeth, and Thomas G. Walker. 2007. *The Supreme Court Compendium: Data, Decisions, and Developments*. 4th ed. Washington, DC: Congressional Quarterly Press.

Epstein, Lee, Jeffrey A. Segal, and Timothy Johnson. 1996. "The Claim of Issue Creation on the U.S. Supreme Court." *American Political Science Review* 90 (4): 845–52.

Epstein, Lee, and Thomas G. Walker. 2005. *Constitutional Law for a Changing America: A Short Course*. Washington, DC: Congressional Quarterly Press.

Eskridge, William N., Jr. 1991. "Reneging on History? Playing the Court/Congress/President Civil Rights Game." *California Law Review* 79 (3): 613–84.

Fahy, Charles. 1942. "The Office of the Solicitor General." *American Bar Association Journal* 28: 20–22.

Fisher, Louis. 1990. "Is the Solicitor General an Executive or Judicial Agent? Caplan's Tenth Justice." *Law and Social Inquiry* 15 (2): 305–20.

Fleiss, Joseph L., and Jacob Cohen. 1973. "The Equivalence of Weighted Kappa and the Intraclass Correlation Coefficient as Measures of Reliability." *Educational and Psychological Measurement* 33 (3): 613–19.

Fowler, James H., Timothy R. Johnson, James F. Spriggs II, Sangick Jeon, and Paul J. Wahlbeck. 2007. "Network Analysis and the Law: Measuring the Legal Importance of Supreme Court Precedents." *Political Analysis* 15 (3): 324–46.

Fraley, George. 1996. "Is the Fox Watching the Henhouse? The Administration's Control of FEC Litigation through the Solicitor General." *Administrative Law Journal of the American University* 9: 1215–72.

Franzese, Robert J. 1999. "Partially Independent Central Banks, Politically Responsive Governments, and Inflation." *American Journal of Political Science* 43: 681–706.

Friedman, Barry. 2006. "Taking Law Seriously." *Perspectives on Politics* 4 (2): 261–76.

Galanter, Marc. 1974. "Why the 'Haves' Come Out Ahead: Speculation on the Limits of Legal Changes." *Law and Society Review* 9 (1): 95–160.

Gates, John B., and Glenn A. Phelps. 1996. "Intentionalism in Constitutional Opinions." *Political Research Quarterly* 48: 245–61.

Gelman, Andrew, and Hal Stern. 2006. "The Difference Between "Significant"' and "Not Significant" Is Not Itself Statistically Significant." *American Statistician* 60 (4): 328–31.

Giles, Michael W., Virginia A. Hettinger, and Todd Peppers. 2001. "Picking Federal Judges: A Note on Policy and Partisan Selection Agendas." *Political Research Quarterly* 54 (3): 623–41.

Gillman, Howard. 2001. "What's Law Got to Do with It? Judicial Behavioralists Test the 'Legal Model' of Judicial Decision Making." *Law and Social Inquiry* 26 (2): 465–504.

Goodrich, Herbert F. 1967. *A Case on Appeal – A Judge's View*. Philadelphia, PA: Joint Committee on Continuing Legal Education of the American Law Institute and the American Bar Association.

Greiner, D. James, and Cassandra W. Pattanayak. Forthcoming 2011. "Randomized Evaluation in Legal Assistance: What Difference Does Representation Make?" *Yale Law Journal* 121.

Grilli, Vittorio, Donato Masciandaro, and Guido Tabellini. 1991. "Political and Monetary Institutions and Public Finance Policies in the Industrial Countries." *Economic Policy* 13: 341–92.

Gunning, Robert. 1952. *The Technique of Clear Writing*. New York: McGraw-Hill.

Hamilton, Clyde H. 1999. "Effective Appellate Brief Writing." *South Carolina Law Review* 50: 581–89.

Hansford, Thomas G., and James F. Spriggs II. 2006. *The Politics of Precedent on the U.S. Supreme Court*. Princeton, NJ: Princeton University Press.

Hart, Henry M., Jr. 1959. "The Supreme Court 1958 Term-Forward: The Time Chart of the Justices." *Harvard Law Review* 73: 84–240.

Harvey, Anna, and Barry Friedman. 2006. "Pulling Punches: Congressional Constraint on the Supreme Court's Constitutional Rulings, 1987–2000." *Legislative Studies Quarterly* 31 (4): 533–62.

Hettinger, Virginia A., and Christopher Zorn. 2005. "Explaining the Incidence and Timing of Congressional Responses to the U.S. Supreme Court." *Legislative Studies Quarterly* 30 (1): 5–28.

Ho, Daniel E., Kosuke Imai, Gary King, and Elizabeth A. Stuart. 2006. "Matching as Nonparametric Preprocessing for Reducing Model Dependence in Parametric Causal Inference." Unpublished manuscript.

Hoffer, Peter C., Williamjames H. Hoffer, and N. E. H. Hull. 2007. *The Supreme Court: An Essential History.* Lawrence: University Press of Kansas.

Hume, Robert J. 2007. "Administrative Appeals to the U.S. Supreme Court: The Importance of Legal Signals." *Journal of Empirical Legal Studies* 4 (3): 625–49.

Iacus, Stefano M., Gary King, and Giuseppe Porro. 2009. "CEM: Software for Coarsened Exact Matching." *Journal of Statistical Software* 30 (9): 1–27.

Iacus, Stefano M., Gary King, and Giuseppe Porro. 2010. "CEM: Software for Coarsened Exact Matching." Extended user's guide, February 22. http://gking.harvard.edu/files/cem.pdf.

Iacus, Stefano M., Gary King, and Giuseppe Porro. 2011a. "Multivariate Matching Methods That Are Monotonic Imbalance Bounding." *Journal of the American Statistical Association* 106 (493): 345–61.

Iacus, Stefano M., Gary King, and Giuseppe Porro. 2011b. "Causal Inference without Balance Checking: Coarsened Exact Matching." *Political Analysis* Advance Access published August 23, 2011, accessible at: http://gking.harvard.edu/files/political_analysis-2011-iacus-pan_mpro13.pdf.

Ignagni, Joesph, and James Meernik. 1994. "Explaining Congressional Attempts to Reverse Supreme Court Decisions." *Political Research Quarterly* 47 (2): 353–71.

Jenkins, John A. 1983. "The Solicitor General's Winning Ways." *American Bar Association Journal* 69: 734–39.

Jeong, Gyung-Ho, Gary Miller, and Andrew C. Sobel. 2009. "Political Compromise and Bureaucratic Structure: The Political Origins of the Federal Reserve System." *Journal of Law, Economics, and Organization* 25: 442–98.

Johnson, Timothy R. 2003. "The Supreme Court, the Solicitor General, and the Separation of Powers." *American Politics Research* 31 (4): 426–51.

Johnson, Timothy R. 2004. *Oral Arguments and Decision Making on the United States Supreme Court.* Albany: State University of New York Press.

Johnson, Timothy R., Paul J. Wahlbeck, and James F. Spriggs II. 2006. "The Influence of Oral Argumentation before the U.S. Supreme Court." *American Political Science Review* 100 (1): 99–113.

Johnson, Timothy R., James F. Spriggs II, and Paul J. Wahlbeck. 2007. "Oral Advocacy Before the United State Supreme Court: Does it Affect the Justices' Decisions?" *Washington University Law Review* 85 (3): 457–527.

Jurafsky, Daniel, and James H. Martin. 2008. *Speech and Language Processing: An Introduction to Natural Language Processing, Computational Linguistics, and Speech Recognition.* Upper Saddle River, N.J. Pearson Prentice Hall.

Kam, Cindy D., and Robert J. Franzese Jr. 2007. *Modeling and Interpreting Interactive Hypotheses in Regression Analysis.* Ann Arbor: University of Michigan Press.

Keefer, Philip, and David Stasavage. 2003. "The Limits of Delegation: Veto Players, Central Bank Independence, and the Credibility of Monetary Policy." *American Political Science Review* 97: 407–23.

Kincaid, J. Peter, Robert P. Fishburne, Jr., Richard L. Rogers, and Brad S. Chissom, 1975. *Derivation of New Readability Formulas (Automated Readability Index, Fog*

Count and Flesch Reading Ease Forumla) for Navy Enlisted Personnel. Naval Technical Training Command Research Branch Report 8-75. Springfield, Virginia.

King, Gary, and Langche Zeng. 2001a. "Explaining Rare Events in International Relations." *International Organization* 55 (3): 693–715.

King, Gary, and Langche Zeng. 2001b. "Logistic Regression in Rare Events Data." *Political Analysis* 9 (2): 137–63.

King, Gary, Michael Tomz, and Jason Wittenberg. 2000. "Making the Most of Statistical Analyses: Improving Interpretation and Presentation." *American Journal of Political Science* 44 (2): 347–61.

Klein, David, and Darby Morrisroe. 1999. "The Prestige and Influence of Individual Judges on the U.S. Courts of Appeals." *Journal of Legal Studies* 19 (4): 371–91.

Knight, Jack, and Lee Epstein. 1996. "The Norm of Stare Decisis." *American Journal of Political Science* 40 (4): 1018–35.

Krehbiel, Keith. 1995. "Cosponsors and Wafflers from A to Z." *American Journal of Political Science* 39 (4): 906–23.

Krehbiel, Keith. 1998. *Pivotal Politics.* Chicago: University of Chicago Press.

Kritzer, Herbert M., and Mark J. Richards. 2003. "Jurisprudential Regimes and Supreme Court Decisionmaking: The Lemon Regime and Establishment Clause Cases." *Law and Society Review* 37 (4): 827–40.

Kritzer, Herbert M., and Mark J. Richards. 2005. "The Influence of Law in the Supreme Court's Search-and-Seizure Jurisprudence." *American Politics Research* 33 (1): 33–55.

Landis, J. Richard, and Gary G. Koch. 1977. "The Measurement of Observer Agreement for Categorical Data." *Biometrics* 33 (1): 159–74.

Lax, Jeffrey R., and Charles M. Cameron. 2007. "Bargaining and Opinion Assignment on the U.S. Supreme Court." *Journal of Law, Economics, and Organization* 23 (2): 276–302.

Lax, Jeffrey R., and Kelly Rader. 2010. "Legal Constraints on Supreme Court Decision Making: Do Jurisprudential Regimes Exist?" *Journal of Politics* 71 (2): 273–84.

Lee, Rex. 1986. "Lawyering for the Government: Politics, Polemics, and Principle." *Ohio State Law Journal* 47 (3): 595–601.

Lemos, Margaret H. 2009. "The Solicitor General as Mediator between Court and Agency." *Michigan State Law Review* 2009: 185–223.

Lewis, David E. 2003. *Presidents and the Politics of Agency Design: Political Insulation in the United States Government Bureaucracy, 1946–1997.* Palo Alto, CA: Stanford University Press.

Luse, Jennifer, Geoffrey McGovern, Wendy L. Martinek, and Sara C. Benesh. 2009. "'Such Inferior Courts:' Compliance by Circuits with Jurisprudential Regimes." *American Politics Research* 37 (1): 75–106.

Maltzman, Forrest, James F. Spriggs II, and Paul J. Wahlbeck. 2000. *Crafting Law on the Supreme Court: The Collegial Game.* New York: Cambridge University Press.

Maltzman, Forrest, and Paul J. Wahlbeck. 2003. "Salience or Politics: *New York Times* Coverage of the Supreme Court." Paper presented at the 2003 annual meeting of the Midwest Political Science Association, Chicago, IL.

Martin, Andrew D., and Kevin M. Quinn. 2002. "Dynamic Ideal Point Estimation via Markov Chain Monte Carlo for the U.S. Supreme Court, 1953–99." *Political Analysis* 10 (2): 134–53.

Martineau, Robert J., Kent Sinclair, Michael E. Solomine, and Randy J. Holland. 2005. *Appellate Practice and Procedure.* St. Paul, MN: Thomson West.

McAtee, Andrea, and Kevin T. McGuire. 2007. "Lawyers, Justices, and Issue Salience: When and How Do Legal Arguments Affect the U.S. Supreme Court?" *Law & Society Review* 41 (2): 259–78.

McConnell, Michael W. 1988. "The Rule of Law and the Role of the Solicitor General." *Loyola of Los Angeles Law Review* 21: 1105–18.

McCree, Wade H., Jr. 1981. "The Solicitor General and His Client." *Washington University Law Quarterly* 59: 337–48.

McGuire, Kevin T. 1995. "Repeat Players in the Supreme Court: The Role of Experienced Lawyers in Litigation Success." *Journal of Politics* 57 (1): 187–96.

McGuire, Kevin T. 1998. "Explaining Executive Success in the U.S. Supreme Court." *Political Research Quarterly* 51 (2): 505–26.

McGuire, Kevin T., and Barbara Palmer. 1995. "Issue Fluidity on the U.S. Supreme Court." *American Political Science Review* 89 (3): 691–702.

McGuire, Kevin T., and Barbara Palmer. 1996. "Issues, Agendas, and Decision Making on the Supreme Court." *American Political Science Review* 90 (4): 853–65.

McLaughlin, G. Harry. 1969. "SMOG Grading – A New Readability Formula." *Journal of Reading* 12 (8): 639–46.

Meinhold, Stephen S., and Steven A. Shull. 1998. "Policy Congruence between the President and Solicitor General." *Political Research Quarterly* 51: 527–37.

Michel, Paul R. 1998. "Effective Appellate Advocacy." *Litigation* 24 (4): 19–23.

Miller, Gary. 1989. "Confiscation, Credible Commitment and Progressive Reform." *Journal of Institutional and Theoretical Economics* 145: 686–92.

Moe, Terry M. 1987. "Interests, Institutions, and Positive Theory: The Politics of the NLRB." *Studies in American Political Development* 2: 236–99.

Moe, Terry M., and William G. Howell. 1999. "The Presidential Power of Unitary Action." *Journal of Law, Economics, and Organization* 15 (1): 132–79.

Murphy, Walter F. 1964. *Elements of Judicial Strategy.* Chicago: University of Chicago Press.

Nicholson, Chris, and Paul M. Collins Jr. 2008. "The Solicitor General's Amicus Curiae Strategies in the Supreme Court." *American Politics Research* 36 (3): 382–415.

North, Douglas, and Barry Weingast. 1989. "Constitutions and Commitment: The Evolution of Institutions Governing Public Choice in Seventeenth-Century England." *Journal of Economic History* 49: 803–32.

Owens, Ryan J. 2010. "The Separation of Powers and Supreme Court Agenda Setting." *American Journal of Political Science* 54 (2): 412–27.

Owens, Ryan J., and Lee Epstein. 2005. "Amici Curiae during the Rehnquist Years." *Judicature* 89 (3): 127–33.

Owens, Ryan J., and David A. Simon. Forthcoming 2012. "Explaining the Supreme Courts Docket Size." *William and Mary Law Review* 53(4).

Pacelle, Richard. 2003. *Between Law and Politics: The Solicitor General and the Structuring of Race, Gender, and Reproductive Rights Litigation.* College Station: Texas A&M University Press.

Pacelle, Richard. 2006. "Amicus Curiae or Amicus Praesidentis – Reexamining the Role of the Solicitor General in Filing Amici." *Judicature* 89 (6): 317–25.

Palmer, Jan. 1982. "An Econometric Analysis of the U.S. Supreme Court's Certiorari Decisions." *Public Choice* 39: 387–98.

Perry, H. W., Jr. 1991. *Deciding to Decide: Agenda Setting in the United States Supreme Court.* Cambridge, MA: Harvard University Press.

Peterson, Mark A. 1992. "The Presidency and Organized Interests: White House Patterns of Interest Group Liaison." *American Political Science Review* 86 (3): 612–25.

Phelps, Glenn A., and John B. Gates. 1991. "The Myth of Jurisprudence: Interpretative Theory in the Constitutional Opinions of Justice Rehnquist and Brennan." *Santa Clara Law Review* 31 (3): 567–96.

Pittoni, Mario. 1991. *Brief Writing and Argumentation.* 3rd ed. Brooklyn, NY: Foundation Press.

Pritchett, C. Herman. 1948. *The Roosevelt Court.* New York: Macmillan.

Provine, Doris Marie. 1980. *Case Selection in the United States Supreme Court.* Chicago: University of Chicago Press.

Rehnquist, William H. 2001. *The Supreme Court.* Rev. and updated ed. New York: Vintage Books.

Richards, Mark J. and Herbert M. Kritzer. 2002. "Jurisprudential Regimes in Supreme Court Decision Making." *American Political Science Review* 96 (2): 305–20.

Richards, Mark J., Joseph L. Smith, and Herbert M. Kritzer. 2006. "Does Chevon Matter?" *Law & Policy* 28 (4): 444–69.

Riker, William H. 1962. *The Theory of Political Coalitions.* New Haven, CT: Yale University Press.

Salokar, Rebecca Mae. 1992. *The Solicitor General: The Politics of Law.* Philadelphia: Temple University Press.

Scalia, Antonin, and Bryan A. Garner. 2008. *Making Your Case: The Art of Persuading Judges.* St. Paul, MN Thomson West.

Scheb, John M. II, and William Lyons. 2000. "The Myth of Legality and Public Evaluation of the Supreme Court." *Social Science Quarterly* 81 (4): 928–40.

Scigliano, Robert. 1971. *The Supreme Court and the Presidency.* New York: Free Press.

Segal, Jeffrey. 1988. "Amicus Curiae Briefs by the Solicitor General during the Warren and Burger Court: A Research Note." *Western Political Quarterly* 41 (1): 135–44.

Segal, Jeffrey A., and Cheryl D. Reedy. 1988. "The Supreme Court and Sex Discrimination: The Role of the Solicitor General." *Western Political Quarterly* 41 (3): 553–68.

Segal, Jeffrey A., and Harold J. Spaeth. 1996. "The Influence of Stare Decisis on the Votes of United States Supreme Court Justices." *American Journal of Political Science* 40 (4): 971–1003.

Segal, Jeffrey A., and Harold J. Spaeth. 2002. *The Supreme Court and the Attitudinal Model Revisited.* New York: Cambridge University Press.

Sheehan, Reginald S., William Mishler, and Donald R. Songer. 1992. "Ideology, Status, and the Differential Success of Direct Parties before the Supreme Court." *American Political Science Review* 86 (2): 464–71.

Smith, E. A., and R. J. Senter. 1967. Automated Readability Index. Aerospace Medical Research Laboratories Paper AMRL-TR-66-220.

Smith, Steven S. 1989. *Call to Order: Floor Politics in the House and Senate.* Washington, DC: Brookings Institution Press.

Sokol, Ronald P. 1967. *Language and Litigation: A Portrait of the Appellate Brief.* Charlottesville, VA: The Michie Company.

Songer, Donald R. 1979. "Concern for Policy Outputs as a Cue for Supreme Court Decisions of Certiorari." *Journal of Politics* 41 (4): 1185–94.

Songer, Donald R., Ashlyn Kuersten, and Erin Kaheny. 2000. "Why the Haves Don't Always Come Out Ahead: Repeat Players Meet Amici Curiae for the Disadvantaged." *Political Research Quarterly* 53 (3): 537–56.

Songer, Donald R., and Reginald S. Sheehan. 1992. "Who Wins on Appeal? Upperdogs and Underdogs in the United States Courts of Appeals." *American Journal of Political Science* 36 (1): 235–58.

Songer, Donald R., Reginald S. Sheehan, and Susan Brodie Haire. 1999. "Do the 'Haves' Come Out Ahead over Time? Applying Galanter's Framework to Decisions of the U.S. Courts of Appeals, 1925–1988." *Law and Society Review* 33 (4): 811–32.

Songer, Donald R., and Stefanie A. Lindquist. 1996. "Not the Whole Story: The Impact of Justices' Values on Supreme Court Decision Making." *American Journal of Political Science* 40 (4): 1049–63.

Spaeth, Harold J. 1964. "The Judicial Restraint of Mr. Justice Frankfurter – Myth or Reality." *Midwest Journal of Political Science* 8 (1): 22–38.

Spaeth, Harold J. 2006. *The Original United States Supreme Court Judicial Database 1953–2005 Terms.* East Lansing: Michigan State University Press.

Spaeth, Harold J., and Jeffrey A. Segal. 1999. *Majority Rule Or Minority Will: Adherence To Precedent On The U.S. Supreme Court.* New York: Cambridge University Press.

Spiller, Pablo T., and Rafael Gely. 1992. "Congressional Control or Judicial Independence: The Determinants of U.S. Supreme Court Labor-Relations Decisions, 1949–1988." *RAND Journal of Economics* 23 (4): 463–92.

Spriggs, James F., II. 1996. "The Supreme Court and Federal Administrative Agencies: A Resource-Based Theory and Analysis of Judicial Impact." *American Journal of Political Science* 40 (4): 1122–51.

Spriggs, James F. II, and Thomas G. Hansford. 2000. "Measuring Legal Change: The Reliability and Validity of Shepard's Citations." *Political Research Quarterly* 53 (2): 327–41.

Spriggs, James F. II, and Thomas G. Hansford. 2001. "Explaining the Overruling of U.S. Supreme Court Precedent." *Journal of Politics* 63 (4): 1091–1111.

Spriggs, James F. II, and Thomas G. Hansford. 2002. "The U.S. Supreme Court's Incorporation and Interpretation of Precedent." *Law and Society Review* 36 (1): 139–60.

Spriggs, James F. II, and Paul J. Wahlbeck. 1997. "Amicus Curiae and the Role of Information at the Supreme Court." *Political Research Quarterly* 50 (2): 365–86.

Staton, Jeffrey K., and Georg Vanberg. 2008. "The Value of Vagueness, Delegation, Defiance, and Judicial Opinions." *American Journal of Political Science* 52 (3): 504–19.

Stern, Robert L. 1989. *Appellate Practice in the United States.* Washington, DC: Bureau of National Affairs.

Stern, Robert L., Eugene Gressman, Stephen M. Shapiro, and Kenneth S. Geller. 2002. *Supreme Court Practice.* 8th ed. Washington, DC: Bureau of National Affairs.

Sundquist, Matthew Lee. 2010. "Learned in Litigation: Former Solicitors General in the Supreme Court Bar." *Charleston Law Review* 5 (1): 59–97.

Swisher, Carl B. 1974. *The Taney Period*. New York: Macmillan.

Tanenhaus, Joseph, Marvin Schick, and David Rosen. 1963. "The Supreme Court's Certiorari Jurisdiction: Cue Theory." In *Judicial Decision-Making*, ed. Glendon A. Schubert, 111–32. New York: Free Press.

Tate, Albert, Jr. 1978. "The Art of Brief Writing: What a Judge Wants to Read." *Litigation* 4 (2): 11–15.

Teply, Larry L. 1990. *Legal Writing, Analysis, and Oral Argument*. St. Paul, MN: West.

Thompson, David C., and Melanie F. Watchell. 2009. "An Empirical Analysis of Supreme Court Certiorari Petition Procedures: The Call for Response and the Call for the Views of the Solicitor General." *George Mason Law Review* 16: (2): 237–302.

Totenberg, Nina. 2009. "*Chandler v. Miller*: Double Indemnity." In *A Good Quarrel: America's Top Legal Reporters Share Stories from Inside the Supreme Court*, eds. Timothy R. Johnson and Jerry Goldman, 110–24. Ann Arbor: University of Michigan Press.

Ulmer, S. Sidney, William Hintz, and Louise Kirklosky. 1972. "The Decision to Grant or Deny Certiorari: Further Considerations of Cue Theory." *Law and Society Review* 6 (4): 637–44.

vanR. Springer, James. 1984. "Some Suggestions on Preparing Briefs on the Merits in the Supreme Court of the United States." *Catholic University Law Review* 33: 593–602.

Vose, Clement E. 1959. *Caucasians Only: The Supreme Court, the NAACP, and the Restrictive Covenant Cases*. Berkeley, CA: University of California Press.

Wahlbeck, Paul J. 1997. "The Life of the Law: Judicial Politics and Legal Change." *Journal of Politics* 59 (3): 778–802.

Ward, Artemus, and David L. Weiden. 2006. *Sorcerers' Apprentices: 100 Years of Law Clerks at the United States Supreme Court*. New York: New York University Press.

Waxman, Seth P. 1998. "Presenting the Case of the United States As It Should Be: The Solicitor General in Historical Context." *Journal of Supreme Court History* 1998: 3–25.

Wedeking, Justin P. 2010. "Supreme Court Litigants and Strategic Framing." *American Journal of Political Science* 54 (3): 617–31.

Wohlfarth, Patrick C. 2009. "The Tenth Justice? Consequences of Politicization in the Solicitor General's Office." *Journal of Politics* 70 (1): 224–37.

Woodward, Bob, and Scott Armstrong. 1979. *The Brethren: Inside the Supreme Court*. New York: Simon and Schuster.

Zorn, Christopher J. W. 2002. "U.S. Government Litigation Strategies in the Federal Appellate Courts." *Political Research Quarterly* 55 (1): 145–66.

Index

Index

Made in the USA
Monee, IL
04 September 2020